Hmmm! Who's Speaking?

WAS THAT THE F, S, & HS?

DAVID COX, A BIC

WESTBOW
PRESS®
A DIVISION OF THOMAS NELSON
& ZONDERVAN

Copyright © 2018 David Cox, A BIC.

All rights reserved. No part of this book may be used or reproduced by any means, graphic, electronic, or mechanical, including photocopying, recording, taping or by any information storage retrieval system without the written permission of the author except in the case of brief quotations embodied in critical articles and reviews.

WestBow Press books may be ordered through booksellers or by contacting:

WestBow Press
A Division of Thomas Nelson & Zondervan
1663 Liberty Drive
Bloomington, IN 47403
www.westbowpress.com
1 (866) 928-1240

Because of the dynamic nature of the Internet, any web addresses or links contained in this book may have changed since publication and may no longer be valid. The views expressed in this work are solely those of the author and do not necessarily reflect the views of the publisher, and the publisher hereby disclaims any responsibility for them.

Any people depicted in stock imagery provided by Getty Images are models, and such images are being used for illustrative purposes only.
Certain stock imagery © Getty Images.

ISBN: 978-1-9736-3977-0 (sc)
ISBN: 978-1-9736-3978-7 (hc)
ISBN: 978-1-9736-3976-3 (e)

Library of Congress Control Number: 2018911051

Print information available on the last page.

WestBow Press rev. date: 9/28/2018

Opening Comments

Seeing as how my minister, and basically all ministers, are taking care of their flock on Sundays, they do not have the opportunity to physically visit other churches or other religions that conduct their services on the same day of the week. For some reason, this concerned me and so about 15 years ago I decided (and probably with Gods help) to occasionally start visiting other churches and religions and report my observations back to my minister, Rev. Tom Gray, at Tulsa's Kirk of the Hills Church.

Now one can see TV Services of some local and area religious services and you can also go to many of their web sites and view their more recent services. But that is still not quite the same as physically being there.

Initially I would report my visits directly to Tom but then as time went on I started sending my reports out to others and even to the places I had visited. The reports could be complimentary or suggestions on how maybe to check into some changes that would help visitors feel more welcome and maybe ways to increase attendees.

In a previous book I had written "The Chaplains at Hale Scout Reservation" in 2006, it was with the intent to increase the attendance at the daily chapel services at summer scout camp. When I went on board with a Baptist minister, Pastor Reichman, to help increase attendance – the services were often attracting less than a handful of people. But with new ideas and messages the daily attendance increased to sometimes as many as 400 scouts and scout leaders. The local Scout Headquarters suggested that we write down what we were doing different and share it with others.

Perhaps this new book will inspire non-church attending folks to seek out a Church to visit and start attending on a regular basis and help some Churches grow in size and attendance.

I recently attended a seminar by Mark Vinkler on 'How God speaks to people thru dreams' which I can attest to which you will see in some of my stories. And this is an important way for God to communicate to us now as well as He has since the Beginning. As Dr. Vinkler points out the Bible describes more than 50 dreams in it and in dissecting the dreams and the resulting actions, they compose nearly one-third of the Bible.

Yes! God has communicated with me thru my dreams and sometimes He has used other ways to communicate with me. And maybe thru some of these stories you'll recognize something similar that happened in your life and maybe you'll think – **Hmmm? Was that the Father, Son and Holy Spirit Speaking?**

Contents

With my initial visit reports for only my minister I would sign off with my name. As my reports started to spread out I begin to sign off as the KRR guy. The KRR stood for the Kirk Roving Reporter to signify someone associated with the Kirk of the Hills Church. However, over time I hoped people would see the Scottish meaning of Kirk as being 'Church' so that the KRR would imply the Church Roving Reporter. And in some of the reports you will see me signing off simply as A BIC which is short for A Brother In Christ or A Believer In Christ. This I picked up on by a Brother Boy Scout Chaplain (Carl Amend) from Texas.

I have made literally hundreds of visits to not only Churches, but also Mosques, Temples, Synagogues and cults. In most of my visits I would try to blend in with those in attendance, but of course in some places I would stick out like a sore thumb, either not dressed in a similar manner, not speaking the language or not the same color of skin. Most of the time I was made to feel very comfortable as soon as I was recognized as not a regular attendee. Then there were the times when I was totally ignored.

Some of my stories are about other happenings that may not be related to Church visits but to experiences I have had as a Boy Scout Chaplain, a Billy Graham Emergency Response Chaplain, and a Door Holder for the 268 Generation (Passion) and as a Chaplain for the Tulsa Juvenile Detention Center.

Some stories are about ways and things God used to get my attention. Sometimes it could be physical or with words or music and even animals like foxes, donkey's, frogs, birds and even insects.

Hopefully in some of the stories it will bring back memories of a coincidence that happened to you previously and maybe at the time you just brushed it aside. But now maybe you'll reflect back and see where it was GOD trying to communicate with you.

I like to tell the boys in the Juvenile Detention Center how God loves each and every one of us and He tries to guide us in the right direction but sometimes He has to kick us in the rear end to get our attention. I'd give them an example of how maybe some young man needs a couple of hundred bucks so he figures he'll go rob a convenience store. When he arrives, and starts to walk in – Lo & Behold his 6th Grade English teacher is walking out and she starts talking to him – "Johnny – what a pleasant surprise. I was thinking of you the other day and wondering how you were doing. You were one of my most favorite students and I just knew you had so much potential". As she went on and on Johnny realized this wasn't the right time for a hold up so he goes home. The next day he is back at it and he goes out to get in his car and the car won't start- the battery is dead. The next day he gets the car battery charged up and that night he heads again for the convenience store. As he gets ready to walk in – Lo & Behold two police cars show up and the two cops go in for donuts and coffee and then they go back and sit in their cars. Well – three times God was trying to communicate and connect with Johnny. God was trying to help him but Johnny didn't get the connection. So, Johnny goes back the 4th night and pulls off the hold up. But God decided the only way to get Johnny's attention is to give him a hard kick to the rear end. Yup! People and cameras had picked Johnny out and recognized him and the police went and arrested him. Hmmm? Had God been trying to communicate with Johnny? How about you? Has God tried to connect with you sometime in the past and you just didn't realize it?

Find out in this book how in so many different ways God has connected with me and others. Maybe it will remind you of something similar in your past and you'll say Hmmm?

"And I would like to thank all the folks God used at different times in different ways to get my attention to check something out. And thanks to my family - my 2 sons, Doug & Andy, who are mentioned in the book, and then my 3 daughters, Shelly, Kristy & Adrienne who God also used at different times to lead me in a certain direction. Sometimes even joining me on Mission Trips. And for Kristy who spent a lot of time helping me formulate this book so that it would meet the standards set by WestBow Publishing. Thank you all and may God continue to Bless each and every one of you."

Chapters

All Chapters will start out with my older visits or happenings and end up with my more recent visits and happenings……

Opening Comments v
Contents vii

Chapter One: God Using Living Things 1
    a.   The Fox at the Cross 1
    b.   Sir Isaac Newton on Newton 3
    c.   Molly the Donkey 7
    d.   The Mayfly? – A God Sign? 10

Chapter Two: Church Visits- Baptist 14
    a.   Friendship Baptist & Antioch Baptist 14
    b.   Greater Progressive Baptist 17
    c.   Battle Creek Baptist 19
          i.   Parking in the Hay Fields 19
    d.   The Gathering Church 21
          i.   God Rocks & Born This Way 21
    e.   New Beginnings Baptist 25
    f.   Riverside Baptist 26
          i.   Location-Location-Location 26
    g.   Liberty Baptist 28
          i.   Better Together 28
    h.   Southern Hills Baptist 31
          i.   GPS: God's Positioning System 31
    i.   Metropolitan Baptist 33
          i.   The Vet and the Met 33

Chapter 3: Church Visits - Penecostal 36
    a. Reaching the World at World Outreach 36
    b. Russian River of Life... 38
        i. Big Mouth Billy Bass 38

Chapter Four: Church Visits- Methodists 42
    a. Route 66 – Tulsa Church Route................................. 42
    b. Asbury United Methodist Church 46
        i. BCOC & AUMC.. 46
    c. Centenary United Methodist 49
        i. Centenarian & Centenary & Centennial........... 49
    d. First United Methodist Church................................. 51
        i. A First at the First United Methodist Church ... 51

Chapter Five: Church Visits- Presbyterian 54
    a. The Korean Presbyterian & others............................. 54
    b. College Hill Presbyterian 57
        i. More Light College Hill 57
    c. The Kirk Ramp 59

Chapter Six: Church Visits- Nazarene 62
    a. Route 66 and K.T. & YFC @ JDC 62
    b. LifeChurch & Core Church....................................... 65
        i. Judging or Helping 65
    c. Central Nazarene 67
        i. The Mysterious Phone Call 67

Chapter Seven: Church Visits- Catholics 70
    a. Church of Saint Mary.. 70
        i. Fir mina Times Three....................................... 70
    b. Sacred Heart Catholic Church 72
        i. Sapulpa Church Drive 72

Chapter Eight: Church Visits- Seventh Day Adventist................. 75
    a. Splitting Logs and Jeans on the Sabbath 75

Chapter Nine: Church Visits- Episcopal 78
    a. U2 @ Trinity 78

Chapter Ten: Church Visits- Lutheran 80
    a. Grace Lutheran Church 80
        i. WWOW- Wonderful Wonders of Worship 80

Chapter Eleven: Church Visits-Mennonite 84
    a. Eden Mennonite in Langley, OK 84
        i. The Mennonite Visit.. 84

Chapter Twelve: Church Visits-Assembly Of God................................ 88
    a. Woodlake Assembly of God... 88
        i. The New WC... 88

Chapter Thirteen: Church Visits- United Church Of Christ................ 91
    a. Fellowship Congregational... 91
        i. A Good Parable 91

Chapter Fourteen: Church Visits- Non-Denominational..................... 95
    a. Westmoore in West Moore & New Life in Norman 95
    b. Landing Church in Glenpool, OK.. 98
        i. Cowboy Up 98
    c. Christ's Church of Owasso 99
        i. Hitch 'Em Up and Ride Again 99
    d. Life Church 101
        i. Free Movies & Popcorn...101
        ii. Free Movies & Cookies & Popcorn & Drinks 103
    e. The Rock Church 105
    f. Victory Church... 106
        i. Victory at Victory 106
    g. God's Shining Light... 108
    h. Foundations Church 111
        i. R U AN OU Redneck?.. 111
    i. Redeemed By Grace 113
        i. Diversified But United...113

    j. Discovery Bible in Owasso, OK...116
        i. No French Spoken 116
    k. Cowboy Gatherin' in Inola 118
        i. Cowboy Up 118
    l. Cowboy Church in Talala, OK 121
        i. Talala-Cowboy 121

Chapter Fifteen: Other Religious Visits... 124
    a. Jehovah Witness... 124
    b. Latter Day Saints 129
        i. LDS on New Haven 129
        ii. LDS & LSD: Latter Day Saints & Losing Sanity
            Disorder.. 132
        iii. LDS (Last Days Salvation)..135
        iv. LDS and 3 4 3 139
        v. LDS & Forwarding Address 142
        vi. LDS 1 4 4... 146
        vii. My Note and My Hope for Mormons...................... 148
    c. Muslim 150
        i. Legacy of a Prophet 150
        ii. Letter to Islamic 152
        iii. 7th Century & 21st Century Muslims 154
        iv. Tulsa Mosque: The Happy Mosque 157

Chapter Sixteen: Trip Experiences...165
    a. GOD IS ALIVE AND WELL! 165
    b. BGEA RRT (Billy Graham Evangelistic Association
        and Rapid Response Team)...173
        i. BGEA to Mena, Arkansas..173
        ii. BGEA to Joplin, Missouri..175
            1. Joplin and the Big Breezy 175
        iii. Joplin and the Boogie Woogie Rocks Nursing Home......178
        iv. BGEA to Moore, Oklahoma.....................................182
            1. The Dove Over Moore 182
        v. BGEA to Houston, Texas 186
            1. Houston & Harvey 186
    c. God's Way Is The One Way Always....................................189

Chapter Seventeen: Music 193
    a. Victory and Israel Houghton 193
        i. Israel in Tulsa, Israel Houghton that is 193
    b. Jesus Culture 195
    c. Lyrics for my song- GOOD NEWS 196
    d. Rap Song For Tom 198
    e. U2 Can Know JC 200

Chapter Eighteen: JDC- Juvenile Detention Center 201
    a. The Boogie Woogie Strikes Again! 201
        i. The JDC's at the JDC 204
            1. The Jesus Disciples Crew at the Juvenile
               Detention Center 204
    b. In God We Trust 207
    c. The Attitude Indicator 210
    d. THE ATTITUDE INDICATOR JDC 7/5/2015 211
    e. Illusions, Illustrations, Images 213
    f. Geese & Geezer (What's the Difference?) 216

Chapter Nineteen: Passion 219
    a. Passion 2013 219
    b. Passion and The Toothbrush 222
        i. Toothbrush closes down world's busiest airport 222
    c. PASSION 2016 226
    d. Passion 2017 YES! Or Passion 2017 NO! 228

Chapter Twenty: Scouting 234
    a. God's Bank 234
    b. BAM! BAM! Going for the Gold! BAM! BAM! 237
    c. The Sequel (QT & Muffins) 240
        i. Some things are not what they seem…. The Sequel 240
    d. E-Mail to A Scoutmaster 243
        i. Subject: Camp Tom Hale Chaplain 243

Chapter Twenty-One: Trail Life USA 245
    a. Trail Life Climbing 245

Chapter Twenty-Two: Miscellaneous 247
- a. The Phos Cross 247
- b. Whooooa! Whaaaaat A Weeeeek! 249
  - i. Earthquakes 249
- c. God and the Psychiatrist 251
- d. God's Whirlwind 256
- e. Stranger Payback 259
- f. Does God Still Speak to His People? 263
- g. The Perfect Mistake 264
- h. Tom's Retirement Celebration 265
- i. 3 in 2 & One Missed Skillet 268
- j. Psalm 44:4 270
  - i. "You are my King and my God" 270
- k. Christianity Today-Favorite Verses 272
  - i. Hmmm! Something to think about…. 272
- l. Football Sunday and Lakeview Baptist Church 274
- m. 'Y' God at the 'Y' 276
  - i. And a last name with a 'Y' 276
- n. Where is Paul Harvey and the Rest of the Story? 279
- o. 444 & 333 and the Anthem 281
- p. Post Oak Sewer Station 284

The Epilogue 287

Chapter One: God Using Living Things

The Fox at the Cross

Hello Tom,

I experienced something the other day at the Kirk that I thought you might find interesting. As a matter of fact, I will be using a version of what happened as one of my devotionals at Scout Camp this summer. I think I'll title the devotional: THE FOX AT THE CROSS.

With all the construction going on now at the Kirk and the headaches it creates along with the other problems at the Kirk and in the denomination, a few of us in our accountability group decided to meet at the Cross early one Thursday morning and pray. As you are aware, the hillside where the Cross is at may only be about 1/3rd of an acre. The patch of land there is in more or less a natural state except for a trail and some benches that some Eagle Scouts worked on.

As one member was starting to pray we saw a small, wild, red fox casually walk by us (not more than 20 feet away). The fox didn't bother to look at us but just walked by and on down the hill away from the Cross and out of our sight.

Why the fox was there? We have no idea! Did God plan it?? Maybe so! Why in the world would a fox be living in a small area like that surrounded by houses, streets and people? The fox looked like what they call a cross phase red fox which is native to this part of the country. It is reddish brown in color with a black band across the shoulders and a black line down the back, which forms a cross and gives it that name. Hmmm – a cross on a fox at the Cross. Makes you kind of wonder!

God Using Living Things

I mentioned it to Scott French later that day and he said: "Wow! Wouldn't it have been something if the Wednesday night youth group had met up there the night before like they had been doing? They have been studying 'Song of Solomon' and Wednesday night they were studying the part that included V 2:15 about the "little foxes".

The Bible mentions foxes several times – usually in the context of being devious, cunning and misleading. In Luke 13:32 Jesus compared Herod to a fox, because of his crafty, devious nature. In Judges 15:4 it was Samson who used 300 foxes to destroy the Philistine fields and vineyards. And again, in Song of Solomon in V 2:15 where the young women of Jerusalem are warned: "Quick! Catch all the little foxes before they ruin the vineyard…"

Was God reminding us to watch out for the little foxes in the church that can ruin relationships and destroy a church? Was he telling us to quickly take care of the little problems before they ruin the church? Was the fact that the fox was going away from the cross a hopeful sign?

The incident also brought back memories of my childhood when I was growing up and we had a couple of tracks of land within a half mile of the Kirk. On one track of land, about where the Laureate Center is now, there was a fox den. Could this fox have been one of the descendants?

Boy, God sure can make life interesting. It's Great isn't it.

A Brother in Christ,
David Cox

Sir Isaac Newton on Newton

My Church has a Mission Ministry called the Kirk Karpenters. Just about every weekend a team goes out to build a ramp for someone with a physical handicap that makes it difficult for them to go and come using steps or even a steep incline. Recently we started work on a small ramp for a wonderful Christian lady that usually had no one living with her to help her up and down some steps on her front porch. She didn't have a means of transportation except when she contacted the City of Tulsa and asked for a Handicap bus to pick her up just up Newton Street.

Let me tell you now, what happened on this project and what will get you to wondering if God has a message for us....

The MAN Upstairs showed up again on Newton Street thru our Kirk Karpenter trouble maker Jim S. Our team leader, Richard, had previously checked this project out and had all the materials needed for us to complete the ramp. This time, the project was on Newton, just west of Lewis Street. It was a very active street with an internationally blended neighborhood. I guessed about 50% White and 25% Black and 25% Hispanic, plus 3 horses, a dozen chickens, 1 rooster and a raccoon.

The first weekend on the project Dr. Jim B., an internist, discovered right off a raccoon trapped in a big plastic city trash container. Dr. Jim tilted the container so the Bandit raccoon could escape to its home down in a dark city sewer. Now I wonder what our other Doctor, our DVM, Dr. Paul might have done had he been there. One father, Bill, had shown up with his sons (Justin & Andrew), a couple of Jr. High boys.

The team was able to get a lot done on the first weekend with all the help and the extra help that showed up from the house next door. A couple of Jr. High Hispanic boys, Jose' & Christian, had observed Justin & Andrew in the morning and they wanted to help in the afternoon. Jose', which is Spanish for Joseph, as in Joseph & Mary, was quite the inquisitive one. He wanted to know what we were doing. Why we were doing it, who everybody was, and what did we charge. When I mentioned that Dr. Jim was a doctor, Jose' asked "Doesn't he worry about hurting his hands?" Then when I mentioned that one of the team members, David, has a fantastic voice and sings in the choir, Jose' asked what he sings. So, David sang a song for them a cappella. Our team leader, Richard, then

God Using Living Things

came over to talk to the boys and to try out his broken Spanish. The boys, who spoke perfect English, looked at Richard with a blank look. They either did not understand Spanish, or Richards Spanish was like a foreign language to them.

The ramp was up and useable that first weekend but some handrails and painting and carpet laying would have to wait until the next weekend. On that weekend, the day looked like rain and it did rain some. As we prepared to start to work, lo & behold, we heard the Crow of a Rooster across the street. Hmmm? A little late in the morning for a rooster to be crowing. And what was a rooster doing in the middle of town? Was there a message here? Mark 13:35-37 says: *"Therefore stay awake-for you do not know when the master of the house will come, in the evening, or at midnight,* **or when the rooster crows,** *or in the morning – lest he come suddenly and find you asleep. And what I say to you I say to all:* **Stay awake."**

Well we were hurrying to get as much done as we could before the rain came. Richard had wanted to talk with the lady but it just wasn't working out. THAT was when the MAN Upstairs used Jim S to work it out. Jim S was busy sawing a board with the electric saw when it just stopped working. No power. Jim & I figured that maybe someone had kicked the plug loose where it was plugged in, in the living room of the small house. Richard goes in the house to see. He was in there, and he was in there, and he was in there. When he finally comes out he calls everyone up to the porch so that we can pray with the lady of the house.

It seems when Richard went in the house, the cord was plugged in so the breaker must have blown. Oh! Oh! Jim S must have done something to cause that. The breakers were in the kitchen where the lady was doing some dishes. Richard could tell she was bothered about something and she just unloaded on him. It seems that her ex-husband and his girlfriend had shown up. They were homeless, so the Christian lady had invited them to stay with her. She may have thought it was a one-night thing. Evidently, they had been there for a few days and it looked like they might be settling in for a while, and it was stressing her out. She can hardly get around and it is a small one-bedroom house with one bathroom. And an air mattress was taking up most of the living room now making it even more difficult for her. As she filled us in about her problems, I am standing at the doorway and could see her ex sitting in the living room. I assume he can see us holding hands together and praying with her. This must have been Gods plan.

Richard and I later discuss what happened and Richard said "You know what? The timing was perfect for me to go in and talk with her." Hmmmm? We both reflected on what got him in there at that perfect time. Hmmmm? Surely God didn't use that troublemaker Jim again? Or did HE? And did HE use that rooster to wake us up and make us alert? Well, Well, Well, something to cogitate about, isn't it?

Oh Yes! Newton and Sir Isaac Newton. Now maybe you're very knowledgeable about Sir Isaac. But myself, something made me want to check him out some more. What I learned was that he is called one of the foremost scientific intellects of all times. He lived for 85 years (1642 to 1727). Besides being a mathematician, a physicist, and an astronomer…he was a theologian. As a matter of fact, it is said that he devoted more time to the study of scripture than to science. And he saw God as the Master Creator. Newton believed the system of the sun, planets and comets could only have come about thru an intelligent Being. Hmmm? And Newton was somewhat of a prophet. It seems he was telling people of his day that in about 400 years, but no earlier than the year 2060, that the world may experience a new change. Hmmm? Are Sir Isaac and the rooster and the MAN telling us to **WAKE UP?** And what about the Bandit raccoon running and hiding in the sewer when the Kirk team shows up? Now, the house isn't at 2060 Newton, but it may have been if there hadn't been something else unusual. This is a long street and at the west end, the houses are numbered in the 1900's. At the house at 1954, the next house number is 2104. What happened to 2000??? You go a block or two to the North and South and the houses all have house numbers in the 2000's. Did someone at the Post Office or with the Tulsa Engineering Department mess up about 90 years ago? Did God have a hand in that too?

Oh! And something else. When I made a visit back to the neighborhood about a week later. There was a City Street Warning sign up on Newton. It said 'ROAD CLOSED'. Yup! You couldn't get thru. It seems as though a big hole was being fixed in the middle of the block. Just about where the address of 2060 would have been. Hmmm!

My Oh My! A lot to wonder about, isn't it? But don't stay awake thinking about it, unless you haven't woken up yet. Do you still need to

God Using Living Things

WAKE UP? Then I invite you to check out the web site at www.BGEA.org and then click on 'How to Know Jesus'.

And if you haven't already viewed the documentary HOME-2009 to see how our planet is changing, you might want to check it out. The aerial videos are quite breathtaking and can give you a view of what it may look like from heaven. You may or may not totally agree with the message but you will marvel at the video photography. Our HOME is changing. Is it God? Is it man? In either case, are you READY? Is it time for you to do something? Go to www.youtube.com/watch%3Fv%3DjqxENMKaeCU.

Molly the Donkey

Hey Tom,

This last Wednesday the men's Bible Study at the Kirk was studying Numbers 22 and in particular verses 22 – 34 and Balaam's donkey. All of a sudden it brought back memories from 50 to 60 years ago and things that happened just within blocks of where I was now sitting at the Kirk.

Balaam's donkey story probably happened around 1450 to 1410 B.C., about 3,500 years ago. At that time the donkey was, and still is today in many underdeveloped countries, considered a person's or a families' most prized possession. They have great durability and longevity, living even up to 50 years of age. Their large ears enable them to hear sounds from far away distances. And their loud brays can be heard almost 2 miles away. Many people consider donkeys stubborn, but this can be understood when you realize that donkeys are more concerned about their self-preservation than horses or other animals. Thus, you cannot get a donkey to mind you if the donkey fears a dangerous situation.

I imagine this could be the reason God used Balaam's donkey to get Balaam's attention. The donkey sensed the danger ahead when it saw the Angel with the sword. And three different times the donkey balked and Balaam proceeded to beat it because it was making him look like a fool in front of the Moabites traveling with him. Finally, the donkey spoke up and asked Balaam why he was beating her. It is interesting that Balaam didn't pass out or act dumbfounded when the donkey started talking to him. Had Balaam and the donkey talked before? We do not know for sure. But, maybe you are like me in the fact that I have been known to talk to my pets and to carry on a conversation with them. Not one of them ever talked back to me though, even my pet donkey Molly. But my donkey and other pets had other ways of communicating.

My pet donkey lived on some acreage within a half-mile of the Kirk back 50 to 60 years ago (back before the Kirk was built and 61st & Yale was out in the country). Molly was probably my most favorite pet out of the dozens of different pets I had. On occasion, I would climb on board bareback and ride Molly down to the small airport located on the North-West corner of 61st & Yale. Sometimes I would tie her up and go in and eat

God Using Living Things

at the airport restaurant located in some woods West of the main runway. The building the restaurant was in is still there but has been converted into a residential home. The home is just about a block or two north of the Kirk Church. There were times however when Molly just got tired or maybe upset with me and would proceed to head for the nearest low hanging branch she could find, to walk under, in order to knock me off. Usually she was successful even with me pulling on the reins and doing everything else to prevent it, and in the process, making me look like a fool and she would be busy Hee Hawing! Hmmm! Now, after understanding more about Balaam and his donkey, was God using my donkey to set me straight? As I think back now on why I would ride my donkey bareback to the airport, I realize I was probably trying to show off, attract attention and build up my ego. Not exactly the attributes God would want me to have.

My redemption from being made a fool of by my donkey would come when my Domesticated, but threatening, white goose would get even with Molly for eating some of his food. The goose would clamp on to Molly's short, coarse tail and cause Molly to take off running with the goose hanging on to her tail for dear life. Molly would give an occasional kick with her rear hooves and if and when she connected with the goose you could hear a 'thunk' sound and then see the goose flying up in the air. I wondered how many times the goose would be able to do this and survive. Eventually, one day when I showed up, the goose was no longer to be found. He must have finally 'Cooked his goose'. And/or Molly, who had also been the goose's protector from the foxes that lived nearby, may have decided not to come to his rescue any more. Hmmm! How many times is God going to come to our rescue if we keep treating Him with disrespect?

Something you might not be aware of is that most donkeys have a Cross emblazoned on their back, as did my Molly. Hmmm! And Jesus road into Jerusalem on the back of a donkey with a cross on its back. Hmmm! God is pretty amazing isn't HE!

Now there were also the times that the dry weather had caused cracks in the ground, much like this summer, and Molly was not about to cross over those cracks for fear of possibly hurting herself. I would get off and plead with her and pull and tug on the harness, but all to no avail. Only when I would let her back up and turn right or left to go around the crack would she move on.

Sometimes God uses strange and different ways to try and communicate with us. Are we receptive? Or are we more like Balaam and resist and don't listen and then even get upset when HE is trying to communicate with us. Is God sometimes telling us to turn right, to turn left, or to even back up because there will be danger ahead if we keep on going in the same direction? We all need to get closer to God so that we can understand when HE wants to help us.

If you want to know more about God, then go to www.peacewithgod.net or www.knowJesus.net.

The Mayfly? – A God Sign?

Hey Tom, Wayne & others…. Yup! The KRR guy has some questions….

Check out the attachment showing some weird insect that got my attention on Monday morning Feb. 22, **Washington's Birthday**. As I was getting ready to enter my office, this tiny, tiny white insect caught my attention. The insect was on the outside of my glass window which has venetian blinds. Was it alive? It appeared to not have any wings, but the two arms that extended out from its pencil thin body gave the appearance that it was a glider. Hmmm! An insect that climbs and glides. Was God giving me a sign?

By the end of the day it was still in the same spot. Was it dead? Was it real? The next morning it was still there, but it had moved about six-inches. Jeffery, a Devout Nazarene, was checking in that morning and I pointed it out to him. His immediate comment was that it looks like a **Cross.** Jeffery wanted to see if it was alive so he gently blew on it and sure enough the little guy raised up on his legs about $1/8^{th}$ inch.

I decided to take a picture of it and pulled out a coin and stuck it on the window for size comparison. Hmmm! The coin has printed on it… ***IN GOD WE TRUST.*** And the face on the coin is **George Washington**. Hmmm! That's when the little guy appeared, on George's Birthday. God… What are you trying to tell me? Wednesday comes and the little guy is still there. Is God going to keep the little guy there until I figure out what HE's communicating to me? Also, on Wednesday the Tulsa World had an article headlined **Jenks Crossing** www.tulsaworld.com/business/jenks-crossing. The article didn't mention anything about the **Kirk Crossing Church** www.kirkcrossing.com but it appears that a new commercial and apartment development is about to be built on the property just east of the Church blocking the view from Highway 75. Thursday comes and the little guy is still there. By now I'm really concentrating more & more to what this is all about. You might remember my telling you about some of the ways God has communicated in the past… The Fox at the Cross, where a Cross Phase Red Fox appeared at the Kirk Cross in the middle of Tulsa in front of 4 of us when we were praying for the church because of some conflicts in the congregation. The Frog appearing in My Bedroom…right after I had read a religious message about a Million Frogs. The Mourning Dove.... that appeared to about 30 of us, in a single surviving tree after the tornado in Moore as we prepared to pray. It is absolutely amazing how many different and exciting ways God can give you a sign.

Well, early Friday morning, around 2 a.m., God finally got thru to me. I woke up feeling like HE wanted me to visit the **Kirk Crossing** on Sunday to see what was going on there. Then later Friday morning when I get to my office, the little guy is gone. I guess God figured I had finally got the message. So, Sunday finds me at **Kirk Crossing** and Pastor Dan is visiting that Sunday and giving the message from Exodus 10:1-6. The first comment from Pastor Dan was that he was glad to see the new sign out near the highway that tells people where the church is. Then he goes into the message about the Power, the Purpose and the Perpetuation of **Gods Signs.** Whoa! Exodus 10 and previous Exodus Chapters talk about some of Gods Signs.... the shepherd's staff becoming a snake, the frogs, the gnats, the flies., the boils, the hail, the locusts and then others throughout the Bible.

Pastor Dan went on to talk about the Book of John and 1:18 and 20:30-31 where Jesus' miraculous signs and the sign of the Cross tell us that He Himself is God, the One True God. Hmmm! Wasn't there a rumor not too long ago that maybe the Kirk Crossing could put up a 50' tall Cross to help people find the **way.** And then where did this new development come up with the name **Jenks Crossing.** Someone told me to check with Brother Steve who was in the lobby that morning. Brother Steve told me about the project and the 3-story apartments to be built out in front of the church. And then he said something interesting about the developer who was really impressed with the **Kirk Crossing** and had decided to tie-in with the name **Jenks Crossing.** But the next thing Brother Steve said really floored me. He said the developer is a God-fearing Mormon. What? You never see a Cross inside or outside a Mormon Temple or building. They have a reason. Are some of their members seeing a New Light? Hmmm! Over and over in the New Testament it mentions that the Cross represents the Living Christ.

After showing Brother Steve a pic of the little white insect, he suggested I talk with Brother Paul, a veterinarian. Brother Paul, when shown the picture, first said it was a dragon fly but then when he realized the smallness of it, he replied it must be of the Mayfly family. I looked them up on my search engine and did not see one pictured like my little guy. But then there are over 3,000 species of Mayflies and they look different in the different phases of their short life span. Dr. Paul also mentioned Mayflies are good for killing mosquito's. Hmmm! Maybe we need more of them right now with the Zika virus spreading as it is.

Hey! Everyone have a great day…and always be on the lookout for a sign from God.

Your KRR guy…. A BIC

And Oh! Also, on Washington's Birthday news about the officer who wrote the book about the Angel who rescued baby Lily and him a year ago. www.desertnews.com/She-rescued-me-officer-says. This officer, one of four on the scene, said the incident has transformed his faith. A Mormon, he admitted he was losing his faith and his religious background because of some prior experiences on the police force. But this experience has turned his life around. He now knows God in a more personal way.

Chapter Two: Church Visits- Baptist

Friendship Baptist & Antioch Baptist

Hello Tom,

Well this is your Roving Reporter. I've been staying out of trouble for the most part lately, but I thought I would fill you in on a couple of Church visits I made this spring here in Tulsa. North Tulsa, that is. Since you can't get away on Sundays to visit other Churches very often, I thought I would fill you in on what I see is going on. My real purpose for visiting some North Tulsa churches was to size them up and see if I could recommend some of them to some possible converts from my Laid-back Sidewalk Ministry here at Mall 31.

    I have visited Pastor Bumpers Church a few times in the past as well as Willie George's Church on the Move and their youth ministry, but I wanted to see if I could find a couple more churches. I visited a couple of Baptist churches thinking they would be similar, BUT Boy! what a difference between the two.

    The first one was Friendship Missionary Baptist Church where Weldon Tisdale is the Pastor. Sunday worship starts at 10:30. I figured 10:30 to noon, a little longer than the Kirk's. BOY! Was I wrong? I should have taken a sack lunch. It was 1:45 when I got out of there. I immediately felt comfortable when I entered; even though it was quite obvious I was the only White person there in a congregation of about 350. A nice lady usher greeted me and helped me find a seat. She seated me fairly close to the front and I slid in next to a guy who didn't look up until I sat down. HA! You should have seen the look on his face when he looked around and saw me.

Hmmm! Who's Speaking?

It was like he just saw a 'White Ghost'. We got to know each other fairly well over the next three & one-quarter hours though. There was a lot of congregational singing and praising with contemporary music and I felt I blended right in. The congregation was asked to stand up and be sociable and greet the others around you. Then Pastor Tisdale asked all the 1st time visitors to stand up and be recognized. Well, I didn't feel like I needed to stand up to be recognized (I was pretty recognizable as it was), but after 2 or 3 requests he looked at me and said: "Well if you don't want to stand up, then at least raise your arm up and turn and wave to everybody." I obliged. Just as he was getting ready to start his sermon, he said: "I had a prepared sermon, but God just asked me to do another one, so if the choir would sing another 2 or 3 hymns I'll prepare for another sermon." Well this 1-hour sermon was on tithing, and it was pretty hard hitting and yet with humor tossed in. The piano player kept a close eye on the Pastor and when it was needed (maybe on signal) a little drum roll was played. After the sermon it was time for the offering and Pastor Tisdale asked everyone to come forward and put their offering in the bucket…. But the first to come forward would be the 'Tithers'. After the 'Tithers' then he said "all you want-a-be tithers can come up now." This is a 'Loving' Church and you feel loved almost immediately regardless of your race or dress (by the way, I was underdressed…everybody else had on their Sunday Best).

The next church I visited a couple of weeks later was Antioch Baptist on 56th St. North where the Pastor is M.C. Potter. About the only similarities between these two Baptist churches was that each one had a choir of about 14 women and one man and about 350 in the congregation. Tom, do you remember Louis Farahkhan? I think he grew up in this church. I immediately felt I was not welcome. No one greeted me. No one acknowledged me. When I entered the sanctuary, everyone was sitting down listening to the choir. There were about 6 ushers who were all dressed the same and standing at attention. Long sleeve white shirts with black ties, black pants and shoes. They stood at attention with their left arm behind their back with no expression on their faces. As you started down an aisle they would bring their right arm up and point to a row for you to sit in. Only the Choir would sing the whole time while the congregation remained in their seats. When it came time to recognize visitors, I was not recognized, only those who had previously been welcomed and had their names presented to the Pastor. Pastor Potter announced from the pulpit that it was time to formally recognize the visitors. He said: "As I call out your name, stand and be recognized." He would call out a name and a visitor would stand up and the congregation clapped 3 times. There were three sections of pews and when it came time for the offering Pastor Potter announced that everyone would come forward and put their offering in the bucket. He announced for: "the two outside sections to Stand Up, turn to the right, and starting with the back row first, march forward, and the next row to fall in behind them." After they finished he announced for: "the Center Section to Stand Up, turn to the right, and starting with the back row first, march forward." Tom, I thought I was in the Army again. There were many young families there and I can tell you this…the kids of these families are so well structured that I do not believe a one of them will be getting into any drugs or trouble. However, after being there, I did not feel this was the place to suggest any of my possible New Converts to visit.

Well, there it is for now Tom. My next assignment is to visit a couple of Hispanic Churches. With the little knowledge of Spanish, I have, I'm thinking of keeping my mouth shut for fear if I attempt something it will be sooo wrong that I could get thrown out.

Your Brother in Christ,
David Cox

Post Note… You know, I have visited several African-American Churches and by far the majority of them welcomed me with open arms and friendliness. Probably fully realizing that I may be a one-time visitor, they wanted me to know that I was welcome anytime and I appreciated that. I hope and pray that all White-American Churches reciprocate that feeling of welcoming too when obvious visitors attend their services

Greater Progressive Baptist

Hey Tom & Wayne, your KRR again,

I was able to visit a real neat Church at 1970 N. Boston today. It is the Greater Progressive Baptist Church, known as 'The Church on the Island'. Does that have a familiar ring to it?? It is literally right in the middle of a round-about. It was built in 1915 and the architecture is still very appealing. It has a red brick exterior, trimmed in white. The Chapel has seating for about 150.

Services were to start at 11 a.m. and I walked in right at 11. Guess What? There was no one there. So, I started looking around at the inside of the Church and it was so neat and clean you could tell the members take a real interest in keeping it looking that way. About 5 after, one of the members comes walking in and asked me if I was looking for someone. I said I was thinking about attending services and if they were going to have services today. She said yes but it would be a little while yet. I went back outside, got in my SUV and thought I'd go visit another Church, but something held me back (could it have been God?). We never know do we? In about 10 minutes a distinguished gentleman comes walking out of another building attached to the Chapel, catches my eye and I get out to greet him. I could tell by the pictures I had seen inside that it was Reverend James Smith Sr. I told him I was thinking about attending services there today and explained how much I enjoy visiting other Churches. He said this is a small church with older members. He invited me to stay (probably because I looked old and would blend right in, except for the color of my skin). I jokingly mentioned attending Rev. Tisdale's church a while back and the services went until 2 p.m. and I probably would not be able to stay that long. He said services usually go until about 1:30 and that I was sure welcome to stay.

Service got started about 11:30 and there were 7 members in attendance and 4 grandchildren. One little boy about 4, attached himself to me and filled me in on everything he knew and could do. He was a real livewire. All 7 members had one or more responsibilities…2 in the choir, 1 usher, 1 for announcements, 2 for the offering, and then the Pastor.

This church is a 'Blessing' Church. They Bless God for everything

Church Visits- Baptist

in their lives...no matter however small we think it might be. Three of the members were using canes and yet they Blessed God too. This is the second Black Church I've been to where the minister said he had a sermon prepared but he was changing it today. Hey Tom & Wayne how often do you do that? Anyway, he said he was going to make his sermon shorter today (and everyone said Amen!) Hmmm! You don't think I had anything to do with that do you?

Well sure enough, he was finished by 12:50.

The brick on the Church still looks to be in great condition, but the white trim is in dire need of a good paint job. Do you think our Church could help out this Church with a paint crew? It would probably take a couple of hundred dollars in material and about 100 hours of labor. This could be a great opportunity for a small group, or the Kirk Karpenters, or the Bob Class to make a real difference in this little Church and its members. Maybe a two week-end project and then we go on our way, but what a difference it would make with our members and their members. Churches Helping Churches.

Hey, this is just a thought. If you feel it has some merit, then have someone check it out.

Your BIC,

p.s. Tom, this guy has a Great Preaching and Singing Voice…. Well of course, not quite as good as yours Tom…But Almost

Battle Creek Baptist

Parking in the Hay Fields

Hey Tom & Wayne, guess who? Yep! The KRR guy......

Things to come?? Sunday, I visited The Church At Battle Creek (CABC). About 5 years ago I visited there shortly after Alex Mihaya became the pastor. At that time, they had about 500 members. They now are at over 5,000. They just added a new sanctuary about a year ago that seats about 2,000 and they have outgrown it. As you may recall, they originally had purchased a vacated mini-mall shopping center on 129th East Ave. near the B.A. Expressway.

Well Sunday at the 11 a.m. service, I had to park in the hay fields because the paved parking lot was full. The 2,000-seat sanctuary was full and they had TV screens set up in another room for the overflow crowd. They hold two services at 9 & 11 a.m. Alex said that on Easter Sunday they had over 300 people to inquire about membership.

CABC is affiliated with the Southern Baptist and they have a second location in Pryor. As I was leaving their services I walked thru the Mall and discovered several Hispanics coming out of another room. What I figured out is that they must have a Hispanic group that meets at the same time and watches the main service on video while someone interprets the message into Spanish for them. That way they do not distract from the main service and yet hear the same message with their family and friends.

The worship music and message are contemporary with lots of new electronic enhancements. Chris Pyron might want to check some of it out. Several times they were showing the scripture on the screen when Alex was talking about it and when Alex mentioned that this certain word meant this.... well a pencil would show up on the screen and write in above the word what he was saying.

Not that I am implying anything, but for your own information.... Alex had a long sleeve shirt on with the sleeves rolled up and the tail hanging out over his slacks. And Tom, he had on sandals with no socks. There were several props on the stage that tied in with his message (The Little Red Wagon) and to me the message was geared to the local congregation and not a canned Southern California message. The congregation was largely young families with lots of kids. 85% white and 15% Hispanic and black. The church is in an area of newer homes, many of them very nice, and yet an area that is not too far from apartment dwellers and an area where Hispanics are moving to.

Five years ago, I could get a free coffee at a small area in the middle of the mall. Now, they have a large Cappuccino bar next to their book store in a large area just before you go into the new sanctuary. And the Cappuccino is not Free any more. Oh Well! It looks like they don't need the Free coffee to get members anymore anyway. And it might keep Freeloaders like me away too.

As Always…. Your BIC…the KRR guy

Oh Yes! Wouldn't you know it. Right after the paper comes out with our Church expansion plans, the 1st Presbyterian has to announce their $30 mil remodeling plans. Their membership declines with very little expectation of increasing and they use the money on something unnecessary. My Oh My! Could that money have been used for the Glory of God in some other way?

The Gathering Church

God Rocks & Born This Way

Hey Tom and Wayne, the KRR guy out Rockin Again….

I made it to 'The Gathering' Church Sunday. They meet at Thoreau School on 71st St on Sundays from 10:30 to noon. They are in the middle of a series called 'God Rocks' right now. What got me there was interesting. I had heard that possibly a Wiccan Church had come to Tulsa so I got on my search engine to check it out. I typed out Wiccan Churches in Oklahoma and then Wiccan Churches in Tulsa. In both instances, the Gathering Church popped up at the top of the page under 'Sponsored Links'. Now I was pretty sure they weren't Wiccan, but when I saw a short blurb about God Rocks and messages of artists coming up from Coldplay to Lady Gaga, I got to wondering.

I am pleased to say that they are a Very Christ Centered Church. Pastor Brad Jenkins is just giving a message each week about the lyrics in certain popular songs and tying them to Scripture. This Sunday it was the song "If I Die Young", a popular Country Western song with some of the lyrics attributed to the poet Tennyson. Brad started off with the music video of the song. Then Brad had several scriptures he referred to (Job 14:5, Psalm 139:16, James 4:14, Psalm 90:12, Philippians 1:21 and 1st Corinthians 15:55-58). He also tied it in to a Rick Warren quote and Psalm 39:4-5.

I'm tempted to go back next week when the song is 'Born This Way' by Lady Gaga. Brad says the timing of this message is appropriate with all the Hubbub about Chick-Fil-A.

I did talk to a couple of the techies about the 'Sponsoring' thing with the Wiccans and sent an email to Brad. Hey, they ought to check it out. It could be a Positive + or a Negative -. A (-) if it turns Christians or would-be Christians away from coming, but if it happens to get some Wiccan seekers there and the Gathering can set them straight, then it could be a (+).

They had about 70 people in attendance in an auditorium for 450 so they are going to experiment with some room dividers for the time being so that it will not look too empty. Very casual dress, mostly blue jeans, and everyone had hair and the hair wasn't grey either… if you catch my drift.

Church Visits- Baptist

Oh Yes.... I was out on a Kirk Karpenter job Saturday. It was a handicap ramp for a fantastic Christian family. Richard's email invite had said something about the family fixing lunch for the team. Now, that wasn't the only reason I showed up. BUT, it may have been the most important reason. When we got there Richard wanted to know if I wanted to do some 'Rioting' and I got all excited. I could see me going up and down the street shouting out "Do you know Jesus?" and causing a public uproar about Jesus Christ and the 2nd Coming. But then it turned out he said 'Routing' as in carpenter work. That type of 'Routing' is shaping unfinished wood to produce a fine finished product. Some similarity to what our Jewish Carpenter does. Oh Well! I guess I had better get my hearing aids checked.

Keep on 'Truckin' for Jesus guys, and watch out for me.... I'll be out here Rockin and Rioting... Your BIC, the KRR guy.

Hmmm! Who's Speaking?

Hey Tom....Hey Wayne, the KRR guy again...

I had to go back. Yup! I couldn't stay away from the 2nd Part of the Series of 'GOD ROCKS' at The Gathering Church. I know. I know. I may have sinned but I WAS BORN THIS WAY. The temptation by the tempter, the witchcraft by Lucifer, the fascination and enticement by the ruler of darkness drew me back. I had to find out about Lady Gaga and her song "Born This Way".

Well, Hands Up for the Pastor, Brad Jenkins. He did it again. A great and timely message. He started it off with the ? of what we should ask ourselves. "What do I need to do to follow Jesus?" Then he said "What does the song say and then what does the Bible say?" Brad filled us in a little about Lady Gaga (real name Stephanie). Born in 1986 (26 years old now). She went to a Catholic school and maybe some of her school experience influenced this song. Some of the lyrics may be right on, but some of them are not Scripture based. The song deals with homosexuality and Brad pointed out that in the First Book in the Bible and in the First Chapter (Genesis 1:27-28) that God created people as a male and a female and to go and multiply.

We all have inclinations and some will lead us down the wrong path. If broke...Do we steal? If we're running late...Do we speed? In John 3:3 Jesus says: "I assure you, unless you are born again, you can never see the Kingdom of God." We are first born from our mother and we may have certain inclinations. Yes, we may each be born a certain way, but we must be Born Again to change those inclinations. And the inclinations are not sins. It is the 'Acting Out' of those inclinations that is the sin.

Brad said that Christians should speak the Truth to others. But still show our Love. What is Love? What is Judging? In John 1:14, John tells us that Jesus came full of GRACE (Love) and TRUTH. Jesus walked and talked with sinners. He loved them and He wanted them to know the truth.

Brad suggested that everyone look up and read other Scriptures such as:

Genesis 1:27-28; 2:18-24; 19:4-9
Leviticus 18:22; 20:13

Matthew 19:4-6
Romans 1:20-27
1 Corinthians 5:9-13; 6:9-20
Ephesians 5:22-33
1 Timothy 1:9-10

God's Desire is...1 man & 1 woman and to have a lifelong commitment. Sexual Sin is not only wrong, it is Destructive. The <u>Sin is the Action</u> – Not the inclination. God wants us to Judge Not, but to help people get out of sin.

Brad reminded us that God loves homosexuals just as much as everyone else. And he reminded us of other sexual sins and in John 8:3-11 where Jesus forgives the adulterous woman.

A Billy Graham quote when he was asked his opinion on homosexuality..." *I'm going to quote the Bible now, not myself. That if Homosexuality is wrong, it's a sin. But there are other sins, so why do we jump on that sin as though it is the Greatest sin?"*

I pulled up www.catholic.com and the Catholic answers to Homosexuality and it is interesting reading. They even (in 2004 when Lady Gaga was 18) approached the argument "I Was Born This Way". Hmmm.... Interesting isn't it?

Hey Hey.... your BIC, the KRR guy

New Beginnings Baptist

Hey Tom, Wayne & Dan.... the KRR guy one more time,

I visited the New Beginnings Church on 151st off of Hwy 75 today. They are listed as a Southern Baptist Church in the yellow pages but I did not see any mention of that on their web site nor on any of the printed material I saw or picked up at the church. And from my visit there I certainly did not get the feel that it was Southern Baptist.

    I attended their 9:30 service which was light in attendance because of Spring Break I am sure. The sanctuary would seat about 800 I would say and there were about 100 in attendance at the 9:30 service. If you have driven down Hwy 67 (151st St.) between Bixby & Glenpool in the last couple of years you would have noticed this new church on the south side. From its appearance and location, I guessed the membership would be mainly young families. And just outside the sanctuary there were some climbing towers and slides for the little ones and a coffee and refreshment bar for the more mature. To my surprise however, at the 9:30 service, there were more old and retired people than young families. AND, the music was Contemporary with a Worship Band of young people. AND a few members were lifting their arms up in Praise of God. This certainly didn't resemble the old Southern Baptist Churches I've visited in the past. Maybe that is their reason for not really publicizing their association with the SBC.

    I noticed they have a regular Wednesday evening dinner before their classes and studies. Hmmm! Maybe I should check that out. (The classes of course! And well, maybe the dinner too!) A BIC.... the KRR guy.

Riverside Baptist

Location-Location-Location

Hey Tom, Wayne & others….the KRR guy out and about again,

I had an invite to visit a Baptist Church recently and I took the invite up. It seems the Church has a dwindling membership and they have been trying to figure out what to do. The inviter perhaps wanted to get some input from an outsider.

As my headline states Location is important in many areas in the business world and that often wholes true for Churches too. When Eastland Mall was first being developed it was expected to attract nearby housing development and customers from out of town from the near north like Owasso. From the mid-80's to mid-90's it was in its heydays, but then housing didn't sprout up because of Limestone problems in the area and then towns like Owasso begin to build their own big shopping complexes and new highways made it easier to get to other shopping areas like Woodland Hills. Eastland became a ghost Mall but finally a new use for it came along and now it is the Eastgate Complex.

Recently a Vietnamese Restaurant closed on 51St near Yale and moved to Admiral & Garnett in order to be closer to where the majority of the Vietnamese live in Tulsa which would be better for their business. These are just a couple of examples in the business world where things can change and affect your business and attendance. This can be very true in the Church world too.

The Riverside Baptist Church at 64th & South Peoria opened around 1955 and was literally out in the country at the time but as time went on Tulsa expanded to the South and the Church had its heydays so to speak for many years. The heydays and the days of growth are behind it now however and it needs to revamp and look to its future. Traffic on Peoria got diverted to Riverside Drive and this section of Peoria is a narrow unattractive two-lane street. The make-up of the neighborhood has also changed and is not an area that attracts as many younger or older church friendly families that it used to.

The Minister, Pastor Jonathan, had a good message and a good presentation that day but unfortunately it only reached out to 25 people, mostly retirees and a couple of the retirees' children who now are adults themselves. They were all very friendly and welcoming and it was obvious that I was the only stranger among them and they all wanted to greet me.

They do need to continue to get together and discuss their future as the maintenance and attendance will continue to get worse and become an even bigger problem. I understand that a Burmese Church is now meeting there at another time on Sundays and since there are around 3,000 Burmese in Tulsa, and maybe many in this area, that maybe they should be considered a good prospect to purchase the Church property. Then the remaining Baptist members could continue meeting there at another time or maybe they could seek another location that could even be more convenient to their residences and more attractive to new members. I wish them well and pray that God will guide them in their decision.

The KRR guy.... A BIC

Post script ... This last Sunday I visited the Bixby Life Church on 121st between Sheridan & Memorial at 8:30 a.m. A new church in a new area filled with big beautiful homes and nice streets. They had about 150 in attendance at this early service and I would say about 1/3rd of them were in their 50's & up and many of them with grey hair like me. I think this is pretty good considering the contemporary service and the loud & jumping worship. This Life Church (1 of 25 now) will be having 11 Services on Easter Weekend. This Church Pastor had an interesting testimony... he was not a Church-goer for years, but had a friend who kept inviting him & his wife and finally after two years they attended and found Christ in their lives. So, his advice was to invite someone to church on Easter and if they don't come...don't give up on them.

Liberty Baptist

Better Together

Hey Tom, Wayne, & Others…the KRR guy out and about

Well God directed me to another church this last Sunday. A couple of weeks back my son and I had received a coupon for a buy one fish dinner and get another one for half price. Well we couldn't pass that up. The restaurant is on 71st near Garnett Rd. and after enjoying our dinner we headed home and the shortest & less busy route was South on Garnett Rd. Well at 77th & Garnett Rd. on the East side was a new temporary sign that said **Ethiopian Church Meets Here Sunday @ 10:30. What**? An Ethiopian Church right here in Tulsa? So, the next day I got busy on the web to see what I could find out about Ethiopians. Well you will find in Ethiopia, located on the Horn of Africa, that about 2/3rds of the population are Christians. Very interesting, but you know I couldn't find any information about this Tulsa Ethiopian Church. Something came up about Ethiopian Church nyc but that turned out to be New York City. And an Evangelical Ethiopian Church is affiliated with Victory Bible College in Tulsa. And there is a new Ethiopian Café in Tulsa. Hmmm! I might have to check that out too. Since I was totally confused now I sort of put the Church aside and thought the next time I was in that area I would re-check that sign. Now I'm maybe on that stretch of Garnett Rd. maybe once a year or maybe every other year, but God wanted me back sooner than that.

Yup! Just about a week later I had to go back down that stretch of Garnett Rd. to pick up a sick Grandfather, a clock that is. This time I noticed a more permanent sign that said **Liberty Church** but nothing else. I'm thinking what's going on here. Is Liberty an Ethiopian Church? I had better look that up. Well things were getting a little clearer now. Did you know that stretch of Garnett Rd. is the dividing line between Tulsa & Broken Arrow? If I had typed in Ethiopian Church Broken Arrow I could have found it. But now, Liberty Church Broken Arrow has got my attention. It is affiliated with the Southern Baptists and just recently the minister there, Pastor Paul, after being the minister there for 30 years was thinking that the Church should be looking for a new Pastor. Well God had the whole thing planned out but Pastor Paul wasn't aware of it yet. With the help of Trinity Broadcasting Network (TBN) Pastor Paul was introduced to a young Lead Pastor, Brad Jenkins in Tulsa. Brad is the Pastor with the Gathering Church that was formed with the help of Tulsa's Southern Hills Baptist Church. Now the Gathering Church is not to be confused with the Gathering Place being built on the River except that the Church is an exciting place to go to also and will be even more so in the near future. The Gathering Church is on 71st just West of Memorial St. and has been meeting in the Thoreau School for the last several years.

You might remember back in 2012 when I visited the Gathering Church a couple of times and was so impressed with Pastor Brad that I promised to pray for them that they would find a permanent Church Building. At that time, Pastor Brad was doing a series of messages entitled GOD ROCKS (two messages attached). Now I've driven past that Church about once or twice a month for the last 4 years and I always Lift them up that they will soon find a permanent building. Well God is now Bringing Two Great Churches together and they will be BETTER TOGETHER. You can find more information about what has happened and what the timeline is by going to www.libertychurchba.com. It is exciting to see how quickly God is putting this altogether. They will have their Inaugural Service as one New Church on Sunday, August 7th. When the Bible says as in *2nd Peter 3:14…And so, dear friends, while you are waiting for things to happen, make every effort to live a pure and blameless life. And be at peace with God.* Well, the Gathering Church has been patiently waiting for several years and now when God says the time is now…Watch out because HE's moving fast.

My personal concerns were completely alleviated when I visited Liberty Church this last Sunday. The Gathering is a young church with nary a grey hair in the place. I remember that when I visited there before and enjoyed the contemporary worship and noticed everyone being in their 20's and 30's. Now how is a Church like Liberty going to blend in? WELL, Liberty already has a contemporary worship and the dress is very similar to what was at the Gathering. Even one young man on the Worship team had on shorts. The Worship leader even talked about a song written by Chris Tomlin (*The Only One*). Tomlin is one of my favorite Worship leaders connected with Passion which reaches out to hundreds of thousands of

Church Visits- Baptist

College age students. And even though Liberty had more grey hair, most of it was still mixed in with natural color, so folks mainly in their 40's & 50's and few grey hairs for those in their 60's. What a perfect blend this New Church is going to be.

Since the Liberty 10:30 Service had about 200 people in attendance and seating for about 300 I questioned how they could fit in another 150 to 200 from the Gathering. A nice couple filled me in and said they can re-arrange the chairs and get more in or they can go to a 9:00 a.m. and 10:30 service year-round or add more services or build a new building (they have 20 acres to expand upon). They said "Oh! How wonderful it is to have a problem like this for the future." How true that is.

And Oh! Now about the Ethiopian Church? They do meet there at Liberty on Sundays at 10:30 too but in another part of the building. I asked one young man about that and if he had ever attended and he said yes, he had. But he said they speak in Ethiopian. Well that leaves me out unless they can accommodate visitors with a translator like other Churches have done for me in the past. And Oh! That helps explain why I saw three Yellow Cabs in the parking lot too. May God Bless these Christian Ethiopians and help them grow too.

Hey Hey......your BIC, the KRR guy

Southern Hills Baptist

GPS: God's Positioning System

Hey Wayne, Dan and Others…. the KRR Guy out and about again,

Last week I made it to the 9:30 Contemporary Worship service at the Kirk and I planned on visiting another Church I had been invited to that had services beginning at 11. The early Service at the Kirk was well attended. By 9:30 it was practically full with about 200 in attendance. They had about 12 rows of seating with sections of 5, 10, 10 & 5 seating. Well a family of 5 came walking in late and in my observance, they were going to have to split up. BUT, God had other plans. One of the ushers that morning, Alex, saw them coming in and recognized them as First Time Visitors. Now there were plenty of empty seats on the front row, BUT who, ever wants to be seated on the front row and especially when you're late and a First-Time visitor. Well maybe you would if you were of High School or College age. Well God must have had this all planned out because lo & behold there was one 5 chair section about half way down that no one had sat in.

    I could tell that Alex was excited about having the perfect seating for this family. I hit him up later and asked him if he had known they were coming and if he had this seating all planned out or if GPS was somehow involved. He immediately replied that this family were First Timer's and that God had it all planned out. God's Positioning System (GPS) works out every time.

    You know I visit Churches all the time and I have visited several hundred or so and when I am late I can always sneak in the back and will hardly be noticed. But recently I visited the Southern Hills Baptist Church and thank goodness, I was on time because if I had been late, everyone would have noticed. Yup! This is the only Church I know where you enter the Sanctuary immediately to the left or right of the stage & podium. Whoa! I did notice that nobody arrived late at their Service and this may be why. And, get this, most of the front row seating was filled. Maybe it's because those are the first seats you come to but I also noticed those seats were basically filled with High Schoolers. And this is something else I have observed at various Churches. Whenever I see the front rows filled, it is usually with young people. What is it with them? Are they prouder of their relationship with Jesus than the rest of us and not afraid to show it? Hmmm! ~ Something to check into.

And Oh! The GPS (God's Positioning System) kept me from making it to the Methodist Church I had been invited to. This Church is located right in the center of a square mile of nothing but homes between 31st & 41st and Memorial Rd. & Mingo Rd. Signage to the Church was pitiful and the streets turn and curve every which way and so I got turned around and was going to be late by the time I located it. And then by the time I found it, guess what? I was having terrible indigestion pains. Now that never happens to me, so I finally decided the 'GPS' was positioning me to go on and sure enough as soon as I headed off, my indigestion got better. Hmmm! Oh Well! Maybe God's GPS will lead me there another time.

Psalm 5.8… *Lead me in the right path, O LORD, or my enemies will conquer me. Tell me clearly what to do, and show me which way to turn.*

The KRR guy….. A BIC and remember to use your GPS (God's Positioning System) whenever and wherever you go

Metropolitan Baptist

The Vet and the Met

Hey Wayne, Dan and others…. the KRR guy out and about….

A couple of Sundays' ago, God used one of the Kirk's Veterinarians, the horse vet, to catch my attention. He suggested I check out a Black Church near where he lives out on Apache. He told me when he leaves his place to head for the Kirk 9:30 Service he drives by this Metropolitan Baptist Church and the lot is always full around 9 a.m. And then when he goes back by after attending the Kirk, and it may be as late as 12 or 12:30, the Church lot is still full. I commented that I have visited several Black Churches and some of their services run 2 to 3 hours, but this one sounds like it may run 3 to 4 hours. I told him I would have to think about that and see if I can figure out if God really wants me to visit there. I was not familiar with this Church at all and had not heard of its name.

Well, God got my attention about a week later when I heard the Church's name brought up on the news on TV. Yes! This was one of the first Churches to reach out to the community after the Crutcher shooting by the Tulsa Police. Crutcher nor his family belonged to this Church but this Church, the Tulsa Metropolitan Baptist Church was reaching out to the community. They invited the community to a vigil, a sort of devotional alertness to what had happened. The Church Sanctuary will seat 700 but they had about twice that many show up for the vigil. OK God! You used the Vet and the Met news to get my attention. And then on Sunday (9/25), everything just clicked off and the timing was perfect for me to arrive at their 9 a.m. Service. And in my checking it out before my visit, I discovered that they have two Sunday Services…one @ 9 and one @ 11, so they do not have one 3 or 4-hour service, but two services. Hey, that could give me time to attend another Church with an 11 o'clock Service.

In arriving on time, the first thing I observed was that every vehicle was parked forward facing the Church. Hmmm! That wasn't an easy thing to do unless you were one of the early arrivals, but I managed to park my

Church Visits- Baptist

car in the appropriate direction like the rest of them. I am curious why they park this way but after Attending their Great Service I think it could be that the whole congregation looks <u>forward</u> to attending the Church. Or maybe it could be that they respect God and they do not want to have their back turned to HIM but to always be ready to go <u>forward</u> with HIM. Or maybe it is to show that they are looking <u>forward</u> to being with God forever.

Out of the about 300 or so for the 9 o'clock Service, I was the only one there with white hair. That didn't mean that I was the oldest one there, but by far the majority were younger than me, and those who may have been around my age had bald heads. I noticed a couple of men sitting toward the back who did not have on a coat & tie so I asked if I could join them figuring that section was reserved for those of us who did not blend in with the predominate attire. There were a couple of ladies near me who offered me breath mints and kindly kept me informed on when to stand up and when to sit down.

The music ministry was amazing as usual as with all the Black Churches I have attended. The minister, Dr. Ray Owens, then opened up with a short brief on the vigil held the last week. He then went on and led everyone in Prayer for the city, for the police dept., the Crutcher family, the Police Officer Shelby and her family and the whole country. Then his message for the day was all about the **Power of Prayer** and related it to Hezekiah in 2 Kings 20:1-6. He mentioned the comparison here of the **Power of Prayer** as opposed to the violence in North Carolina. Prayer is always stronger than violence. And not just with Hezekiah but in other parts of the Bible God has changed his mind about punishing people when they turn directly to Him in Prayer and ask for His help.

Well God led me to the MET at a 'Special' time, not just for the recent unfortunate incident here in Tulsa but also for the MET's 100th Anniversary in Tulsa coming up next September (2017). You can check them out at <u>www.metropolitanbc.org</u> or attend a Service there at 1228 West Apache St. Just remember if you attend to park facing <u>Forward.</u>

Hey God…Thanks for using the Vet & the Met to get me to this Great Place of Prayer.

The KRR guy…. A BIC

And Oh! I might mention to our Horse Vet… that on this same Sunday, my 13-year-old Grand Daughter got her Prayers of several years answered on this her 13th Birthday with the gift of a horse from some of her friends.

Chapter 3: Church Visits - Penecostal

Reaching the World at World Outreach

Hey Tom…. Hey Wayne…the KRR guy again, out and around,

God directed me and my son to visit the World Outreach Church on 91st St. a couple of weeks ago. We had planned on going to a Lifechurch.TV but when we noticed we would be late because it was a little after 10:30, my son mentioned about visiting somewhere else. He doesn't like to be late for Church (he doesn't take after me). Well then something hit me about visiting World Outreach since it was close by and I figured they might start at 11. We drive up and 3 or 4 cars in front of us pull into the drive so I figured we were right on time. But, lo & behold the whole parking lot was full and we had to park way out in the North forty. But, just as we got out a guy in a golf cart offered us ride to the entrance door.

Well when we get inside we discovered that the Worship had already started at 10:30. My son remembered being in this building before several years ago when our Cub Pack visited there when I believe it was called the International Church. Mark & Janet Brazee, the Ministers with World Outreach, moved into the building a couple of years ago.

The Worship, led by Janet, went until about 11:30 and then Mark gave about a 45-minute message with some announcements. The music was contemporary with about 15 singers and band players. There were about 750 in attendance and everyone was dressed casually, but conservative. No jeans, no ties, no coats, mostly slacks and a dress shirt.

I got the impression that they were Pentecostal and Mark mentioned they were Full Gospel. My son didn't think they were Pentecostal though because he had visited a Pentecostal Church in Purcell, OK a few years back and at that Church most of the men had crew cuts and the women all had long hair, many with a bun. And they didn't talk or pray in tongues like they were doing at World Outreach.

I ran into Bill Collier, an ORU Professor, in the salad line the following Wednesday at the Kirk and asked him about that. About 15 minutes later Wayne comes up and joins in the conversation. Here I was caught between these two theological intellectuals and hearing more than I ever planned on knowing about Full Gospel, Pentecostal, Nazarene and Assembly of God Churches. As it turned out, the Pentecostals have several different divisions within their denomination like the Presbyterians, Baptists and other denominations and like other religions like the Muslims. For instance, if you have ever checked the Yellow Pages under Baptists you will find American, Free Will, Independent, Fundamental, Missionary, National, Reformed and Southern Baptist. They may have some similarities and then some differences too. And some religions and denominations may have some radical differences among them.

Well that's all the news for now…bundle up, stay warm and spread the Good News for all…. the KRR guy, a BIC

Russian River of Life

Big Mouth Billy Bass

Hey Tom, Wayne and others…. the KRR guy out and about again

Do you all remember the popular wall plaque with the singing fish? Very popular around the years 2000 to 2005. It could make you happy hearing and watching it no matter how bad your day was. It had a couple of songs…" Don't Worry, Be Happy" by Bobby McFerrin and "Take Me to The River" by Al Green. I happen to have one at my office and recently I was trying to figure out what Worship songs to play for the boys at the Juvenile Detention Center…and God must have got my attention as someone walked by and tripped Big Mouth Billy Bass to sing his two songs, so I decided to take Billy Bass to the JDC and tie it in with what God is always trying to tell us. Hey! Get to know Me and I will take your worries away and make you happy. You can go to the web and type in 'Don't Worry Be Happy' by Bobby McFerrin and watch him and Robin Williams sing it on YouTube.

    I also told the boys about the other song and the lyrics "Take me to the river and throw me in the water" and how again this song ties into scripture in the Bible. Now K.T. was there that Sunday to give the message and God must have planned this all out because K.T. and I never communicate what we are going to be saying or doing, but K.T. was flabbergasted because his message was about Acts 22:16 *"And now, why delay? Get up and be baptized, and have your sins **washed away, calling on the name of the Lord.**"* And also, in 1 Corinthians 6:9-11 when Paul tells us that our sins have been **washed away** by our Lord Jesus Christ. Hmmmm! Do you think God had this all planned out??

Well, all this happening got me more inquisitive about the River of Life and Lo & Behold there are several <u>River of Life</u> Pentecostal Churches in the country and one right here in Broken Arrow. It is a Russian Church and they hold services on Sunday at 10:30 in Russian. Well Kirk of the Hills has sponsored a Church in Russia and presently supports a couple of Missionary's in Russia and has had a couple of Mission trips to Russia. Hmmm! Does God want me to check this out? Well weather and other things kept me from visiting and I had kind of forgotten about it. And then Lo & Behold, a couple of days ago I got notice on my email that Jesus Culture was coming out with a new CD "Let it Echo' and the first song you could preview was "In the River". Wow! What a Great Worship song. Hmmm? Was God communicating something to me? Well on Saturday evening I get home and pick up a recent Billy Graham Decision Magazine which I hadn't had time to read and what should I see but on the front cover and a featured article about Franklin Graham visiting Moscow in Oct/Nov and meeting with Vladimir Putin and preaching at three Churches in Moscow (the Greater Baptist church of Moscow, the Church in the Big City and the **Word of Life Pentecostal** Church). What?? God finally got thru to me so Sunday I visited the **River of Life Pentecostal** Church in Broken Arrow.

Now they are way out East of Broken Arrow on 71st and So. 305th E. Ave. It will take you a while to get there, but not nearly as long as it would if you visited a Church in Russia. The Worship & Service was in Russian with an occasional translation in English on the front screen. The building looks more like a warehouse and the parking is on a grassy field but inside it is brand spanking new. It appears to seat about 200 and there were about 125 in attendance. Mainly young families with lots of

Church Visits - Penecostal

children. It was a contemporary worship with 3 guitarists, a drummer, electric keyboard, grand piano and 3 vocalists. No blue jeans, but no ties either. For a change, I blended in pretty well except for the gray hair and no Russian language knowledge.

During the Worship songs, there was a mixture of some holding their hands up and moving with the music. During prayer time, there were those kneeling down and those speaking in tongues. They had all the children come up front and everyone prayed for them aloud and then a couple of more times they prayed aloud for the church. A couple of young guys across the aisle from me had a couple of new hi-tech I-pads and I questioned them later if the pads translated for them. They informed me that they controlled the sound volume in the room. They then explained to me why I heard what was an enormous amount of speaking in tongues during the prayers. They were pitching in with maybe pre-recorded sounds. It did make me feel more comfortable because I would not have stood out as much by not having the gift of tongues. I would have liked an interpreter and they might want to check into it. The Korean Church I visited in Bixby a few years back provided me with ear phones and an interpreter when they realized I did not understand Korean.

Well later Sunday I got notice on my email that Hillsong Music has come out with a new album called 'Open Heaven' and one of their featured songs is "River Wild". You might want to check it out on YouTube by typing in 'Open Heaven' (River Wild) in either the lyric video or the acoustic video. Hillsong is a great worship group with the mega Church Hillsong Pentecostal out of Australia.

Now some of you might want to check out the River of Life Church yourself but you might want to find out first if they have an interpreter. Go to your search and type in River of Life Broken Arrow - Facebook.

Hey! I tell you God can sure make things interesting and exciting some times.

Your KRR guy.... A BIC

More info you can go to and check out:
    www.Hillsong.com and scroll down to Music and click on Worship

Hmmm! Who's Speaking?

www.jesusculture.com and see Kim Walker live with 'In the River' or go to YouTube and see other live versions at worship venues

www.billygraham.org/decision-magazine and click 'past issues', click Dec. 2015 and scroll to 'Franklin Graham – The Real Story of Christmas'

And if you're not familiar with Big Mouth Billy Bass then go to your search engine and type in YouTube and Billy Bass and click on either 'Take Me to the River' or 'Don't Worry Be Happy'

Chapter Four: Church Visits- Methodists

Route 66 – Tulsa Church Route

Hey Tom & Wayne.... the KRR guy again, out and about & checking things out,

SOME<u>ONE</u> (it had to be THE MAN) got my attention and wanted me to check out the Will Rogers United Methodist Church at 11th & Yale a few weeks back. At one time, there were a lot of businesses in and around that area that had the name Will Rogers because of their nearness to the Will Rogers High School. Besides the Church & School there were the cleaners, pharmacy, barber shop, beauty shop, variety store, fabric shop and bar. They were all established before there was a law passed that you had to get permission to use a famous person's name. After the law took effect Will Rogers Jr. came to town to check out who was using his dad's name. Everyone was actually 'Grandfathered' in because they were using the name before the law took effect. Will Jr. approved of everyone except one business...the Will Rogers Bar. The Bar soon dropped the name and I never did hear if it was out of the graciousness of their heart or if Will Jr. had to pay them something.

But back to the Will Rogers UMC. It was built in 1943 and of course is still in existence. I wanted to see how they were doing so I went by there the last Sunday in December. They have an 8:20 Traditional Service and a 10:45 Contemporary Service. I pulled into the Church lot just b/4 the 10:45 Service and was surprised to see the lot so full. Parking for 75 to 100 cars and almost every spot taken. And then I saw some people carrying some Styrofoam food boxes and I thought WOW! I'm in luck. It must be food Sunday. Well you can imagine my surprise once I got into the Church and saw only a few people in the Sanctuary and no food to be found. From the attendees, I saw in the Contemporary Service, I am fearful the church may be struggling and then recently I heard where they may be going to sell some of their property. Why all the cars? And what about the food containers?? Well when I was leaving it all came to light. Nearby is Tally's Retro Route 66 Diner and there were people lined up on the sidewalk all waiting to get in. And I understand they serve huge portions and you may need two doggy bags when you eat there. Hmmm! Is there some way the Church could get some of that crowd? Maybe attend Church Services and get a discount coupon to Tally's or a drawing each Sunday for a Free Meal? Tally's customers are already filling up the Church parking lot. Hmmm! Food for Thought? Food for the Stomach and Food for the Soul. *Isaiah 55:2..." Why spend your money on food that does not give you strength? Why pay for food that does you no good? Listen, and I will tell you where to get food that is good for the soul!"*

The 11th Street Baptist Church at 11th & Louisville was built in 1949 but their membership dwindled down until a few years ago they only had a handful of members and GracePoint Church joined up with them. However, in the last year GracePoint left that location and joined up with a Hispanic Church that meets in the old (1941) Braden Park Baptist Building at 5th & Yale. The 11th Street building is now vacant and boarded up.

Still on 11th at Sandusky is the Sandusky Avenue Christian Church. I visited there and they appear to be growing. They have a young contemporary worship team and a good mix of ages among whites, blacks and Hispanics. Paul Ortiz is the Senior Minister there. They have a fairly new building that was put up after they tore down the old Will Rogers Theatre. I hated to see the artistic look of the Theatre torn down with the tall tower and the Western theme look of the interior but it had become too expensive to maintain. The Theatre was built in 1941 and vacated in 1976 and then the Church took it over but had to tear it down in 1986. You can see and learn more about the Theatre by typing in Will Rogers Theatre Tulsa on your search engine and clicking on cinema treasures. The cost of upkeep & maintenance is a problem with the older Church properties. They have new regulations and codes to contend with from the City, Fire, Security, Disability and Insurance carriers.

Church Visits- Methodists

Well today I wanted to visit the Braden Park Church where GracePoint moved to and shares the building with the Hispanic Church. I thought their services started at 10:30 but when I got there I found out they had started at 10 a.m. The Hispanic Church was meeting in the main Chapel and appeared to have about 125 in attendance (mostly young and middle age families). GracePoint was meeting in the dining hall with about 50 in attendance (almost all white senior citizens). Since I was late and would be a distraction by entering I elected to go across the street to the Yale Avenue Presbyterian Church (YAPB) which started at 10:45. You might remember I visited them a few years back and commented that they appeared to be going downhill in membership. I recall then that there were about 50 in attendance and they were all seniors. They haven't been able to turn it around. Today there were 20 in attendance and last year they lost another 6 members. Seven died and they had one incoming transfer. Total membership is now 68. They did offer Free Coupons for What-a-Burger however when you left. Hmmm!

Oh Yes! Yesterday I was out with the Kirk Karpenters and 10 of our great Junior & Senior High youth. We were building a ramp for a lady near Admiral & Lewis. Her house was only about 300 feet from the 2nd Presbyterian Church Building that was built in 1917. It brought back memories of my visit to them a few years back at a Christmastime Concert. There were about 15 visitors that performed in the concert and only 8 members of the church and me who got to enjoy it. I mentioned it didn't look too good for the Church to be in existence much longer. I heard that the building was sold and there is a new church meeting there now but the exterior needs some maintenance done and no telling what the interior needs.

And one quick God communication to me. Two Sundays ago, it was my turn to do Worship service for the boys at the Juvenile Detention Center. That was the Sunday that the streets were iced over and most area churches cancelled services. I was determined to try and get out and go. First attempt I pulled out of the garage into the street and my car started sliding sideways so I crept back into the garage. God was saying either don't go or wait awhile. One hour later to try again I go to the laundry room door to go into the garage and that door would not open. I tried everything and even my son came and couldn't get it open. That door had worked for over 20 years. Why now? But I was nudged by SOMEONE (The MAN upstairs) and told to try again in 5 minutes. I told my son that God said to try again in 5 minutes. He waited about 5 minutes and tried again and the door opened up with no problem what-so-ever and it has worked ever since. Hmmm? Did SOMEONE keep me from crashing into something?

Hey Everyone Have a Blessed Day…. your KRR guy, A BIC

Asbury United Methodist Church

BCOC & AUMC

Hey Tom, Wayne & others.... the KRR guy out and about,

Sunday, Sept. 6th, I made a visit to AUMC (Asbury United Methodist Church). God had been wanting me to visit there I was sure and I kept putting it off. So, HE finally impeded my personal vehicle and it forced me into my company van that has *timely* (Will Rogers Clock Store) advertising all over it. I felt awkward driving it into any church parking lot with all the advertising on it so I had planned on even not attending any church that day. And then lo & behold God reminded me I could park on the Mardel Christian Bookstore parking lot and walk over to Asbury.

I hadn't been to a service at their new location but I had been there for a few meetings and funerals. Rev. Bill Mason and I were acquainted thru Rotary many years ago. He was the President of his club the same year I was President of my club and we got to know each other. Bill retired in 1992 *(if a Pastor can ever really retire)*. I had never met the new Pastor Tom Harrison and I think God kept *bugging* me to go check them out. Well what a beautiful Sanctuary they have. I went to the 9:15 a.m. service and God must have reserved a seat for me and other first timers in the rear. Right next to me were some other first timers, a couple from the Kirk and another couple. I would say the sanctuary seats around 2,500. The church now has a membership of over 8,000 with about 3,000 attending one of the 3 services on a weekly basis. The Traditional 9:15 Service is followed up with an 11 a.m. Contemporary Service, so now I will need to go back some time to check on it. The traditional service reminded me of my younger days of attending both Boston Avenue United Methodist and Tulsa First United Methodist.

One reason I felt God wanted me to attend that day was because of the advertising on the front of the Church Program. The next Sunday was to be **Asbury's Day of Service**. I got excited when I saw what they had planned for the next Sunday and decided to check it out. They were holding their 5th annual Day of Service and this time they had 33 different sites that needed some kind of loving attention and they needed over 1,500 volunteers. They were in areas all over Tulsa, the surrounding communities and even a day trip to Camp Egan in Tahlequah. By the time, I got ready to sign up with one, most were already complete with all the volunteers needed. I was utterly amazed at how well organized this event is. Details for each location as to what was needed, the age requirement, how light or heavy the labor would require and all the tools and supplies were to be at the site. You did not need to be a member of Asbury. As a matter of fact, they encouraged members to bring friends and neighbors. 30 manned tables were set up on Sunday the 13th to check in at and to pick up your T-shirt, to get a lunch ticket and where your bus or church van would be located for boarding to get you to and from the ministry project.

Well I found a site in my neck of the woods in Bixby. Recently the old building for the First United Methodist Church of Bixby had been turned into the Bixby Community Outreach Center which provides food, clothing, school supplies, financial assistance and other services for people in need in Bixby, Jenks and four other surrounding towns. The building still needed a lot of inside and outside repairs. I signed up for painting parking lot stripes. An Asbury member and old Rotary friend and A BIC was on the team too doing ceiling tile replacement. The 46 on our team were comprised mostly of retirees and young families. One little girl, about 6, was asked what she would like to help with and she replied she was good at washing windows…and it so happened that all the windows needed washing. Now this is a big 2-story building with about 17,000 sq. ft. and full of donated clothing, food and school supplies and other basic necessities. They normally have about 80 volunteers helping out each week at the facility.

What an uplifting day for me and all those involved I am sure and God provided wonderful weather. Hey! Next year some of you might want to check this out.

That's all for now, however if any of you could enlighten me on the most unusual *bug* (a moth or caterpillar) I have ever seen, I would greatly appreciate it. I know God can do all sorts of things and this *bug* had to be from an alien planet. It looked like something right out of these space age movies. It was resting on a brick wall and it was about 4 inches in length, 2 inches in width and bronze in color all over. AND there were no wings (unless they could pop from the body someway). The body had absolutely

Church Visits- Methodists

no curves what so ever. The body was completely formed at right angles in shapes of squares or rectangles. Now, understand that I have had my eyes checked recently, I can paint a straight line for a parking stripe and the Church team only provided cold water for drinking.

And something else some of you might be interested in if you like Great Barbeque prepared by some of the Greatest folks in Tulsa. It's the *Badges, Blazes & Barbeque Cook-Off* on Sunday Sept. 27th from 5 to 7 p.m. at the Kirk of the Hills Church on 61St between Yale & Harvard. It is a cook-off between the local fire and police with some of Tulsa's Courtroom Judges actually judging who are the winners. I understand people from the Mayor's and District Attorney's office may be in attendance too. And all proceeds will be going to help YFC (Youth For Christ) in their mission at the Tulsa Juvenile Detention Center. Call K.T. Johnson @ 918-269-7800 to reserve your $25 tickets. And you better hurry as there is only so much food our area Fire & Police Teams can cook.

And if you know of someone who is undecided what to do about Boy Scouting.... have them check out the New TrailLife USA Organization, www.TrailLifeUSA.com. They have been set up by some of the top officials who broke away from Boy Scouts and are Scripture based and based upon the same moral principles that the Boy Scouts originally started with.

You all have a Blessed Day.... A BIC

Centenary United Methodist

Centenarian & Centenary & Centennial

Hey Tom, Wayne & others.... the KRR guy out and about again,

The three words above all have something in common and that is that they all refer to something 100 years old. Now I'm not 100 years old yet, but I did visit the Centenary United Methodist Church on North Denver a couple of times recently and that Church is over 100 years old. It actually began as the Tigert Memorial Methodist Church in 1906 but built a new Church building in 1921 and was renamed Centenary in honor of the Centenary National Methodist Movement that was building new Methodist churches at that time.

On Sunday, 9/27/2015, I and my son visited the Brady Heights Historical Tour and our first stop was at Centenary. An Elder of the church almost literally jumped on me and started telling me all about the church. I saw a set of drums up front so I asked if they had a contemporary service. I was quickly and politely informed that the church is strictly traditional in every shape and form and that I must come and visit their Services some time to see for myself. He made me promise that I would re-visit. Sooo, I did, the following Sunday.

The Pastor there is Keith McArtor, who is a past Tulsa County Assistant District Attorney and still is a present-day Attorney and Adjunct Professor @ Tulsa Community College.

Being brought up in other local Methodist Churches (Boston Avenue & First United) I thought I was prepared for the order of worship. Wrong! My Oh My! Being away from the old-style traditional service for a while threw me for a loop. And it was also Communion Sunday and I wasn't prepared for how they did that either. I noticed a couple of other first-time visitors and they were as lost as I was in the order of worship.

Now being a beautiful Historical Church building with 124 stained glass windows and with the original curved solid walnut pews donated by Waite Phillips and filigree in the front of the sanctuary...you would not want to distract from all that beauty with a big projection screen to guide you thru the service. So, the order of worship was all printed out on the

Church Visits- Methodists

program and referring you to different parts of the Bible and the UMH (United Methodist Hymnal).

Feeling uncomfortable all during the service because I wasn't that familiar with it and not being able to find my way around quick enough in the Bible and the UMH, prepared me for the very next day however. On Monday I was to pick up a 'sick' Grandfather (a clock that is) way outside of Pryor, OK and bring it in and get it 'ticking' again. The owners had given me verbal and email instructions on how to get to their place. BUT, often what they tell you is perfectly clear to them but not to a new comer. It is also like your GPS which is sometimes not always correct or throws you for a loop when there is an unsuspected Detour. It always works out much better if you have someone in the car that's familiar with the area and can guide you. So, I might suggest to Pastor McArtor that they might think about seating a regular church member next to or close by any new attendees. I can imagine how much more welcome that visitor would feel with someone greeting them with a smile, a conversation and an offer to help guide them thru the service if they would like. As a matter of fact…. maybe other churches should consider doing that too. In smaller congregations it is easier to recognize someone new but in larger churches, then we, ourselves, the members should be observant enough and Christian enough to make every visitor feel comfortable and welcome. You'll generally find first time visitors in the back half of the sanctuary and looking a little confused.

And from my experience in visiting churches, what an impression the small Southwest Church of the Nazarene in Tulsa made on my visit there when a couple of the youth recognized me as a visitor and brought me a nice fresh small homemade banana-nut loaf of bread with the note 'God Loves You'.

Well that's all the KRR guy has for now…
Be Blessed and Bless Others…. A BIC

First United Methodist Church

A First at the First United Methodist Church

Hey Wayne, Dan and others… the KRR guy out and about

I'll talk about the First at the First, but first and let me tell you about the MAN and how HE got my attention recently. I want to tell you about someone who's First name starts with the last letter of the alphabet and whose last name starts with the First letter of the alphabet, Zach Annett. He's the drummer on the Contemporary Worship team at Kirk of the Hills, a family man and a great **B**rother **I**n **C**hrist. God wanted to get my attention about Zach for some reason and HE did it in a different way as usual. In 8 short days, this is what happened.

I was visiting my 17-year-old granddaughter in Skiatook who happens to be on the Worship team at her church. She was standing next to a young man about her age and she introduced the young man to me and said his name was Zach. I jokingly said." You don't happen to play the drums, do you?" And he came right back and said "I sure do". Well I explained to him about the guy I know from Kirk Church whose name is Zach and he plays the drums. Well…What a coincidence? Hmmm!

My granddaughter then tells me about another teenage young man at the Church in Owasso she used to attend whose name is Zach and he plays the drums on the Worship team at that church. Hmmm!

Well 2 for 2. Is God trying to communicate something to me? Well the following Sunday I was doing Chapel Services for about 20 boys at the Juvenile Detention Center and at the end we always invite any boys who may be in need of prayer to come speak with us. I had a couple of boys come up and then we were running out of time when a third boy came up. Well here comes 3 for 3. When I asked his name, he said it was Zach. Again, I jokingly asked if he happened to play the drums, and he came right back and said "Yes, how did you know?" OK God you got my attention but what does it mean? Three teenagers, three Zach's and three drummers in 8 days. What are the odds of that happening? I'd hate to try and figure that out. 3 Million to 3? 3 Hundred Million to 3???

Someone might have a different guess what God is trying to get across,

Church Visits- Methodists

but my thought is that God is so impressed with Zach at the Kirk that HE wants more Zach's just like him.

Now back to the First at the First. On Sunday, Nov. 13th, I attended the Kirk Contemporary Service and thought I would fit in a second service at another church if it worked out. God had gotten my attention a couple of weeks prior when I was visiting Kirk Crossing and happened to see Rev. Wade Paschal visiting there too. When I saw him, I thought what is he doing here, he's supposed to be preaching at Tulsa's First Methodist. Obviously, some local Church news had gotten by me and in checking him out I found out he had retired in June and someone else I knew, Rev. Jessica Moffatt from the Bixby Methodist Church at one time was now the minister at First. Hmmm! Maybe I should visit there sometime.

Well, Pastor Wayne at the Kirk held the Contemporary services on Sunday the 13th and God must have used him to prepare me for my visit to First United Methodist. Pastor Wayne talked about the history of the Kirk Church and how it has grown and how some Churches are struggling with attendance and how all Church members need to get out and invite their neighbors, friends and co-workers to come to Church. The Kirk Contemporary service ended about 5 minutes early (10:25) and I felt that would give me time to make it downtown to attend the 10:55 a.m. Blended Service at First Methodist.

Well, I made it there with 5 minutes to spare and thank goodness I got there early or else I would not have been able to get in. Not because they lock the doors, BUT because there was no place to sit or even stand when it came time for the Service to start. They were packed out. Everyone was given a colorful crown to wear upon entry and I was questioning myself as to what was going on. I was not aware that on this Sunday they were celebrating their 130th Anniversary in Tulsa. They were established in 1886 before Oklahoma was even a State.

This Sunday they started out with the traditional service, Cathedral Choir and all and then went into the history of the Church with the Regeneration Worship Band playing intermittingly and the congregation joining in with many outstretched and raised high arms. Rev. Jessica Moffatt then presented the message and started right off with a picture and message about Louie Giglio with Passion Church. I felt right at home as I've known Louie and his involvement with 'Passion' Worship events since I started attending in 2003. I've volunteered and helped out at a 'Passion' gathering ever since then as they have reached out to hundreds of thousands of young adults (age 18 to 25) all over the world.

Well Services ended around 1 p.m. and it reminded me of many of the Black Churches I have attended where the Services may go for a couple hours or more. My Oh My.... A two-hour Service for First United Methodist may be a First for them. Or maybe it isn't? I might need to go back and double check on that. See a pic at www.facebook.com/FUMCTulsa.

The KRR guy.....A BIC

And Oh, I got to talk with Rev. Paschal briefly and mentioned I had seen him at Kirk Crossing and he replied "Yes I was there. I have a couple of Granddaughters who go there". Hmmm! That reminded me of when I was a member of First United Methodist Church in the eighties and one of my pre-teenage daughters just didn't feel comfortable there because she didn't have any friends her age there. We were living in Jenks then and she attended Jenks schools. Well it is important for your kids to feel comfortable in Church and since I can feel comfortable in just about any 3in1 Believing Church, I asked her to pick out a Church she would like to visit. Well, that is how we wound up at Kirk of the Hills. She picked a winner and had lots of her friends and my friends there too.

Chapter Five: Church Visits- Presbyterian

The Korean Presbyterian & others

Hey Tom & Wayne,

It's me…..your KRR. Hey, have I been busy the last couple of weeks. Yup! Visited 3 churches and made it to the Tulsa Mission Mobilizers luncheon. I was about 5 minutes late to every church service but I was early to the luncheon. I'm beginning to see a pattern to my timeliness. I seem to be late to all meetings except those that are serving food. I'm thinking that food may be one of the driving forces in my life. What do you think?

Anyway, a couple of weeks ago I visited Paradise Baptist Church on East King Street where San Holmes, Jr. is the Pastor. WOW! What a performance. This service was like a Broadway Play. The choreography was great. There were about 250 in attendance and all were black and dressed to the hilt…except for me. More about them on another report.

Then I attended the Mission luncheon on Wednesday noon, held at Christ Presbyterian. About 25 in attendance and 20 churches represented. I mentioned that I was with the Kirk and that we are sort of non-denominational right now. They accepted that and mentioned that we are in their prayers. I sat with Roger Nix, the minister at Believers, and he wanted to know how things were progressing, and that they have us on their prayer list.

Sunday the 12th, I made my way to the Korean Presbyterian Church PCUSA in Bixby (on 126th St. at Memorial). Services started at 10:45 and ended at noon. This church is alive and well too. I could tell by the music and watching the congregation, even though I could not understand a

Hmmm! Who's Speaking?

thing that was said. Yup! It was all in Korean. About 30 to 35 in attendance, and all Koreans except for me. Sort of Contemporary in style with musical instruments. I could tell at one point that they must have asked for any visitors or guests to be recognized because everyone turned and looked at me. Hey! What am I supposed to do? I just smiled. Then there was some discussion about something and I noticed the minister motioning to some people. And then someone handed me an earphone and motioned for me to use it. Then a very nice woman's voice came on and asked if I could hear her. So, I gave a thumbs up. She said she had just been asked to interpret the sermon for me. A great sermon it was too. All about Joshua and the importance of listening to and obeying God.

As I was about to leave, several of them came up to me including the minister and invited me to stay for lunch. They were having authentic home style Korean food. They serve a lunch every Sunday. I could see and smell the food and my taste buds were beginning to go into overdrive, but I tried to graciously excuse myself. Honestly! But just as I reached the door to leave, one of the members grabbed my arm and sat me down in front of a plate of delicious looking food. Now Tom and Wayne, what would you have done? I know, I know, you probably could have resisted. BUT WOW! That was good stuff, and they told me it was healthy too. The only problem was that I couldn't eat it as fast as they could. You see, I was the only one with a spoon, everyone else had chopsticks.

I had an opportunity to talk to the minister at lunch and found out he has been the minister there for 2 years & 2 months. The church started out at John Knox, and met there for 10 years, before moving to the present location about 9 years ago. They are a PCUSA member and I think the minister said something about being ordained along with Cathy Hamrick? at Trinity Presbyterian. His English was not really good and my Korean was totally non-existent. We talked some about South Korea and North Korea. He became a Believer while in South Korea. He understands what the Kirk is doing and I explained to him the reason. He was aware of the video and what happened at the Korean church in California. He was also aware of the 'Secret' paper put out by the headquarters in Louisville. He said the South Korean Presbyterian Church in Korea does not agree with the PCUSA. He also mentioned that he knew the Presbyterian Church in Africa feels the same way. There are a couple of other Korean Churches in

Tulsa, neither one PCUSA, but I might visit them sometime. First, I will find out if they serve lunch though. Hey!! I deserve some perks with this reporting work.

Well, that's all the news that is news worth reporting for now.

Your BIC,

Ps…if you know of any other churches that serve lunch after service, please let me know.

College Hill Presbyterian

More Light College Hill

Hey Tom, Wayne and Dan…. the KRR guy again,

God directed me to College Hill Presbyterian today. It has been a few years since I've visited them. They have a new minister, Todd Freeman. I pulled them up on the web just before I left and discovered that they also have a Spanish service that meets at the same time now, so I kind of wanted to check them out.

The parking lot was pretty full by the time I got there just before 11 a.m., so I was expecting to see more people there than the last time I visited. There were a few more people but not that many more. About 60 all together in the English service and I guess about ½ dozen in the Spanish service. Todd led the Children's worship about the Potter and there were 9 Elementary kids for that. Only one family appeared young enough to have some Elementary kids so it appeared the rest were at the service with their grandparents. Something else interesting was that I did not see any Jr. or Sr. High kids and not one college student either in the whole place which was interesting since College Hill is practically on the Tulsa University Campus. There were about 12 couples in attendance, 10 of them in the older bracket and then a middle-age Lesbian couple and a middle-age Gay couple. The Gay and Lesbian couple were quite obvious by their actions.

They had several traditional Presbyterian duties to begin with, as you can see by the Sunday Bulletin, before they came to the *Passing the Peace. Here everyone was asked to get up and greet everyone else…and they literally did that. We all walked all over the place saying "Hi and Peace Be with You" until everyone had greeted everyone else. This took about 10 minutes. And with the time spent for 'The Response' and 'The Sending Forth', that only left the minister about 10 minutes for his Sermon. It was about the shortest Sermon I have heard in a long time and then the acoustics in the chapel are so bad that I couldn't really hear it anyway.

Among the News was that the Church's Bluegrass & BBQ Party for 9/28 had been cancelled because of lack of interest and ticket sales. Hmmmm!

Church Visits- Presbyterian

WELL the Bright Light, instead of the More Light, is that the UKIRK Ministries, a TU campus ministry, started by First Presbyterian a few years back is growing by leaps and bounds. They hold Chapel at the TU Sharp Chapel on campus and have other weekly events at noon and in the evenings. They started out with 10 to 15 participants and have grown to between 500 to 600 overall. Hmmmm!

Hey! I know you guys can't get away on Sundays to see all this stuff going on, so I'll just keep on 'Truckin' and feeding you the news the way I see it.... The KRR guy

The Kirk Ramp

Scripture: Psalm 127:1….*" Unless the LORD builds a house, the work of the builders is useless"*.

Life without God is meaningless. All of life's work, building a home, establishing a career, or raising a family – must have God as the builder and the foundation.

Ephesians 2:20-21…. *"We are his house, built on the foundation of the apostles and the prophets. And the cornerstone is Christ Jesus himself. We who believe are carefully joined together, becoming a holy temple for the Lord"*.

If we build our lives on the blueprint of the word of God, as found in the Bible, then we will not wander off in the wrong direction, remaining strong and sturdy all the days of our lives.

'The Kirk Ramp' may not mean anything to you unless maybe you've got some Scottish blood in you. The word 'Kirk' comes from Scottish English meaning "Church". Now the Scots derived the word from the Greek language where it meant the "Lord's House". So instead of saying 'Kirk Ramp', we could say 'Church Ramp'.

The word 'Ramp', in the dictionary, means an inclined surface which is to help one get from one level to another level.

At my Church, we have a team of devoted volunteers who go out almost every weekend to build ramps for handicapped individuals. The ramps, once completed, make it easier for the people to come and go. They even find it is easier to leave their house and to go to the Lord's House.

What is interesting about the Kirk Ramp team is that the team leader is who we call "Our Jewish Carpenter". Richard is his name and he was Jewish by birth and then later became a Christian, after much encouragement by his wife and a lot of research and learning on his own.

Some of us on the team are not the greatest carpenters in the world, and I include myself in that category. What I like about Richard is that when I make a mistake, he simply points it out and tells me how to correct it, or he'll take care of the mistake himself, without any complaining. Richard is pretty particular about the slope of the ramp. He doesn't want the ramp to be too steep or out of kilter so he continually checks it with a level. Sometimes a mistake is as simple as not using the right nail in the right place. There are short nails and long nails, thin nails and fat nails,

Church Visits- Presbyterian

twisted nails and straight nails. Richard guides us as to which nails we need to use in order to build a strong ramp. He knows all about nails. And if he has a chance he will tell you about his best friend who was nailed to a Cross. Richard's friend is 'THE JEWISH CARPENTER'.

Now, when the team goes out to build a ramp, they have a blueprint that Richard has drawn up. Each ramp is a little different because of where the doors, steps or porches are, and the slope of the land, and other things. BUT, with a set of blueprints and the guidance of our 'Jewish Carpenter', each ramp is built to perfection for the particular individual.

You know, blueprints are important in the construction field, whether you're building maybe a ramp, a house, or even a Church. Whatever you build, you want it to hold up over a period of time. You don't necessarily want it coming apart in a storm, or a tornado, or even a tsunami. You want it to hold up and to endure.

Sometimes in our lives we too are going to have our own personal storms or tsunami's. Are you built to withstand those storms? Maybe your life is not fitting together the way you planned. Maybe things just seem out of kilter. If you'll study the BIBLE (God's Blueprint) and follow the instructions, you'll be built to weather the storms in your life. You'll figure out what to do to get things straightened out and lined up again. And the more you study the BIBLE (**B**asic **I**nstructions **B**efore **L**eaving **E**arth), the more you will realize when that JEWISH CARPENTER is right there alongside of you and is helping and guiding you.

If you don't have a Church you're attending, you might want to check one out. See what kind of ramps they have. Will they help you get to a higher spiritual level? Find a Church that is built on a strong foundation and one that is using a good blueprint.

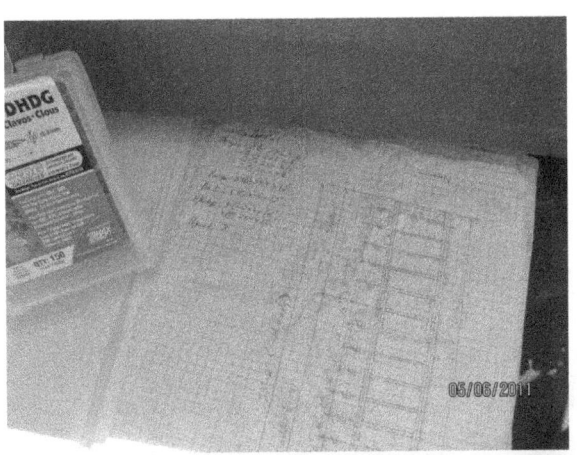

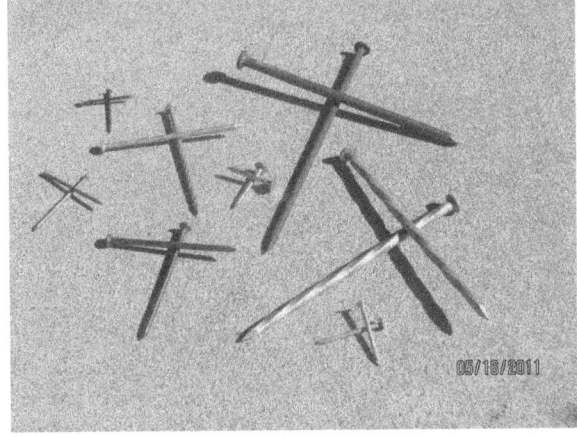

Chapter Six: Church Visits- Nazarene

Route 66 and K.T. & YFC @ JDC

Hey Tom, Wayne and others....the KRR guy out and about again,

This Sunday God had some plans for me but I wasn't exactly sure what. I thought He might want me to help out at the Juvenile Detention Center or to visit another Church. Sometimes on the 5th Sunday of a month they are short on Chaplains at the JDC so I thought I would check it out. First, I went by the Kirk and listened to Dante and the Worship team and then took off (sorry Dan I couldn't stay but the MAN had something else planned). When I get to the JDC K.T. and Alec were there for the "B" Section and a Gideon was there for the "A" Section. So, I told K.T. it looked like I wasn't needed so I wanted to visit a Church nearby. But K.T. said he could use one more. But then God sent Ben and he showed up and so they didn't need me and I took off about 10:30 to find a Church to visit. I had preplanned 4 or 5 Churches but was going to let God lead me to which one. When heading to JDC along I-244 I had seen a Church off on my right at about West 21st so I thought I would seek it out. It was on my list as the Southwest Church of the Nazarene at 1302 W. 22nd St. I was thinking they got the name from being South & West of downtown Tulsa, but I was wrong, they got the name from the Street, Southwest Blvd. which is the 'Mother Road' or Historic Route 66.

    I got fooled on where to get off of I-244. The sign said W. 21st Exit so I took that Exit. Lo & behold I was going the wrong direction. I had to make a U-Turn to get going the right direction. You know sometimes God tells us to make a U-Turn when we're going the wrong way. After I got turned around I thought I was on W. 21st but as I got to the intersection and was about to make a right turn…Lo & Behold I would be going the wrong direction again so God had me make a turn around right in the middle of the intersection.

It was now 10:40 and I figured I would be late for a 10:30 Service so maybe I should skip it. But I see their marquee sign & it says Services at 10:40. WHAT? 10:40? who ever heard of a Church having services start at 10:40. Well you know WHO had that planned out and so I was right on time. Now this Church doesn't have any paved parking, it was grass & gravel. It was probably built in the late 20's or early 30's and they didn't need paved parking then. It was horse & buggies or horseless carriages back then and members who lived within walking distance. And I would say that even today, most of their members live within walking distance.

God knew I needed a break after my last two Church visits and HE sent me to a Great little church. About 40 people in attendance, both young families and grandparents. All were good ol common folks with good ol common sense and a Love of God. One member sitting next to me commented that about 4 years ago they realized they needed to make a turn-around. What all they have done I do not know, but I did notice on the stage where the pulpit was that probably it used to hold a choir. But now there was one piano player, two guitarist and 12 huge speaker boxes. There were two large screens for video and then what I thought was a 3-dimensional picture in the center with a river and mountains. Another member informed me that's their baptismal.

Before they got started some youth brought me a nice fresh small homemade banana-nut loaf of bread with the note 'God Loves You'. I had to struggle to not eat it thru the rest of the service. Later I found out that they have a continental breakfast every Sunday from 9:15 to 10:30 a.m.

It was the first Advent Sunday and Pastor Wayde Normandin had 3 of the youth to light the first candle and then he talked about Isaiah 40:3-5. There were a couple of girls at the service that had development disability and they were as friendly as all get out and you could tell the members loved them too. Before I left I had probably 5 or 6 members and the Pastor also to tell me to come back Wednesday evening at 5:30 because they have a great dinner. My Oh My, they certainly knew my weakness. These folks would give you the shirt off their back even if they couldn't afford it. The

Church reminded me of Jesus story of the Widows Mite in Luke 21:1-4. This is a great God Loving Church and God Loves them too.

Hey, I might check out their Wednesday night dinners and I can get there on time since I now know that they are at West 22nd and Route 66.

Now you all need to go to www.safehousemusic.com and click on Juvenile Justice Ministry. This is a new website that K.T. has just put up and it is Fantastic. He and his Troops are doing Great things for the boys & girls at the Juvenile Detention Center and you may want to get involved.

Hey! That's all for now, your KRR guy, A BIC

LifeChurch & Core Church

Judging or Helping

Hey Tom, Wayne & others…the KRR guy out and around again,

A couple of weeks ago someone I know suggested I might want to check out a Church in Broken Arrow that is reaching out to people like God's Shining Light Church is doing on 11th Street here in Tulsa. These are people that may be homeless or need some kind of Recovery Program and may have even been in prison or jail and there are people in the Church wanting to help them.

Sunday, I first checked out the Life Church (non-denominational) in Bixby at their 8:30 a.m. Service and Pastor Craig was talking about his series of "Most Misused Verses of the Bible" and this week it was what he says is the Most common Twisted or Misused Verse by both Christians and non-Christians…. Matt. 7:1-2… *Do not judge, or you too will be judged…*

And Pastor Craig went on then and explained what is clear About Judging in the Bible…

John 7:24…. *Stop judging by mere appearances, but instead judge correctly*

Romans 2:1…Use God's example and be kind, tolerant and patient as He is with our own sins

1 Corinthians 5:12…*God will judge those outside the church. We are to help those inside the church.*

Galatians 6:1-2…*Brothers and sisters, we are to restore those caught in a sin gently. And we must watch out that we do not also become tempted.*

Now I do not want to sound like I am judging, but I thought it was interesting that Pastor Craig was wearing white sneakers or tennis shoes. Hmmm! More about this later.

After Life Church I was off for the Core Church (www.corechurch.com), just north of the Creek Turnpike on 145th E. Ave (better known as Aspen to Broken Arrowans). They are Nazarene affiliated. Their service starts at 10:30 and they have a young Contemporary Worship Team. The new building seats about 325 and I would say there were about 275 in attendance. This Sunday Pastor Brad and his wife, Laura, were presenting the message on lasting friendships, marriages and family relationships.

Church Visits- Nazarene

Those in attendance were mainly in the under 40 bracket and a mix of nationalities.... American, African American, Hispanics and Far Eastern. And each and every one just as friendly as all get out. As I walked in and introduced myself a Hispanic greeter immediately told me how much this church has changed his life. He has moved to Colorado but whenever he gets back to Tulsa he visits this church and wants to share his testimony and to help others like he was helped.

At one point during the announcements, one or two people who were hurting and needing prayers went to the front and immediately were surrounded by members who surrounded them and lifted them up in prayer. I got the impression that the church has Communion every Sunday because at the end of the service everyone stood up and walked down the aisle to the front and picked up a communion wafer and dipped it in a juice cup and partook of the elements right then. There was not a uniform Scripture prayer with the elements.

Now, back to the tennis shoes. Pastor Brad had on sneakers too...beige in color. Hmmm! So, I started looking around.... **every male** I saw, age 10 to 60 or so, had on sneakers or tennis shoes. Some in bright colors, some multi-colors, some in basic colors. Wow! I was sure glad that no one was judging me by my appearance. You see I had on black loafers. Hmmm! Maybe the LDS churches could pick up on this some?

Hey, your BIC....Let's lift up those Churches that are reaching out to the homeless, the needy and the hurting and ask God to continue to Bless them.

Central Nazarene

The Mysterious Phone Call

Hey Tom, Wayne & Others…....the KRR guy out and about again,

I got the opportunity to visit a couple of churches last Sunday. A couple of people, several weeks back, had invited me to visit their church sometime and I had probably commented that I would when God called me to. It seems their church membership has been dropping off for the last few years and maybe they were looking for some suggestions. Well, last week I felt God was calling me to visit their church so I checked them out. Their Sunday church service was at 10:30 so I thought I would drop by the Bixby Life (non-denominational) Church beforehand. The early service at Bixby Life begins at 8:30 a.m.

As I pull in to Bixby Life there were a couple of guys out on 121St waving away and acting excited to see me pull in the parking lot. Then Bixby Life had a couple of door entrances and both of them had 3 or 4 greeters standing outside holding the doors open, reaching to shake your hand and greeting you with a smile. Hey! It's 8:30 in the morning on a Sunday, you need that! Once inside, I noticed most of those in attendance (about 150 or so) were of a more mature age….no wonder they were up bright & early. I've been to other Life Church services later in the morning or even in the afternoon and evening services and then I generally see younger families. This time some of those in attendance even looked like early riser Bixby area farmers. This Life Church continues to pull the crowds in at all 8 services they have on the weekend. After enjoying the services here I head off for the Central Nazarene Church, www.tulsacentral.church on 81st between Memorial & Sheridan.

Central Nazarene is located as their name suggests, in the Central part of South Tulsa right on a major street and between two other major streets (Memorial & Sheridan). They are in a great area where there are a lot of young families. As a World-Wide Denomination, the Nazarenes are growing. They grew almost 50% in the decade 2004-2014 (1.5 million to 2.3 million). However, this particular location is losing membership. I remember visiting there several years back and the 600+ sanctuary was

Church Visits- Nazarene

practically full. Today there were about 200 in attendance but the number of cars in their lot implied that there were more. I found out later that a Hispanic congregation meets there too at the same time in a different part of the church and that they have about 100 in attendance. That also partially explains why the service I attended was lacking a racial & ethnic diversification even though the Nazarene Denomination is well diversified.

The Church building is contemporary in style however the service was more traditional. Of the 200 in attendance it was weighted toward retirees and even though the musical instruments included some drums and guitars the songs were more traditional. I commend them for including a couple of solos by Jr. & Sr. High youth. Every Church needs to get their youth involved someway for they are the future. I had difficulty figuring out where to park and where to enter. Perhaps they need to check into getting volunteers like other growing churches are doing and get more greeters in more visual areas.

I have visited hundreds of Churches of many denominations and even checked out a few Mosques, Temples and cults. Of the Churches, I have visited I have found those that are reaching out to young families are the ones growing the most. And that means that in order to grow you generally need some kind of contemporary service. I have also seen those that tried to combine traditional & contemporary into one service and it was just not successful. If a Church has the space and the staff then they can have both a traditional and a contemporary at the same time in different locations like at Kirk of the Hills. If the Church does not have the appropriate space or enough staff and ministers then they can do what Asbury Methodist does where they hold two traditional services at 8 & 9:15 and the contemporary at 11. If you notice, most Churches will hold the traditional services earlier for the older earlier risers and the contemporary at the later time for the families with kids. And maybe like Asbury, the senior minister can do both the traditional & contemporary services just dress down a little for the contemporary. If nothing else just take off the robe or coat & tie.

And Oh! That phone call? Now, nobody calls me on my cell phone on Sunday mornings, but at 11:45 right in the middle of the Service I heard something and it wasn't until the lady in front of me turned around and looked at me that I realized it was my phone. Well, well, well. A business tenant of mine was calling to tell me that there was no *Light* in their space and they wanted to know how to get a hold of Jeff who had fixed a breaker for them not too long ago and brought them *More Light*. Well, Well, Well. Just about this time, about 8 rows down from me a guy stands up…..and Lo & Behold it is Jeff! Hmmmm? Was God calling??? Did He call me to attend this Church on this particular day at this particular time? Did God want Jeff to go and fix the *Light so there would be more Light?* Hmmmm? And, does God want this Church to share the *Light with more people?* Hmmmm? Something to think about.

Let's all lift this Church up in our prayers and pray for God's guidance for them.

The KRR guy… A BIC

Chapter Seven: Church Visits- Catholics

Church of Saint Mary

Fir mina Times Three

Well God got my attention early Sunday morning about 3 a.m. and I had no idea what it pertained to. I had asked Him on Saturday if He wanted me to visit a church or something on Sunday. Sometimes He directs me and other times I hear or sense nothing. But my 2-year-old grandson was taken to the Emergency Room at St. Johns in Owasso on Friday and they admitted him to the hospital for dehydration and probably would hold him for 2 or 3 days. I was going to go visit when I remembered I had told Scott French I would visit the Discovery Bible Church in Collinsville/Owasso sometime. So, I figured this was God's thoughts too. I told my daughter I would go to the Kirk 9:30 service on Sunday, then skip up to see Scott at their 11 a.m. service and then come by the Hospital. Well my daughter calls me at 9:15 a.m. Sunday and told me the hospital had just released my grandson. That changed my plans some, but for the better since my grandson was out of the hospital.

I went by the Kirk 9:30 service and then proceeded to Discovery Bible for the 11 a.m. service and got to hear Scott's message from Nehemiah to get the people in the church to use their gifts to rebuild not just their church but the Kingdom of God.

Then that afternoon I get to my office and try to figure out why He woke me up at 3 a.m. and spelt out **Fir min a,** three times to me. He did not pronounce it and I still am not sure how it is properly pronounced. My 1st thought was that maybe I was supposed to check on a tenant that leases from me in the Wellness space whose name is F**a**rmina. I'm thinking maybe I didn't hear Him right… but He did spell it out for me three times. I go to my search engine and type in exactly how He spelt it and sure enough, up pops St. Fir mina. A woman who was martyred around 275 – 300 AD. Why was she hung & burned to death? She had changed a high official with the Roman Empire (which was a body of non-elected officials) and others, from a cult religion that worshiped all sorts of things to the Christian faith. Whoa! Where did I find this information? On a Catholic website! www.catholic.org. What else did I see on this site on Catholic Online? The whole story about some of America's female entertainers who were totally disgraceful during the Women's March on Washington which our National News press did not go into detail about. Where are our Fir mina's? Where are our women that Nehemiah refers too? They are out there. They need to be encouraged. Some like Carmen LaBerge. Read her blog about 'Nasty Women Unite' at https://reconnectwithcarmen.com.

Well God got my attention, plus I noticed where the Church of Saint Mary was having Mass at 5 p.m. It was 4:30. I quickly checked out a Mass held that morning in New York State to familiarize myself then head off for Saint Mary's. Watching the Mass in NY, I figured I was not dressed properly. I did not have on a coat & tie. Well, maybe they would let me in anyway. Lo & Behold, at Saint Mary's no one, about 300 in attendance, had on a coat & tie. I blended right in except for not kneeling, bowing, raising hands and saying the right words at the right time. It was a beautiful service but I would have felt a little more comfortable if someone could have guided me some. And maybe they could use some Door Holders like Passion (www.268generation.com) does to welcome you.

Hey! Hey! Everyone have a Blessed Day. Your KRR guy, A BIC

And oh! One of my grandson's older sisters who was homeschooled just got a Full Scholarship to Oral Roberts University. Maybe the future does not look so bleak with girls like her and those thousands upon thousands from all over the world connecting with Passion.

Sacred Heart Catholic Church

Sapulpa Church Drive

November 1, 2017

Hey Wayne, Dan, and others…. the KRR guy out and about,

Last Friday I was making my way to a call in Sapulpa on Highway 75 and as I was passing by the Kirk Crossing Church I remembered I needed to ask God if there was a church He wanted me to visit the coming Sunday. Well it didn't take long for Him to get my attention. In just about 3 or 4 miles, after getting on to West 121st (Highway 117 and Sapulpa East Taft Street) I catch a glimpse of what I thought was a red metal barn roof with a white cross painted on it. I just barely saw it because of the trees and the rolling hillside in that part of Sapulpa. Well, well, well…. I figured I had better check it out, so the first street I could turn right on…. I did. There was a small sign saying turn right to Sacred Heart Catholic Church. After entering this neighborhood, the next street where I could turn right on was another small sign pointing to the right saying Sacred Heart Church. This road was really narrow and I had to squeeze by a truck that was parked on the side. In about a block, I came upon a beautiful piece of scenery. Here was a beautiful church building with a view of the trees and rolling hills around it. Okay God! I'll visit them on Sunday.

I've visited a couple of churches nearby in the past and have noticed several other churches in the immediate area but this was the first time this one caught my attention. I would call this the Sapulpa Church Drive because there must be 10 to 12 churches within about a 2-mile area here. And this church is celebrating its 110th anniversary this year. It was first established in 1907, the same year that Oklahoma became a state. It started out in another location in a white frame building and then in 1922 it moved into a Gothic brick structure. It was in 1989, or 28 years ago that this new location became its home.

I checked to see when their Sunday services were and they have an 8:00am (Spanish) Mass and a 10:30am Mass. So, I figured I would go to

Hmmm! Who's Speaking?

the Kirk Crossing Contemporary Services at 9:30 and then skip over to the 10:30 Mass at the Sacred Heart Catholic Church.

Well on Sunday I went to the Kirk Crossing and the first thing I see are a bunch of excited little kids running from the parking lot to get to the church. You could see the excitement on their faces. Once inside, the church was packed with little kids. I understand when there is a 5th Sunday in a month, all preschool up through elementary kids are invited into the main church for worship and announcements. The seating accommodated about 300 and it was packed out. When the kids were excused to go to their respective classrooms after worship and announcements, the sanctuary diminished in size to about 200. Yes! One-third of the attendance were excited kids. I saw families with one, two, three and even four kids in this age bracket. Why so many? Lots of young families going to this new church with lots of new homes in the area and I'm sure offering a preschool program helps too.

You can check out the preschool by going to www.jenkschamber.com/kirk-crossing-expands-preschool

Well, I skipped out a little early to go down the road to Sacred Heart Catholic Church. Now, I've visited a few Catholic churches in the past and I know I would have a hard time keeping up with the order of worship but I was going to tackle it again anyway. I did a little review on the web and discovered the Catholic churches may have a Closed Communion or an Open Communion. What I discovered is that it is mainly a Closed Communion when it is for those members only of that particular church or maybe anyone who is Catholic. Open Communion can be for anyone who is a Christian.

When I arrive, they had already begun. Obviously, promptly right on schedule. I didn't see a program that would help me follow the service so I knew I was in trouble. As I walked in my hearing started giving me problems. There was a loud humming noise in my head. I attempted adjusting my hearing aids but it was not helping. Later, I realized God most likely had something to do with that. They had about 75 in attendance and even though they had an earlier Spanish Mass, about 1/4th of this Mass were Hispanic attendees.

Like the Catholic Churches I have visited previously, everything is in a traditional ritualistic order and you need to be a Catholic through

Church Visits- Catholics

and through to keep up with it. They even asked everyone to greet others around them and they told you exactly what to say to them. When it came time for communion I turned to the retired couple next to me and asked the gentleman if this parish had a Closed or Open Communion. He said he didn't know for sure because they were from Texas. He then informed me that his wife said it is a Closed Communion, so I said I'll move so you both can go up front. After the Mass he came up and said he had checked further and that all Catholic Communions are closed to only Catholics. I didn't say anything but when one goes to their search engine you will find all sorts of explanations. And even Pope Francis, has implied that changes may be coming. Evidently, there are several families where one is a Catholic and the spouse is of another Christian faith and they say they feel very uncomfortable when their spouse cannot join them for communion.

After the service, I went outside to check out the beautiful Devotional Garden they have and the scenic beauty around them. That was when I realized my hearing problem had completely disappeared. Hmmm? Did God plan that? Did He want me to only observe and not try to join in? He probably knew I would mess the service up and attract attention. He saved me from embarrassment and enabled the Pastor and the Church to have a decent, typical Sunday Mass.

Hey! Check them out at www.sacredheartsapulpa.com

Your KRR guy.... A BIC

Chapter Eight: Church Visits- Seventh Day Adventist

Splitting Logs and Jeans on the Sabbath

Hey Tom & Wayne and others….the KRR guy out & about

I recently contacted someone I knew in the custodial business to help me do some major clean-up in a vacant restaurant location. I was hoping he could do it on a Saturday but he informed me that he was a Seventh Day Adventist and that Saturday was his day of rest and worship. He said he could help me on the following day, Sunday. Whoa! I informed him that Sunday was my day of rest and worship. So, after some discussion we decided on a weekday. We're both Christians but my day of rest & worship is on Sunday like the majority of Christians. But some Christians observe Saturday as their day of rest and worship like the Jews do.

But this incident caused me to start thinking about making a visit to a Seventh Day Adventist (SDA) Church. And then when I heard that Dr. Ben Carson is an SDA and when my son mentioned that he met a girl thru work that is an SDA from the Philippines, I begin to feel God was strongly hinting for me to make a visit. I did a little more research before making a visit and found that they are the most racially diversified religious group in the U.S. According to a recent Pew Research report they are about 1/3rd white, 1/3rd black and 1/3rd others. The Tulsa First SDA church celebrated 100 years this last April and is now located near Tulsa University just off 11th on S. New Haven. Their web site www.tulsasda.org is very informative and is actually the first church web site I've found that addressed 1st time

Church Visits- Seventh Day Adventist

visitors and 'What to Expect'. It informed me as to how to dress, what kind of music I'd most likely hear, times of service (10:45 a.m.) and type of meals. Everything I usually have to guess about.

Being near TU I figured there may be some students there and with the Pastor being a youthful International Black man I thought the congregation may be heavily Black. And from the web info I felt comfortable wearing my khakis and a shirt. Wrong! Wrong! Wrong! With about 75 in attendance there were no TU students that I could tell (probably preparing for a football game or some other TU event). The congregation was about 20% Black & Asian (not the expected PEW report of 2/3rds). And with a more Senior type congregation like myself.... the dress was mainly coat & tie. But even being mainly underdressed for my age, I was made to feel very welcome by everyone in attendance. And I must say the Pastor, Michael Smith, had a great presentation on a great message and the Church Bulletin was full of information and very helpful in following the Worship Service. They have a separate building next door for a Christian school Pre-K thru 12th and another building for a Community Service operation. They had a Spanish Service going on at the same time in another location in the Church building I think, and a Burmese Service follows the English Service at 1 p.m.

Now, on to the Splitting Logs and Jeans on my Sabbath. Yep! On a recent Sunday I decided to split some logs up for firewood the old-fashioned way with an axe and sledge hammer. After splitting up one tree and thinking about heading for another, God intervened and He was either playing a joke on me, upset with this type of work on His Sabbath or telling me to stop before I had a heart attack. You might remember when about 7 years ago the Doctors said I should have died at Boy Scout Camp when I was weed eating the Chapel but God made the weed eater unexpectedly run out of gas and I had to stop, not realizing I myself was also running out of gas. And later finding out my heart arteries were 99, 99, 90 and 50% closed and having to have emergency triple by-pass surgery. Sooo! Just as I was finishing up splitting my first tree and thinking about the 2nd tree, I heard and felt a real big split in my favorite Blue Jeans. Now have you ever heard of Blue Jeans splitting apart? And I'm not overweight and my jeans were loose fitting too. So, with my jeans falling apart and a couple of granddaughters laughing at what has happened, I decided God wanted my attention and I stopped. Hmmm? God has a funny way of communicating, sometimes doesn't He?

All Right! That's all for now but I think God is wanting me to visit a Russian Christian Church way out east of Broken Arrow next. I'll fill you in on that visit when He works it out.

Your KRR guy… A BIC

And Oh! You remember once when I commented it would be interesting if some Churches would invite Guest Pastors from different Churches and different races to exchange Church services every now and then? Well they might want to check out Pastor Smith. I like his qualifications and his presentation.

Chapter Nine: Church Visits- Episcopal

U2 @ Trinity

Hey Tom & Wayne,

Your KRR guy had Holy Communion with U2 at Trinity Episcopal Sunday. I don't think U2 and the Eucharist are ready to Rock and Roll together yet. They had about 100 people there and the sanctuary could have held 300. Of course, I don't know if this is a better attendance than what they normally have or not. I didn't recognize anyone there except for Rick Wells and his wife and son.

    Everyone was asked to sing along with U2, but if you are familiar with Bono and U2, it is hard to sing along with them. So, no one was singing along except for the Minister. To start at 5 p.m., it actually started 10 minutes early and finished promptly at 6 p.m. Everything that was sung, said and done was in the program, except for the sermon by Rev. Kristina Maulden. By the way, FYI, her sermon was only 5 minutes long. Of course, she only made one point.

    I've only been to Episcopal Churches for funeral services, so I had difficulty keeping up with their Traditional Customs. I was wanting to pick the pillow up that was on the floor and put it on the wooden pew to sit on or to lay my head on, but I noticed that no one else was using the pillows for that. Unfortunately, I didn't realize that I was supposed to walk to the front when I entered and do the traditional Father, Son, and Holy Spirit sign. Now I was concerned when I noticed during Holy Communion that everyone drank from the same cup and it wasn't being wiped clean after each participant. You will be happy to know though that I didn't make a scene about this. And, you will be proud of me when I didn't ask for a second sip of wine when I tasted it and found out it was the Real Thing and not just grape juice. After Holy Communion and the Wine, I felt a lot better about things and even started to sing along. Everyone must have appreciated my singing because they were all turning and looking at me. Surely it wasn't the Wine?

Your KRR on the road again,

Chapter Ten: Church Visits- Lutheran

Grace Lutheran Church

WWOW- Wonderful Wonders of Worship

Hey Tom, Wayne & Others.... the KRR guy out and about again,

I got to visit a couple of Churches this last Sunday and what an uplifting day it was after not such a day the day before. As normal, a couple of days earlier, I was asking God to direct me to what Church He would like me to visit, if He actually wanted me to make a visit, and to make it as plain as possible so I would know.

    Saturday morning my son was to fly out to Lima, Peru (fyi...Lima's population is about the same as New York City). He was going to visit a strong Christian family there and he needed a ride to the airport so he could board about 5:30 a.m. That meant getting him to the airport about 3:30 a.m. Well, at 11 p.m., mid-night and then again at 12:30 a.m. I was awakened by Security calling to tell me that they had not received an arming for the shopping center. I kept hoping someone was there late and would eventually set the alarm or otherwise I would have to drop by there on the way to the airport about 3 a.m. and set it myself. Needless to say, I couldn't sleep anyway after those calls. After getting him to the airport I decided I would just stay up and go help the Kirk Karpenters finish up a handicap ramp for someone living in the Tulsa University neighborhood. Now I thought I remembered where the project was but after driving around the neighborhood for about 20 minutes and not locating it I decided that maybe God had other plans for me or I was in no condition to be of any help anyway. So, since being in the Kendall-Whittier Square area (K-W Sq.) I decided to drive by a home that my son has recently contracted to buy in K-W Sq. and check it out. And then a couple of days earlier a customer friend of mine had asked me to bring a clock to his recently purchased vintage home in K-W Sq. which he said was on the same street as the Church at 5th & Lewis. As I drove by I noticed the Church was the Grace Lutheran Church and they had Sunday services at **8 a.m.** and 10:30 a.m. Hmmm? My son's home would be just a couple of blocks away. Hmmm? God is this the Church I'm supposed to visit?

I finally stop driving around and pick up the Tulsa World and pause to read it in my car. Well to my surprise, the big headline in the Faith Section says…**Tulsa church to close its doors in May**. It wasn't Grace Lutheran, but it was another Lutheran Church…. the Ascension Lutheran on Lewis too but near 48th & Lewis and not 5th & Lewis. But what did this mean for Grace Lutheran? And what about Second Presbyterian, now gone, that had been just North down Lewis about 5 or 6 blocks. They had 6 attendees the last time I visited them a few years back, but now a New Church (Redeemed by Grace) has moved in and it is a growing Church. Hmmm! Maybe I should check them out.

A second article in that Tulsa World talked about Swinney Hardware on Lewis & 1st St. that had closed, BUT now will be remodeled and a new tenant opening up. And what about the two elementary schools, Kendall & Whittier that were mentioned but now have both been torn down and combined into one new building (Kendall-Whittier Elementary). O. K. God…. I got the message. I'll go visit Grace Lutheran at 8 a.m. Sunday.

At 8 a.m. I'm thinking older folks. Their web site www.glctulsa.org mentioned services are ritualistic. Oh my! Does that mean coat & tie too? Well I was wrong on the older folks and wrong on the coat & tie, but they were right on the Ancient Ritualistic Service. I should have gotten there earlier or prepared myself better thru their web site because I had an awful time of keeping up with their order of service. There were times when you stood, times when you kneeled, times when you sit, times when you turned to face the participants, times when you crossed your heart, times when you spoke, times when you listened, times when you sang and times when you were quiet. There were times when candles were lit and times when the incense was lit and there was a time when I was wondering what was that

Church Visits- Lutheran

unusual aroma I smelt. And then there was the time for the Sacraments and the order in which it was done and the surprising taste of real wine (I later found out that certain cups contained de-alcoholized wine – Oh Well, the real wine added to the beauty of the ritualistic service).

The traditional Sanctuary would not adhere to a contemporary type service but with the beauty of the building and the beauty and wonder of the ritualistic liturgy, why change? They should just continue to reach out to those in our community who Love and Adore God with reverence and awe in a liturgical way.

The Sanctuary seats around 250 and there were about 50 in attendance at the 8 a.m. service including some young families. A parishioner, Larry, I talked to the next day said the 10:30 service usually has about twice that many in attendance and it is usually loaded with kids. At the 8 a.m. service I set myself down in one of the wooden pews right behind a young family with 3 little ones and asked them if that was OK. They said that was fine if I didn't mind their kids climbing and squirming the whole time. The father of the 3 kids had obviously been brought up in the Lutheran denomination because even with one child in his arms and eyes on another one he was able to sing and follow the liturgy of about 24 different parts of the order of worship without looking at the words in the Hymnal or printed on the handout. And even when the Sacraments were offered, both the mom and dad carried one child in their arms up front and participated and then stopped to light a Prayer candle. Boy! I was impressed.

Hey! This type of church service might not be for everyone but you might want to visit it sometime just to view and realize the wonder and beauty of a traditional ritualistic service.

After visiting this Church, I had time to make the 9:30 Contemporary Service at Kirk of the Hills. They had about 150 in attendance and some families with small kids too. Again, I was pretty near a family with kids and one small boy about 2 was having a great time enjoying the Contemporary Worship music. He was swinging back and forth in his mother's arms and having a great time. However, when the Preacher man came he must have lost interest because then he became a little rowdy and his mom had to escort him to the nursery. Hey! I've been there before myself, when the Worship music & message meant more to me than the Preaching. However, this Sunday, Preacher Dan, had a great message too. I enjoyed both. Preacher Dan was talking about sin in our lives and it made me feel a little guilty when I left the church with two big homemade delicious cinnamon rolls. But hey I could justify eating them because the money to buy them was going to help the high school youth go on their mission trip.

Hey, let's keep getting the Good News out to those who haven't heard the Word.

The KRR guy... A BIC

And Oh! I've just finished a couple of great books by Chauncey Crandall, MD. A well- known Cardiologist out of West Palm Beach Florida. His 2nd book just came out a few months ago *'Touching Heaven'*. Here he was a Yale graduate, highly intellectual and trained for heart surgery. How could he choose faith over science? Everything had to be explained thru science. But then time after time he witnessed those who had flat-lined coming back to life and hearing what they had to say convinced him of the evidence of heaven. You might want to check his book out.

Chapter Eleven: Church Visits-Mennonite

Eden Mennonite in Langley, OK

The Mennonite Visit

Well…Well…. Well Tom, Wayne and others…. the KRR guy had the wrong conception about the Mennonites in Inola and I'm sure glad God straightened me out.

With all my Church visits over the years, my son asked me a couple of weeks back if I had ever visited an Amish Mennonite Church. I responded that I hadn't and that I wasn't even sure I would be welcome. I thought they met in their homes and you had to be personally invited. And I thought since I didn't have a horse & buggy I wouldn't fit in. In years past I would occasionally see them in their horse & buggies on Hwy 412 (the Dan P. Holmes Hwy) when I traveled back and forth from Tulsa to the University of Arkansas. But my son's question did get me to thinking and I thought if God wanted me to visit one He would work it out.

Well, Lo & Behold, maybe you noticed the same news article I did last week in the Tulsa paper about the 'New Gentlemen's Club' with nude dancers on Hwy 412 just down the road from the Eden Mennonite Church. The article mentioned David Wiens, the Pastor of the Church. Oh God! Do you really want me to visit? As the week went along I thought of a couple of other churches close by that I might visit on Mother's Day Sunday. Eden Mennonite was a 35-minute drive away and rain and hail and maybe tornadoes were being forecast for Sunday. Anyway, how would my car fit in with all the horse & buggies? And I didn't have a real large beard (not a beard at all). And what would I wear? I didn't have a hat that

Hmmm! Who's Speaking?

would work and I didn't have any plain black clothing. Surely God you don't want me to go?

I did pull the Church up on MapQuest and pulled up the Satellite view and Lo & Behold I saw pickups and cars parked on the lot and in the open field. Hmmm! I bet the horse & buggies were in the big barn like structure I could see. OK! OK! Maybe I wouldn't stand out like a sore thumb too much. But still the weather forecast Saturday night didn't look promising for Sunday for the 10:30 Service. I get up Sunday and the weather still doesn't sound good, BUT there was a receipt in my pocket from grocery buying a day or so before and as I started to throw it in the trash…. Guess What! I glanced at it and the first thing I saw was 'AMISH MAC'. WHAT? I had to look at that closer and sure enough that was what it said and then it dawned on me that I had purchased some Amish Macaroni. Oh! My! Come on God! It's going to be raining Cats & Dogs and no telling what else. The church is off on a side road S 425 and East 600 Road and it will probably be flooded.

At 10 a.m. when I should be leaving it starts raining in Tulsa. That's it…I'm not going. But then something pokes me and makes me get out of my chair. OK! OK! I'm going. I get in my car and take off just as the rain starts coming down harder. I tell God if it's still raining by the time I get to the Hard Rock Casino I'm getting off the Hwy. It was still raining at Hard Rock and even harder and I could hardly see. Some truck passed me and made so much water spray I couldn't see and I missed the turn off. OK! OK! God! I'm going on but I don't want to. BUT! You Know What? When I reach Road 425 South to turn right, it immediately Stopped Raining and by the time I reach the Church, 1.5 miles down the road, the sky was clearing. Hmmm!

And I didn't get a drop of rain on me as I parked my car in the open field and walked into the Church. Two-thirds of the vehicles were SUVs and sedans and the other third were pick-ups. I was 5 minutes late in arriving and a nice young man, Vernon, greeted me and welcomed me. He said the Pastor was giving the prayer right at the moment and I could go in as soon as he finished. Vernon didn't have a beard. Neither did the next two guys I saw. When I entered into the Sanctuary everyone was dressed contemporary. The women didn't have any white bonnets. They were dressed just like most women I see in most of my Church visits. Most of the men had on clean & pressed blue jeans. The only person with a suit & tie was Pastor Wiens. Hey, I blended right in with the rest of the congregation of around 120.

Up front was the American Flag with a brass eagle finial on top. Opposite the U.S. Flag was the Christian Flag with a brass cross finial on top. There was one Grand Piano, an organ, and then one guy with a regular guitar (not electric). As I read later about the Mennonites, Worship is a big part of their program and what a delight it was. Besides the congregation singing some songs, the Pastors wife played a beautiful song on the Grand Piano. She should be in Carnegie Hall. She got an ovation. And then there was the Young Men's Quartet who also got an ovation.

Then it was time for the Children's Lesson led by Pastor Dave. All of a sudden about 20 little kids popped up from all over the Church and went down front to hear Pastor Dave. And when he finished he gave each one a sucker and you must have heard 20 times, "Thank You".

Now, I didn't see any African Americans nor any Hispanics, but as I read later about the Mennonites around the world (1.3 million) about 50% of them are people of color. In the U.S. about 20% are African-Americans, Hispanics and Asians. Now about Pastor Dave, what can I say? He should be on T.V. but many of the Mennonites refrain from accepting a lot of modern technology and feel a lot of the TV programs are more harmful than good. And I say Good for them.

Pastor Dave started off with his concern on how our country and some of our churches and pastors are trending now. They are moving away from what the Bible says and going along with the vocal minority who accept Abortion and Gay Marriages. He talked about a Black TV Minister that he likes and watches and wishes that he could have the presentation the way the Black Minister does. Well as far as I'm concerned Pastor Dave has a great presentation too. And I figure that the Rogers County Sheriff must like the presentations too because it appeared that he must be a member there.

In research after the fact, I discovered that maybe I wasn't the only one mixed up about the Mennonites and the Amish. One can go to www.FAQ-ThirdWay or type in on your search engine Who's Amish & Who's Not. The Amish and the Mennonites are not the same, but both have roots with the Anabaptist back in the 1500's who put the emphasis on Scripture rather than tradition or new interpretations. Both became two different branches in the late 1600's and when they came to North America they tended to settle near each other. And now the Mennonites are roughly divided into two types, the Traditional or the Assimilated. The Traditional generally grow beards, dress very plainly, the women wear bonnets, still use horse & buggies for transportation, live in rural areas, mainly are farmers and have church services in their homes. The Assimilated more often pursue a higher education and engage in everyday professions and thus live in or near urban areas and wear contemporary dress. They look and act just like ordinary folks except for the fact that they truly live for Jesus Christ. You can read a little more about this Church at www.edenmennonite.com.

As I was leaving, shortly after 12, I discovered that the sun was shining brightly outside now. And inside the Church the SON was beaming down on each and every soul. On the way back to Tulsa I felt an impulse to pull off and go inside the Hard Rock Casino. A beautiful building with lots of lights and sounds but as I walked around inside the people there looked so serious and lonely. They were putting their hope in some one-arm bandits while where I had just come from the people were full of Hope because God was reaching out to them with open arms.

I can understand the Churches concern about the Gentlemen's Club being so nearby, but maybe God put it there so that the young girls working there could be ministered to by this Church and others in the vicinity. For all intent and purposes, you have to consider that a club like this would be involved in Human Sex Trafficking. Close by my office is an Abortion Clinic and about 7 years ago the Roman Catholic Diocese of Tulsa purchased some property right across the street from the Clinic and put up the Garden of Hope where literally thousands of people come over the year and pray for the young women across the street. The Garden is open to any and all Pro-Life Advocates of all faiths and I have witnessed Church vans of Baptists, Methodists and many other faiths on the property. They can be checked out at www.unplannedhope.com.

Well Brothers, Thanks for letting me share this bit of news with you... maybe a few of you were as confused as I was about the Amish & the Mennonites...Your KRR guy...A BIC

Chapter Twelve: Church Visits-Assembly Of God

Woodlake Assembly of God

The New WC

Hey Tom, Wayne & others….the KRR guy out and about again,

I received an oversized postcard a couple of weeks back addressed to 'Friend of Woodlake' at my address in Bixby. Nowhere on the card did it mention the Assembly of God Denomination unless you were alert enough to decipher that from their web site www.woodlake**ag**.org. Also, there was no signage on the new location pertaining to the AG denomination. I had been driving by their new location at 104th & Mingo for the last year while it was under construction and was interested in accepting their invitation to come check out their first service.

I was familiar with their home location in Tulsa on 31st just east of Sheridan having visited there once before. About 10 years ago they purchased around 25 acres in Bixby on an old tree farm and at that time the plan was to build and move there. And their original location was even put on the market for a while. However, along the way, plans changed and they decided to expand by opening up campus sites like several churches are doing now. WC (Woodlake Church) has been around for almost 100 years and now they have three locations with their second location opening in Glenpool last year.

Remembering way back from my previous visits to AG Churches I figured I should be dressed with at least some khaki slacks and a white shirt and I should take along a tie just in case. I was going to attend their

Saturday evening 6 pm service and didn't know how formal or traditional it might be. Well, I was overdressed in my khakis and white shirt. The largest percentage were in blue jeans and colorful shirts. And the parking lot had a good number of pickups. I discovered both Saturday & Sunday Bixby Services are casual & contemporary while they still have one traditional service at their home church on Sundays at 9:30.

I had previewed what I could on the web and found an article by Bill Sherman (the Tulsa World Religion Editor) about Historic Woodlake back in January of this year.

Now, by reading the article, I should have guessed that the dress would have been casual and the service would be contemporary. Why? Well, there was a picture of Rev. Jamie Austin in his church office with some hunting trophies from his hunting trips in Africa. The Zebra stood out really well. Probably too well for a few folks who capsized and made some derogatory comments on the website. I don't know if Sherman had warned Rev. Austin about probably receiving some negative comments or not, but in today's world it is to be expected. You know, wouldn't it be something if when a news article about providing abortions, eliminating school prayer before football games or at graduation, eliminating saying Merry Christmas in public places, removing the Ten Commandments from public view and taking off 'In God We Trust' on our coins and currency would all cause Jesus followers to become suddenly vocal in a loving and caring way. We could tell people about The WAY just like Paul did in Acts. And Acts and Paul was what Rev. Austin's message was about this day.

The article by Sherman in the Tulsa World can be found by typing in Historic Woodlake Assembly Bixby on your search engine.

The new location for Woodlake is not too far from a couple of other Churches and so you may wonder where their members will come from. But I noticed the other day when I was driving by a couple of BBQ places just a block apart, that both were very busy. Obviously, some people prefer one over the other, maybe how the BBQ is served or in the preparation or the friendliness or the folks you may know there. In either case the customers are being fed some good stuff. It can be the same with churches. Each church can feed the Word of God to their members but in a different manner. And hopefully more people will find the WAY.

I noticed the new WC did not have a Cross on the exterior yet. Maybe it's on the Way? I wasn't confused but an LDS Mormon or Jehovah Witness might thank it's one of their locations since they never show a Cross on their exterior or interior. And since I had a little difficulty in figuring what to wear, maybe they could show Contemporary or Traditional somewhere in small type on the exterior signage.

The folks I met and talked with were as friendly as all get out and maybe they had been brought up in an AG Church because it seems like most of the ones I met had names like Paul, Mark, John and David. And in a way now the land, where the church is, was used to plant a seed or a sapling and a mighty tree would grow. Now as a church they can plant some seeds of JC and watch them grow into a mighty & only WAY.

That's all for now from the KRR guy…. A BIC, Have a Blessed Day

Chapter Thirteen: Church Visits- United Church Of Christ

Fellowship Congregational

A Good Parable

Brothers Tom, Wayne & others, the KRR guy....

I hadn't planned on it, BUT God had other plans. Sunday, I attended the 9:30 Contemporary Service with Pastor Dan and left there about 10:35 to go do some paper work. But God directed me onto Harvard Ave. and literally led me right down to Fellowship Congregational Church. I had never attended a Service there and would have gone into the building with the Cross on the top but then I noticed 3 obvious younger visitors who were coming out of there and going to a building that I thought were the Church offices. I did not see a sign telling when their Church services were but as I walked into the building about 10:45 I could immediately see the Services were in progress. I started not to go in but a lady happened by and I asked her what time the Services were and she said they started at 10:30 and so I tried to excuse myself by saying I would come back when I wasn't late, but she insisted that I come in and she opened the door for me. Well, quiet a difference here than with my Mormon Church visits.

There were about 50 people present plus 10 more for the choir. I got there just as the Children's program was starting. About 8 kids were up front listening to a short message. I quickly went over the Church program to prepare myself. The message for the day was titled "Coming Out". There was a strange rumbling noise in the Church and at first, I thought it was thunder but then it was like God telling me that this is what "Hell"

Church Visits- United Church Of Christ

sounds like. Just as the Scripture was about to be read, two obvious young visitors got up and left. Hmmm! Should I take a hint? Soon the Scripture for the day was read: *Matthew 22:1-14*. Then the Rev.? Chris Moore started with the message. The very 1st thing he said was: "This is one of the most ridiculous Parable's in the Bible". He got a chuckle from about half of the attendees'. He then asked "What in the world does this parable mean?" Another chuckle. He went on to say that he thought that Jesus was not the originator of this parable, but that Matthew probably came up with it while he was speaking to a specific audience. He talked about how some Parable's "Stink". He was elated and surprised about the national decision on Monday about gay rights and how our governmental system is finally working positively and that we now have Freedom. He said he went home Monday to tell his two sons about the Great Historical decision that had been made for the World but his sons interrupted him and said mom "has already told us all about it"

His Church has already had a Gay Marriage this last week and that there is a big cake in the foyer to celebrate and enjoy right after the service. He also went on to say that wasn't it ironic that National Coming Out Day was Saturday. This had to be too consequential for even God to have planned it. Another chuckle from the attendees. He said all the churches should now start having a 'Coming Out Day' of their own and start joining in on what is right in Jesus eyes. Rev? Chris said he's tired of debating about what the Bible says. Chris says that Science has proven that homosexuality is natural and not learned. It sounded to me like the Rumble in the building was getting louder.

I briefly checked on Rev? Chris? Credentials and lo & behold he got his degree from Phillips Theological Seminary right here in Tulsa. I looked them up briefly and lo & behold they too performed a Gay Marriage this week at the school.

WHOA! My Brothers and Sisters, we need a 'Whole Lot of Prayer Goin On' Right Now!

Rev? Chris introduced himself to me as I was leaving and I just gave him my first name, but you know I sensed he was aware of something when we shook hands. Maybe there was something Good in that Parable after all.... *Those who do not come to God will not enjoy eternal life.* And maybe Rev? Chris should have gone on to Matthew 22:29 where Jesus says *"Your problem is that you don't know the Scripture, and you don't know the power of God"*. And maybe Rev? Chris has a reason why he doesn't hold his services in the building with the Cross on it. Hmmm!

Well on to some good news...Last Sunday God again directed me. It was my day to hold Worship with the kids at the Juvenile Detention Center. God gave me a message to share with the boys' courtesy of Lecrae Moore, the Christian rapper. I had talked about some of Lecrae's lyrics to them about 3 weeks ago, but then this last week Lecrae came out with a new CD called 'Anomaly' and it went right out and was Number 1 on the Billboard 200. Only the 5th time in about 50 years that a Christian Album came out as Number 1 on the Billboard. Hmmm? Anomaly?...." something out of the ordinary; something rare; something unusual." Some 'Christian leaders?' are downplaying Lecrae, but I tell you he is reaching out to the hurting. He recently toured with Franklin Graham. Lecrae has a "Message" that he is getting out and another Worship song on his album is called "Calling All Messengers". I explained to the boys that what Lecrae is saying here is what Jesus tells us to do in Matthew 28:19-20. At the end of my message I asked the boys if any of them wanted to be a 'Messenger' and every hand went up! [Of the 15 rap songs on the CD, I personally like the last half more than the 1st half.]

Another God thing just hit me.... isn't it interesting that God had me listening and talking about two Moore's? Rev? Chris and Lecrae. And one Moore is much more in tune with God and is Thankfully reaching hundreds of thousands more than the other Moore.

And one more sign from God on this last Saturday. A long story but I will get right to the point. A 'Sick' lady, we believe High on Drugs, contacted me at the shop and said I had to come right away and unlock her Grandfather clock because her medicine was inside and she had lost her key. We had been dealing with her for several weeks but now she sounded desperate. She told me I had to come immediately or she would die. If when I got there I found her on the floor, to immediately call the ambulance because she might be dead. I told her I would Pray for her on the way and that she needed to Pray to God too. She thanked me for that. Well, just b'4 I got there my office called and said she had called and she had found her clock key in her dirty laundry basket. Well, a lot of symbolism there, but I think God answered her prayer and maybe she will figure that out. My staff now thinks that I should be on the 911 Emergency Assistance List for Grandfather Clock Emergencies. We have helped several 'Grandfathers' start "Ticking" again. Ugh! I know, I know, sometimes I get carried away.

Hey, I'm Praying for you guys…. your BIC

Chapter Fourteen: Church Visits- Non-Denominational

Westmoore in West Moore & New Life in Norman

Hey Tom,

Here's your roving reporter again. I still haven't made it to any Hispanic Churches here in Tulsa yet, but I did attend a couple of Non-Denominational Churches today. One in Moore, OK, the Westmoore Community Church, and one in Norman, the New Life Bible Church. Our traditional members who joke about our New Age Contemporary Service in the Upper Room should visit one or both of these churches and then realize how conservative our contemporary service is.

At 9 a.m., my son and I visited www.westmoorechurch.com or WCC, "The flock that rocks". I had an idea what we were getting ourselves into when I saw about a third of the lot filled with Harley's. It was a brand-new building with all the whistle's and bells and flashing lights. Do you remember when I told you I felt underdressed when I visited the two black churches in North Tulsa? Well, this time, my son and I were way overdressed in our khakis and short sleeve shirts. The appropriate dress was Blue Jeans and T-shirts. And, I'm not only talking about the men but the women too. I did not see one woman in a dress, they were in blue jeans or slacks. A lot of Harley & Nike, or the like, T-shirts. And the Preacher? Well Tom, the congregation loved him. He was one of them, in his blue jeans, Nike T-shirt (not tucked in), and Nike tennis shoes. This church is in a medium to up-scale neighborhood. Everyone, and all Caucasian, had clean blue jeans and pressed t-shirts. Obviously, this is a church that's reaching out to a part of society that would not feel comfortable or welcome to a lot of mainstream churches. The Pastors message was also appropriate and I'm sure understood by the congregation "Just Do It". I understand that this is the commercial message that Nike uses and the Pastor was able to tie it into the commercial by James 2000 years ago. James 1:23-25, where James says.... *"And if you do what it says and don't forget what you heard, then God will bless you for doing it."*

Now Tom, I'm not suggesting that you should start wearing blue jeans and a t-shirt when you preach, but this church and the next church I visited did offer something that you might want to check into. They both offered CD's. The Moore church offered the Sunday message on a CD and the next church offered a Free CD to all new visitors. I liked the one particularly from New Life because it seems like a personal invitation to join the church.

The New Life church, www.newlife.info, has been around since 1979 in Norman but just moved into a Brand-New Building 4 weeks ago. In talking to one of the Staff before church, I found out that this church primarily is reaching out to the seekers and new believers. And this was the message by the Pastor too. They stress Small Groups and they do not have Sunday School Classes. They have Contemporary music and have a Drama skit every Sunday (personally, I didn't care for either one, but the audience seemed to). This new building seats about 750, and as far as I could tell it was pretty full. New Life's Pastor was also wearing blue jeans, but had on a shirt (not tucked in). I'm telling you Tom...Blue Jeans are the In Thing!

Both of these churches have an open foyer for refreshments and conversation. Moore's refreshments are free and New Life charges for theirs. Both offer a variety of T-shirts for sale, and evidently the members eat that up, by the number of t-shirts I saw being worn. New Life seemed to have mainly low to medium income families and the church is not close to any homes. It is on Hwy 77 North in a mainly Industrial/warehouse area. I'd say about 5% to 10% of the people at New Life were black. I'd say New Life is effective in bringing in un-churched people. The music at New Life was loud and upbeat. It reminded me of a church in San Jose, Costa Rica that I visited once with our High Schoolers from Kirk. On the CD, the Pastor gives the message of atonement and salvation, which he can't do every Sunday in Church, but it is available on the CD for first time visitors

By the way Tom….I want to say how Proud I was of the Kirk and particularly Tammy Gill at a recent early morning meeting of the Tulsa Mission Mobilizers. I had attended a couple of these meetings in the past and this time the Kirk was well represented by Tammy, Bob Biederman, Carol Davis, and Vicky Vultee. There were about 25 different churches represented and the Kirk had not just one, but five in attendance. It was a panel discussion on what four different churches were doing and how they were doing Mission Outreach. Tammy represented the Kirk. Oh Tom! The Kirk is so far ahead of everybody else in Mission Outreach and how we do it, it is unbelievable. And Tammy, Bless Her Heart, did her part in such a humble way. If it had been me, I'm afraid I would have laughed out loud at some of the other churches and told them how they are doing it all wrong. Tammy showed so much dignity. I was so proud of her and the Kirk. The Kirk is blessed with a wonderful Staff.

Your brother in Christ

Landing Church in Glenpool, OK

Cowboy Up
(Or when things get tough you have to get back up, dust yourself off and keep on trying.)

Hey Tom & Wayne…. the KRR guy rides again….

Well you may have read about the Cowboy Churches in Vinita and Claremore, but let me tell you about what's going on in Glenpool. Have you heard of "The Landings' Church?" It's on 141St just west of Highway 75. Joe Jones is the Worship Leader, the Minister, and I guess handles about everything else. He has had extensive experience in the music industry in bookings, promoting and management of several contemporary Christian Artists and most significantly Carmen. The church first started in a Jenks school on Sept. 9th in 2001, two days before 9/11/2001. About six months later it moved to Bixby, and then in 2008 it moved to the present vacant building.

Anyway, I made it by there last week. Services start at 10 a.m. and the Worship goes on for the first 45 minutes with Pastor Joe leading (and everyone was standing the whole time). Then Pastor Joe goes into the sermon for the next 45 minutes with the services ending at around 11:30. About 150 people in attendance. I was in khakis and everyone else was in Wranglers or Rustlers. Part of the worship music was country/western and the congregation really got into that style of music.

My observations…I do not see the church growing very fast. The location and visibility are not the greatest and the style of worship probably does not attract a high percentage of the population in the area. I would also be concerned about the life of the church if something happened to Pastor Joe who is a graduate of ORU. There does not seem to be much, if any, accountability in place. The church and Pastor Joe are reaching out though to a limited but very loyal constituency in Glenpool and the surrounding area.

You guys are doing a good job of Cowboying It Up with some help from the Man above…so keep it up. Your KRR guy…A BIC

Christ's Church of Owasso

Hitch 'Em Up and Ride Again

Hey Tom, Hey Wayne....the KRR guy rides again,

Is God trying to tell me something or what? Last Sunday He sent me to the Cowboy Church in Glenpool. This Sunday, my daughter invites me to visit her Church, Christ's Church of Owasso, for their 'Western Days' Special Event. Very similar to the Glenpool Church Services except this 'Cowboy' Event only happens one Sunday in the year whereas the Glenpool Church Services are the same 52 Sundays a year, unless Glenpool celebrates with a 'Traditional Days' Special Event once a year. For some reason, I think that is very unlikely to happen.

Once a year though, I think this could be a great event, especially for Kirk Crossing. They didn't have Sunday School. They wanted all the youth in the main sanctuary with their parents for this event. Again, everyone was in their Wranglers and Rustlers (including me this time). Boots, cowboy hats and all sorts of Western Wear. Décor included Hay bales and saddles. Services started at 10 a.m. and ended about 11:30. They had songs like "I'll Fly Away" and "When the Roll up Yonder is Called, Will you be there?"

They had a 'Best Western Dressed' contest and a contest to see who could name the 'Cowboy' movie or TV show the quickest. Then the Pastor, Dale Jones, went into the message. You know, the Glenpool Pastors last name was Jones too. And this Jones was musically talented too and would play the piano for background music while he prayed. His message was tied into a Western Theme on discipleship and 4 points. Ride 'em, Rope 'em, Brand 'em, and Corral 'em.

After the Service, it was Chuck Wagon time. Yup! Barbeque beef, Cole slaw, baked beans, fried potatoes and homemade desserts. Now, why else do you think I would go to two Cowboy Services in a row? After stuffing ourselves, it was then time for Fun & Games. Horse Shoes/ Sack Races/ Hay Wagon rides/ Goat petting/ Pie Eating contests/ Western Quick-Draw shoot-out/ Pony rides/ Sno-cones and Inflatable's for the wee ones.

For a fun Fund Raiser, they had a Jail. And you could have somebody

Church Visits- Non-Denominational

locked up for $1 per minute. And if someone got locked up for a long time, then someone else could bail them out with a similar donation. The funds raised were for a building project.

Now there is one more Cowboy Church in the area that I might attend just to see how it is handled. That is the one where the Minister sits tall in the saddle on a horse for his message. Our DVM David Mitchell raised my curiosity about this. Mitchell said a horse can only stand still for so long and if you have a long-winded preacher, you're going to have problems like Horse flies & tail swattin, gas emittin & other emittin stuff …if you know what I mean.

I think I had better be gettin along…. You all had better get busy and start checkin to see if everybody's name will be on the Roll Call Up Yonder…. The KRR Guy, A BIC

Life Church

Free Movies & Popcorn

Hey Tom, Wayne & others.... the KRR guy again,

Well its' Sunday and what's better than a Free Movie and Free Popcorn. Yup! I found both at LIFECHURCH.TV. I heard about their 4-week series last year from my son, but I didn't get to make one then. So, this year when I got home one day this week and found a flyer on my front door with a Free Bag of Popcorn inviting me to attend one of their 8 Services on Saturday at either 5 or 6:30 p.m. or on Sunday at 8:30, 10, 11:30 a.m. or at 1 p.m., Well.... What did you expect me to do? I know. I know what you are thinking but it wasn't only the popcorn that got me there.

I was planning on doing my Worship thing at the Juvenile Detention Center Sunday a.m. and then skipping over to Life Church on 41st near Sheridan for the 11 a.m. showing. But God had other plans which I will tell you about later.

When I pulled into the back lot at Life Church at 1 p.m. the first thing I saw was a huge Viking Ship with a huge working catapult. Now that will catch your eye when you're in the middle of Tulsa. I asked a volunteer if all Life Church locations in the area had gone to this extreme. He said they all had something, but he thought each one was different. So that means I will need to go visit all 5 of them. Well, once I got past the crowd of kids and young families and inside to the lobby, but what to my surprise BUT there was a 2-story waterfall and a stream running nearby. Whoa! Ho! And then there was the Free Popcorn and Free Drinks for all.

Well for 1 p.m. it was pretty full. They could seat 650 I understand but had set up for about 400. They had regular Worship, a brief introduction and then right into the movie. They emphasized that this movie, based upon the 2004 Tsunami in Asia, was really not quite appropriate for the little ones and invited them to the Kids Life Church instead. They didn't show the whole movie but they keyed in on the religious aspect of certain parts. Very, Very effective.... they could have passed out tissues too. I certainly could have used a few. Well I invite everyone to check this movie

Church Visits- Non-Denominational

out if you have time today or you can catch another movie each of the next 3 weeks. You can still go to your regular church and then sneak this in at another time. Now some of you could probably use two church services anyway. And if you haven't been able to get your friends or neighbors or co-workers to your church then this is an opportune time to invite them to a Movie and Popcorn and tell them you'll foot the whole bill.

Now, what happened at JDC you ask? Well Ben was out of town and Peggy was sick. So, I showed up at my usual time about 9:30 and lo & behold Vicky showed up in place of Peggy. BUT, as we go to check in.... things had just changed and they hadn't had time to contact us. But, the new director had changed the Chapel time from 9:30 to 10:30 in order to accommodate the lunch time with both Section A & B. Vicky did not think she could stay. I could change my plans for LifeChurch, but Vicky could not change her plans. At least she didn't think she should. She was going to have to go off and pray for God's Direction and said she might see me back at 10:30 or maybe not. Normally two of us handle the older boys in Section A and another organization handles the younger boys and girls in Section B. Well, guess who told Vicky to come back? Yup! The MAN Above. HE knew what was going on and what was going to happen. As Always. Vicky & I go in and just as we're getting started with Section A, the JDC director comes in and says no one has shown up for Section B and could we split up. Well, Well, Well, wouldn't you know it. It's a good thing Vicky knew what the MAN was telling her to do.

Hey, Hey, Hey...we all need to Listen and Do what HE asks us to do. The KRR guy...A BIC

Hmmm! Who's Speaking?

Free Movies & Cookies & Popcorn & Drinks

Hey Tom, Wayne & others….the KRR guy getting filled in and filled up,

I hit LIFECHURCH.TV again as they present their 4-week series of **AT THE MOVIES 2015**. Since last year Life Church as grown some more. Up to 24 churches now in 7 States, including Florida and New York. Craig Groeschel, the Sr. Pastor, majored in Marketing at Oklahoma City University before entering the ministry. He started off in the ministry with the First United Methodist Church in Oklahoma City. Then his Marketing started to play a part as he checked into why some people just do not want to go to a Traditional Church. He started figuring out how to reach the non-church goers and Life Church became the 'Most Innovative Church in the U.S.' for two years in a row and is now the 2nd Largest Church in the U.S.

    I went to the 'Movies' and Church last Saturday evening at 5 and it was packed out. The 2nd Service Showing was to be at 6:30. Then on Sundays they have 5 Services at 8;30, 10:00, 11:30, 1:00 and the '**Late Night**' at 8 at the location near 41st & Sheridan. This location was decked out with the 'Cinderella' theme. The Bixby location is decorated in the Gotham City (Batman) theme and Tulsa Hill's theme is from the science fiction movie 'Avatar'. The Church doesn't go by 'members' but instead refer to everyone as 'Partners'. Well they had a ton of 'Partners' who were Volunteers. Many in costume and little kids hanging around them getting pictures taken. And a bunch of volunteers passed out home door flyers and popcorn to all homes within at least a 3-mile radius of the Church. That's how I found out about this years 'Movie Series'.

    The first weekend featured the movie "The Lost Boys of Sudan'. I had really wanted to see this movie when it came out, but my big problem with movies is that I always feel like I have lost 2 hours of my life while watching one whether it is a good one or one not so good. And if I go into a movie in daylight and come out and its dark, I feel like I have lost a whole day. What a delight this is when I can get the whole theme of the movie in 15 minutes AND get Scripture tied in with it at the same time, **and free popcorn, cookies and a drink.**

    Hey! Now I'm not saying not to attend your own Church service, but

Church Visits- Non-Denominational

you need to check this LifeChurch out and you can do it on a Saturday or one of many other times on Sunday. And if you know a church that is stagnated and needs some ideas on how to start growing again…tell them to check out the FREE info that is found at **LifeChurch.tv Resources.** They offer FREE over 7 million resources.

Hey…I'm off again and maybe I'll see you at **The Movies** this weekend. Your KRR guy…A BIC

The Rock Church

Hey Tom and Wayne…. it's me the KRR guy hiding behind the Rock….

Well I wasn't really hiding, but I did attend **The Rock Church** this morning at the Union High School auditorium. This church is Pastored by Billy Joe and Theresa Watts. They were first meeting at an elementary school but after about a year they outgrew it and moved to UHS. The services started at 10 a.m. and it ended at about 11:50. The first 30 minutes was Worship Music that was really upbeat. A couple of songs by Israel Houghton that got everybody clapping and jumping. You know it is kind of hard to jump very long on a slanted floor like is in the Union Performing Arts Center. They only had an electronic keyboard today, because someone (Pastor Billy Joe) had failed to get their early enough to unlock the storage room for the drums and guitars and speaker boxes.

About 150 people were in attendance and about 70% black and 30% white. Billy Joe started his message about 10:30 and then went on a high-speed message for the next 75 minutes without stopping for a drink or sitting down. There was an assistant that would hand him a towel a time or two so he could wipe his brow. He paced the floor the whole time from one side to the other side and up and down the aisles too. Now I wish my hearing aid had a higher speed on it because I could have used it. Billy Joe is like listening to an auctioneer non-stop for an hour and fifteen minutes, except for several 'Amends' from the congregation.

His message was very upbeat and positive, tying in some of the USA Olympic Champions and putting our Trust in God.

If I attend again, I will get something to record his message and then play it back on slow speed.

Hey, you guys have a Blessed Week and keep on watering the Word so that it will continue to grow and multiply. Your BIC…. the KRR guy

Victory Church

Victory at Victory

Hey Tom, Wayne and others…. the KRR guy again,

This last Sunday I slipped over to Victory Christian. A husband & wife team (the Shibley's) members of Victory Church, hit me up recently to come visit Victory and hear their new Lead Pastors…Paul & Ashley Daugherty. The Shibley's are on fire for Jesus Christ and they are bold in reaching out to others. I just happened to overhear them talking to a young repairman at their house about whether he was a Believer or not and that he ought to come visit Victory. Then I heard the wife talking to someone on the phone and telling them that she and her husband would be by Sunday morning to pick them up and take them to Victory. And then not really knowing me they asked if I had a Church or not. My Oh My! I wish there were literally thousands of others like the Shibley's.

    Anyway, they got my curiosity up to go check out Victory's New Lead Pastors. I had visited Victory a few times in the past when Billy Joe and Sharon Daugherty were the Pastors. And then I visited once since Billy Joe died to see how Sharon was doing and the Church itself since they had some negative publicity with some staff problems. The Shibley's are really excited and really impressed with Paul & Ashley. And after visiting there Sunday I can see why. Paul & Ashley make a great team. They are very young (mid to late 20's). Married 5 ½ years with a small child and one on the way. Paul was the youngest son of Billy Joe & Sharon. My son actually attended Victory Christian School for a couple of years and graduated from there. And I believe it was Paul that was in a class or two with him.

    I attended the 9 a.m. Service and was so impressed I stayed over for the 11 a.m. Service to see and hear it again. The 1st Service had about 1,500 in attendance and most of them were Senior Citizens. Dressed in business attire and yet some still jumping up and down with their hands raised high while the 30-member Worship team performed. I didn't recognize the songs particularly but they were upbeat and may have been written by the Worship Leader. They performed for about 25 minutes and then some announcements by Sharon and Ashley and then Paul came on and talked,

Hmmm! Who's Speaking?

WITHOUT NOTES, for the next hour. Paul even played the guitar and sang solo at one point. He mentioned to the crowd that in his younger days (and that could not have been too long ago) he was a Worship Leader himself and that he could go back to that if he ever gets tired of preaching but he thinks God is calling him to be a Preacher now. And I agree.

Since so many of the early crowd were Seniors I wanted to see what the 11 a.m. crowd was like and if Paul gave the same message. Paul was talking about 1 Corinthians Chpt. 7 about marriage (written by another Paul). Victory's Paul talked about marriage and mentioned that he does some marriage counseling also. Well the 11 a.m. crowd started coming in and I would say there were maybe about 3,000 of them. They were younger and there were a lot of families. All were of the human race but of different nationalities and different skin colors and they had on a lot of bright colored clothing.

Along with what Paul talked about in 1st Corinthians 7 he also mentioned 3 points on how to make your marriage better…

1. Don't get irritated so easily
2. Don't complain too much
3. Don't make comparisons to your father or mother or someone else.

So, I look to see great things happening with God's Church thru this young couple. They remind me of what Billy Joe and Sharon may have been like in their younger days.

And talking about Great Things Happening, I helped out again at Passion 2015 at Houston. 15 thousand 18 to 25-year-old College age youth on Fire for Jesus Christ. They had two previous gatherings in Atlanta in early Jan. with another 30,000. Next year they plan to hold 3 events all at the same time. Then in 2017 they will be back in the Georgia Dome with 60,000.

Hey, Keep the Faith Brothers….Your KRR guy, A BIC

God's Shining Light

Hey Tom, Wayne and others…. the KRR guy here

I made it out last week to another church on Route 66 (11th St) just west of Hwy 169. Hey! This is a growing church that is filling a Special Need for some of our Brothers & Sisters here in Tulsa. One of our good Brothers, Kenny Wamble, has been highly involved with this church thru the Worship Group called 'Broken Yokes'. Kenny is the lead guitarist and you can check him out at their web site www.brokenyokes.com.

God's Shining Light Church (www.gslchurch.com) is led by Pastor Dixie who founded the church along with his wife in 2003 with a membership of eight. They have grown to a membership of over 400 with a weekly attendance of more than 900. They have Bible Study; Recovery Programs & Worship going on 5 to 7 times a week and offer breakfast and meals at each one. They presently provide living quarters for many of their attendees in 107 apartments thru Wings of Freedom (www.freedomranchok.com). These are individuals and families that have an addiction and may have been in prison or jail. These are people who need Jesus in their lives but do not feel comfortable in the more traditional churches.

They have two services on Sunday and I attended the one at 11. I was immediately welcomed into the church even though my appearance didn't exactly fit in. I had on a shirt and khakis while most of the 200 in attendance had on jeans and t-shirts. Some had on leather jackets with appropriate religious overtones of a cross or a saying 'Bikers for Christ'. It was about half men and half women and most of them under age 40. As a matter of fact, there were only 4 grey heads in the whole place and that was me, Brother Kenny & a couple of others. About 1/3rd of the attendees had tattoos and some of those also were of religious nature. Some had small children with them while the older children were attending classes of their own.

Even the seating in the church was laid out appropriately for the members. There were three sections with seating for six in each row so that people could easily excuse themselves without disturbing others. And this was needed as I would say about half of the membership got up, went down front or went out and came back in during the 90-minute service.

One young man sitting behind me asked if this was my first visit too and I said I had been here once before. He was born and raised in New Orleans and moved to Tulsa a couple of years ago and loves Tulsa and is excited to find this church. A lady, 1st time visitor, sitting in my row didn't hear when Pastor Dixie invited people to come down front that needed prayers. Pretty soon she saw people heading up front and asked me what they were doing and I told her they were going up front to be prayed for. She quickly excused herself so she could get by and go up front and said "I need some prayers really bad."

Pastor Dixie can relate really well with those in attendance and commented that he's been right where some of them are right now and he wants them to know that "God Loves each and every one of them and God wants to change their life! No matter where you've been, no matter what you've done, no matter who you are – God still loves YOU!" Pastor Dixie talked about what we want! And what we need! He said God knows what we really Need. We really Need God in our lives and when we have HIM in our lives, HE knows what are Needs are and HE will take care of our Needs. HE might not do anything about Our Wants, but HE will take care of Our Needs.

As Pastor Dixie was closing out he asked if those wanting to accept Jesus Christ into their lives right now, to please stand up. I would say about 2/3rds of those in attendance immediately stood up and repeated the acceptance of Jesus Christ into their lives.

As I was leaving I told the young man from New Orleans to have a Blessed Day and he immediately said he was going to hang around the church all day. He likes it here.

Hey, this Church is doing great things and if you see Kenny, give him a high five and tell him you're praying for him and what he is doing.

And since Kenny is originally from Texas you might want to check out something else in Texas. That's the 19 story Cross right on Route 66 in Groom, Texas. Over 10 million people pass by it each year and over 1,000 people visit it each day. www.crossministries.net

Church Visits- Non-Denominational

Hey the KRR guy got Lifted up on his visit to God's Shining Light Church. Maybe you'd like to check it out sometime too or know of someone else who needs to check it out.

Foundations Church

R U AN OU Redneck?

Hey Tom…Wayne and others…. the KRR guy out checking things out again,

Someone hit me up at the Kirk a week ago Sunday and asked what Church I was planning on checking out next. I just said I'll leave that up to God. Well little did I know that God had it figured out and would lead me to it in a matter of minutes. I was heading to my office when I remembered I had meant to check on something and now I was going to have to turn around and go back. I had just gotten on to Skelly Drive at Yale heading east and I needed to get back to 51st. The first street I saw to turn right on was Darlington Ave. Now I don't ever remember being on this street before but just as soon as I get on it I see an interesting Church directly ahead of me. The Foundations Church TV building (www.foundationschurch.tv). Now it was too late to attend that day, but since they had a 9 and 10:45 a.m. Service I promised God I would make it my next church to visit.

The following Sunday after the Kirk 9:30 Service I whipped over to Pastor Justin Graves Church. Being where it is located I assumed most of their attendees would be walk-ins from the apartments in the surrounding area. My assumption proved wrong. Just about 3 blocks east of this Church is the Muslim Mosque which I have visited 3 or 4 times. There were Church Members out near the curb waving at me and any other drive-bys' to come on in. I did and I noticed the parking lot was pretty full and they were mostly new sedans and SUVs and only about 3 pick-ups. When I pulled in I could easily hear some hip worship music. Yup! They had speakers outside the building enticing people to come on in. Reminded me of Church Services in Mexico.

A contemporary sanctuary with a great contemporary worship band that played several upbeat songs for the first 45 minutes. Bright flashing lights all about and a crowd of cleanly dressed folks with arms lifted high. The sanctuary is rather small and may seat only a couple of hundred so as they grow they will need to add more services, expand or move to a larger building. They just moved into this building in 2012 after growing out of

Church Visits- Non-Denominational

a smaller location where they first began in 2008. This church is reaching out to the new modern Christians with the news of the traditional Bible in a high-tech way. They didn't even have a program to pass out, they just told you to pull it up on your phone. And you can pull the service up on 'live stream'.

Pastor Graves is an OU sports fan thru & thru. I got the impression he went to school there and may have been a basketball player. He and a couple of other young people in the audience were tall enough to be basketball players anyway. They have a weekly sand volleyball get together and a scheduled golf tournament coming up. And Pastor Graves introduced one of their college students (Bryce Robinson) who was on the front page of the Tulsa World Sports just a couple of days later as one of the eighth-fastest runners in the world with a 9.99 second dash in the 100-meter run. It is a great read by Kelly Hines with the Tulsa World how Robinson was headed down the wrong path as a homeless High School sophomore when the Billeter family from the church got involved and became his legal guardians and they Praise God for HIS hands in it. And Robinson now knows that God gave him the gift of speed. For more info, you can go to kelly.hines@tulsaworld.com and find the article.

Pastor Graves message was in his series titled 'Redneck' which was not only informative but highly entertaining. So, Are You AN OU Redneck? If so, you would certainly enjoy this sermon series. To me it appears that most of the members of this Church are coming from a distance farther away than from the immediate area around their location.

And to fill you in on my weekend visit to the Goodland Boys Home near Hugo. We had 9 capable members of the Kirk who were guided by a new houseparent there who is a professional carpenter, electrician and general all-around handyman who had us help build some bunk beds and cabinets for the boys who will be moving into one of the houses. And keep the Dearinger family in your prayers as their granddaughter Catherine is doing well but still needs a lot of therapy for her Seratoma type cancer. You can check her story out at www.catherinethestrong.org.

That's all for now until God gives me another get busy call…. The KRR guy, A BIC

Redeemed By Grace

Diversified But United

Hey Tom, Wayne & Others…the KRR guy out and about again.

A little late in getting this report out but I've been covered up. On Sunday, the 22nd I got to visit two churches…one at 9:30 and one at 11. The one at 11 was in the Tulsa University Kendall-Whittier area again. This is the 3rd church visit in this vicinity, all within a few blocks of each other. The first one I visited a few years back, the St. Francis Xavier at 2515 E. 1st St., continues to grow and now has 7 Holy Mass Services on Sundays with 2 in English and 5 in Spanish. A Catholic Realtor I met in the area said they had recently added another Spanish Mass Service.

Then a couple of weeks ago I attended the Grace Lutheran Church and then last week I made it to the RBG Church (www.redeemedbygrace.com). This is a fairly new location for this church and they have been encouraged and assisted by Grace Church in Broken Arrow. The Church building was originally built in 1917 and housed Tulsa's Second Presbyterian Church. 2nd Presb. had as many as 1500 members at one time, but when I visited it once in Dec. of 2003 there were only 6 people in attendance and no one greeted me or another visitor that came in that day. The Presbytery effectively shut it down in 2004 because of some major structural problems and lack of funding from the congregation. The RBG Church has done a tremendous job of getting the building back in shape and it has a whole new fresh look to the interior.

Now by **Diversified But United**, I must explain that St. Francis Xavier is predominantly Hispanic Christian believers. Grace Lutheran is predominantly White Christian believers and RBG is predominantly Black Christian believers. All three within a few blocks and all near Tulsa University. Having made visits to a half dozen or so Black Churches in the past I was sort of prepared on what to expect. One thing, I sort of expected the service to last a couple of hours. I missed it…this one went for 3 hours. I had expected everyone to be dressed in beautiful attire and I was right on there. I also expected to hear some great worship music and here I underestimated what I saw and heard because it was like a

Church Visits- Non-Denominational

Beautiful Broadway Musical Worship that lasted a full hour. My Oh My, to see something like this on Broadway would cost you a Hundred Bucks a $eat. Sometimes the whole congregation was joining in loudly singing in tongues or shouting words of praise. The whole building was vibrating at times and it made me wonder how long the bricks on the exterior of the building would hold together.

This Church is just West of Lewis and just North of Admiral on Archer (76 North Zunis). The Kirk Karpenters with some High School students recently built a handicap ramp just up the street on Archer from this Church. It seems that most attendees park in the new parking lot just North across Archer and then enter the side door of the Church. It might help newcomers and first-time visitors to have a greeter outside that door. Once I found my way inside I was immediately greeted by several people and made to feel very welcome. And then during some announcements and prayer times you get to enjoy a big old time Christian Hug.

Now Pastor Lewis talked for about two hours. I wouldn't say it was really preaching but he was getting his message across by telling some stories that obviously connected very well with the congregation. And he wasn't behind a pulpit but he was down front and mingling in now and then with members of the congregation. It was quite obvious that the congregation really enjoyed his approach and his message.

Now here within a few blocks of each other are three great churches, Diversified somewhat, But United in their Belief of God, The Son & the Holy Spirit.

And now to add a little Hmmm! to this report. Early that Sunday morning, and by early I say 1:35 a.m., my cell phone starting beeping & glowing. What in the World? I get up in the dark to check it out and it was a text message from someone in Cushing, OK. They were trying to get hold of someone called Martin and to tell him about someone who had died. What in the world? Why were they texting me? They must have made a mistake. AND THEN, my five Phos Crosses that glow in the dark and were stretched out on my bathroom counter top, started glowing and then going dim. They were not in unison but glowing bright and dim at different times. This went on for about 5 minutes. Now I have been wearing and telling a message about these Phos Crosses for about 20 years and this has never happened before and there is no possible way for phosphorus to do this unless God had something to do with it. Was God trying to get my attention again by demonstrating that He too can Glow and He can have a message for me? Hmmm! Was His message to go visit the RBG Church and to see how they Glow??? Hmmm!

The KRR guy... A BIC

Discovery Bible in Owasso, OK

No French Spoken

Hey Wayne, Dan and others….the KRR out on the Hwy again….

Had a great day last Sunday. Knowing that Scott French was leaving Kirk Presbyterian the end of June to join up with **Discovery Bible Fellowship (DBF) in Owasso/Collinsville** and hearing that he would be speaking at that church on Sunday's in July, I was guided to go hear him. Well…. I didn't see Scott there and so I didn't hear **French Speak.**

But I did hear two great messages by two Youth Pastors. Yup! I started out at the 9:30 Service at the Kirk Contemporary Service and I got to hear an exciting message by Kirks' new middle-school pastor, Marc Ragusin. Then I skipped out to make it to the 11:00 Service at Discovery at the German Corner in Owasso. From what I've heard, German Corner got its name because many years ago it was a Mennonite community and the people there spoke mainly German and Dutch. And the DBF Church was originally a Mennonite Church before it became non-denominational. Well…French was not in attendance and so **French did not speak**, but they had their Student Pastor, Mike Benson, giving the message for the day and he too had a great presentation. And after he spoke they had a young woman, a recent High School graduate, give a very moving testimony. Her message was about overcoming and God will be using her in the future. Her testimony reminded me of what the Mormons do at their services. Another impression I got that was similar to the Mormons, was that this Church was very family oriented. Just a whole lot of young families in attendance and all sitting together. Now those were the only similarities with the Mormons. Everything else at Discovery was Christ centered. Everyone just as friendly as all get out, even to strangers like me. The foyer was packed and everyone having something to drink or eat and enjoying conversation with friends. The attire was casual and the worship was contemporary and Communion the way it should be. Scott's position will be to continue to help Discovery to reach out to lost people and lead people into a relationship with Jesus Christ.

Scott & Rondi and their girls will fit right in. Scott came to Tulsa from Buffalo, New York to attend ORU. That is where he met Rondi and I understand that when he proposed to marry her that she agreed but to one condition…that they would live in Oklahoma and not Buffalo, New York. Thanks, Rondi for keeping Scott here.

The first time I met Scott was at an ice cream shop on South Lewis. The Kirk wanted me to check him out before he was hired to be the new youth minister. Well, he certainly impressed me and about a dozen of the high school youth. The youth connected with him immediately. Scott had recently been the drummer with the then new highly popular Contemporary Worship group led by Darrell Evans. Evans is considered a pioneer in the modern worship music movement. Scott has commented that some of the songs like "Your Love is Extravagant" & "Let the River Flow" were actually God produced 'Live at Concerts' just plain ole spontaneously. I remember that Scott, shortly after being hired, took the High School youth to a Darrell Evans concert in Skiatook just a short way down the road from where Scott is going to be now.

That road happens to be Highway 20 and it is populated with Churches on both sides of the road and just off the road in Claremore, Owasso and Skiatook. I have been able to visit about ½ dozen of them in the last few years and that is probably only about 10% of the total. And now with Scott there as Pastor of Community Groups and Teaching at Discovery Bible Fellowship I know that more Churches will be growing and new ones opening up in the surrounding area and beyond.

Well that's it for this report and I hope to catch Scott in the near future so that I can hear **French speaking & preaching.**

Your KRR guy.... A BIC

Cowboy Gatherin' in Inola

Cowboy Up
aries–aries–aries

Hey Wayne, Dan and others… the KRR guy out & about

Well God had been sending me some hints lately about visiting a Cowboy ministry. I had talked with a couple of our Kirk Vets, Mitchell & Welch, and they filled me in on places to check into and maybe what to expect. You know these logo's on pick up's and some cars that show a horse and a cowboy on his knees at the cross (the praying cowboy)? I thought those were neat and did not realize that usually that implies that those folks attend a Cowboy Church. I've been seeing more and more of these logo's and it is because the Cowboy Churches are growing and growing. They first birthed in 1972 and they are all over the place in Texas and Oklahoma and now they are expanding into all the other states, even including New York.

Most of them must meet 5 characteristics: 1. Be non-denominational, 2. Have No offerings collected or solicited, 3. Have no membership, 4. Have No dress code and 5. Hold their services in non-traditional settings. WHAT? How can they survive? Well they are reaching out to an awful lot of folks who do not feel comfortable in main-line denominations just because of these 5 characteristics. These are explained in a little more detail if you go to www.cowboychurchofvirginia.org. Now the Southern Baptist had noticed the growth of the Cowboy Churches so they jumped in and have started their own cowboy churches but they don't go along with all the original 5 characteristics.

Well, I was guided to the Cowboy Gatherin' Church just past Inola on Hwy 412. And now it wasn't just because they had donuts and Cowboy coffee. Some others in our area even offer biscuits & gravy and others offer sausage & biscuits with their Cowboy coffee. Hmmm! Maybe I better check them out too. No, I checked the one out near Inola because I thought it would be the easiest to find. And it was pretty easy to find but I would suggest that they put up a sign a few hundred yards b/4 you get to the road to turn in on. Us city folks just don't know our way around out

Hmmm! Who's Speaking?

in the countryside. I missed the turnoff and had to go about another mile to turn around and go back.

The Gatherin' Church seats about 400 and they had around 300 at the 10:20 service, which from what I read seems to be about their average attendance. They advertised, and that is one of the characteristics of a Cowboy Church, to come as you are. Well, even though I hardly ever wear a coat & tie to any of the churches I visit, I decided I oughta put on my blue jeans instead of khakis and wear a pressed shirt. And guess what, I blended right in. As a matter of fact, I would guess that 90% of the folks there (men & women) had on blue jeans and looked as comfortable as all get out. Now I didn't take my cowboy hat but maybe I should of because there were a bunch of them there. Now they weren't being worn in the modernized arena chapel area but they were hanging on hooks on the back wall.

They had good old Western Worship music too and some little Buckaroo's in the audience were stompin to the rhythm. Now it was interesting that Pastor Roy Shoop tied in the day before about a Mission work trip to New Life Ranch (NLR) with Numbers 13:1-30. Pastor Roy hadn't been looking forward to clearing some of the hillside on the N LR property because it was going to be hard & dirty work. Just like some of the Scouts in Numbers 13 sent to check out the promised land did not want to enter it because of their fears. We all have our fears about certain things in life, but we have to remember God's promise to help us when we are doing His work.

Now they didn't pass an offering plate which is one of the characteristics of a Cowboy Church but they do give you an opportunity to drop something in a boot, hat or bird house on the way out. In this case it was a neatly made bird house. And even though I wasn't in a pick-up, there were still some other SUV's and sedans. One thing I expected but didn't experience was someone to greet me as I drove in or walked into the farm building. They might not get that many visitors but it is always nice to be greeted with a friendly smile and handshake even if you are a regular attendee. And Oh! For any city folks planning on attending and not wearing boots, then you will need to be careful where you step in the parking lot because there are a lot of horses around.

Oh! B4 I forget... **Aries**... Yup! God woke me up again early Sunday morn around 3 a.m. He was doing His best to guide me to this Cowboy Church. Three times He spelt out the letters a-r-i-e-s. I had no idea what that meant but I wrote it down so I could look it up later, which I did after my visit to the Cowboy Gatherin' Church. Now, I'm not a Zodiac follower so Aries meant nothing to me. I did discover that I'm not an Aries but did read where an Aries is resilient and will persevere. Hmmm! That kind of ties in with Numbers 13 in the Bible where we learn God will help us persevere when we are doing His work.

And one more thing before I shuffle on…have you ever asked your spouse or family where they want to go eat and they come back with 'I Don't Care'? Well just a couple of miles away back toward Tulsa is the 'I Don't Care' restaurant. And from the looks of their parking lot and all the pick-ups I'd say it must be pretty good eatin' there.

Hay. Hay, you all have a Great Day… the KRR guy, A BIC

Cowboy Church in Talala, OK

Talala-Cowboy

Hey Wayne, Dan and others… the KRR guy out and about

Thanks to our Kirk Vet, DVM Mitchell, I was guided and directed to another growing Cowboy Church www.cowboycountryfellowship.com up North of Oologah and Owasso. Doc Mitchell actually provided me a list of several Cowboy Churches in Oklahoma and for some reason I was tempted to go to the one in Talala. Could it have been because they offered homemade biscuits, sausage and gravy before their Sunday Services? Surely not?

Anyway, this was a delightful visit and lots of delightful, Christ-centered folks in attendance. And too, this Sunday, someone brought their homemade Bread pudding. My-Oh-My Someone sure knows my weakness for good food.

This Church is only about 4 years old and is growing. They meet in a big open-air barn right now, but have just started ground work on a new enclosed type barn similar to other Cowboy Churches. They are located on the Common Ground Ranch with 217 acres with silos and a rodeo arena. Instead of pews and rows of folding chairs, they have picnic tables all over the barn with country table cloths on them. It makes you feel right at home like out with the family on a picnic. It makes conversation very easy with those around you. You sit there and enjoy the conversation with your breakfast and coffee right in front of you.

They started the service off @ 9 a.m. with the Pledge of Allegiance and then some Happy Birthday and Happy Anniversary songs. Now I did have on my blue jeans and cowboy boots and a big leather belt but I failed to bring a straw western hat so I still was recognized pretty quickly as not a regular. You could wear your hat until it was prayer time. For about the first 45 minutes it was announcements and foot stomping and hand clapping Worship songs and then a 10-minute break to take a stretch and refill your coffee or breakfast plate. Then about 10 o'clock it was time for the Service and Pastors Cletis and Diana Coe went into their series on '7 Hindrances to Healing'. This Sunday it was on 'Preparing for Healing'

Church Visits- Non-Denominational

with several verses in the New Testament tied to it. Again, as common with Cowboy Churches, there was no official offering but there were a couple of 10-gallon milk cans to drop some money in. And before I left they presented me with a neat pocket sized NIV Bible specially printed for Cowboys.

In talking with the folks at my table I asked them what they thought the reason was for the Cowboy Churches to be growing while many of the main-line denominational Churches are in decline. They said they want to be Biblically Correct and not so much Politically Correct as so many of the main-line denominations are becoming. They also like the smaller type more family type size of Church. If they start getting over 300 to 500 in their Church they will go out and start another Cowboy Church down the road. One of the men told me he likes the way you can come dressed to Church. Sometimes he might be out in the pasture taking care of some horses or cattle and his wife will call out and say its time to head for Church and he said he doesn't have to hurry in and shower and clean up and put own fresh clothes…He can just come as he is. No one is trying to present themselves as better than anyone else. And since this is an open barn, you can even bring your pet dog or dogs if you want to. There was one there this day and last week they said there were 3 dogs.

There were several young families there with a lot of little ones who were enjoying the music and clapping and jumping around until time to go to their classroom. I did not see many Junior or Senior High kids there and when I asked about that the folks said at that age the kids don't want to be seen with their parents or the older folks. However, the Church does offer many activities that attract those age kids and those activities involve other Christian kids. The Church may get their kids to invite other kids to go to Christian led events in and around the area like concerts, ball games, rodeo's or even a Fresh Catfish Fish Fry coming up in a couple of weeks. Hmmm! That sounds enticing to me.

The Logo for this Cowboy Church doesn't just show a Cowboy and his horse at the Cross, but it shows a couple of horses and a husband and wife and a couple of little kids at the Cross.

May God continue to Bless this Cowboy Church and others like it…
Until next time… your KRR guy, A BIC
Oh, one more thing, God woke me up at 3:33 Monday morn (hmmm…

The Spiritual meaning which is The Trinity… Father, Son & Holy Spirit) and something about Fishers of Men. I had been wondering about a new barn looking building going up in Broken Arrow on 129th E. Ave., or Olive, just South of the Creek Expressway. To me it was beginning to look like a Cowboy Church so I felt God was wanting me to check it out. Well, Well, Well….in talking to one of the foremen on the job, it is to be a restaurant, bar and Indian casino. A place to go where you can hope to get lifted up for a little bit. Wouldn't it have been better if it was a place to go to and get lifted up forever? Hmmm!

Chapter Fifteen: Other Religious Visits

Jehovah Witness

Easter* at Kingdom Hall with the JW's
*well I know this isn't quite accurate, but it
is a catchy headline. The KRR

Hey Guys,

I had been wanting to visit a Kingdom Hall in my neighborhood ever since it was put up a couple of years ago. I just didn't know how to go about it. Well, a couple of weeks ago I found an 'invitation' stuck on my front door (copy enclosed). So, you know me. I took them up on it. Before I went, I did brush up on the JW's. Tom, your series on the different faiths and religions and the book *So What's the Difference?* was a big help in getting me prepared.

First off, it's not Easter to them. It's a Memorial Service for Jesus' death, which according to the JW's fell on Saturday, March 22nd, this year.

Well, I stuck out like a sore thumb again. Sorry guys, that's just the way I am. This Hall, which I would say is pretty typical, would hold about 150 people. There were probably about 120 there. About 10% black and 20% Hispanic. Evenly mixed 50% male, 50% female. I must have been the only visitor there because I was the only male there without a coat and tie on. Even the smallest kids had on a coat & tie. At least I did have on my black cargo pants which sort of blended in with all the black suits. I didn't question, but maybe the black suits were tied in to 'Black Saturday'? The other reason I stood out was the fact that there was only one other person there with 'grayish' hair and that guy was the 'Chief' Elder. Just about everyone else was under the age of 50, and most were around 40. The women were all dressed up like it was prom night.

Everyone was very friendly and I probably met about 20 of the men. The 'Chief' Elder explained that the JW's do not have a pastor or minister. The Elders do everything and it was his turn to do the service this particular night. The service started at 8:30 p and ended at 9:15 p. This surprised me, but didn't disappoint me.

The 'Chief' and I had a short conversation before the services started. He wanted to know if this was the 1st time I had been to a Kingdom Hall (as if it wasn't obvious enough). I told him I was a Chaplain with the Boy Scouts and that I like to visit different denominations and religions so that I can relate more with the Scouts from different denominations and religions than my own. He wanted to know what denomination I was with. I told him I was from the Kirk which was Presbyterian, then non-denominational for a while, and now Evangelical Presbyterian. I should have told him we broke away from the PCUSA because they are re-interpreting the Bible. Maybe God kept me from saying this.

They found a seat for me in the back row (either they thought I would feel comfortable there since I was a Presbyterian, or in case I got disruptive they could haul me out faster). I felt there were several people keeping an eye on me to take care of every need. It wasn't fair though when they seated me next to two attractive single ladies.

They opened up with a song out of their hymnal called 'Harvest' which mentioned 'Armageddon' in 1914. One of the ladies handed me her hymnal when she saw I didn't have one. The only other song was sung at the closing, and it mentioned the 144,000 and that God sent his Son Jesus and that Jesus would not rival God.

Before the message started someone realized that I did not have a JW Bible so some guy came up behind me and handed one to me. The message was difficult to understand. The 'Chief' Elder referred to the 144,000 as a medical team that took care of their understudies and they in turn took care of the patients. He also pointed out the growth of the JW's by saying that last year at the World-wide memorial services there were 10.7 million in attendance which was about double what it was 10 years ago.

The Elder then started talking about the sacraments or emblems and

Other Religious Visits

the meaning and the *passing* of them. It then came time to pass the bread and wine. And since they started passing the plate of bread on the front row, this gave me time to flip thru the bible. In a little bit, I realized I had better figure out what they were doing. It didn't look like they were eating the bread so I figured they were holding the bread until the wine came. As it got to the row in front of me I noticed No One was taking the bread. They were just looking at it as they *Passed* the plate of bread. So, I did likewise. Then came the wine, and they did the same thing. Later, in the JW bible (1984) in Luke 22:17 I saw where it says Jesus said "Take this and *pass* it from one to the other among yourselves." Whereas in the Christian Bibles in reference to Luke 22:17, Jesus is quoted as saying "Take this, and *share it (or divide it)* among yourselves". Hmmm! This appears to be one of many times the Jehovah's Witness Bible (their Watchtower publication, the NWT-New World Translation 1984) has mistranslated the real Bible in order to promote their doctrines.

I really did not get to look at their bible as much as I wanted too, so I thought I would hint about getting one. I told the two ladies that I would like to get a copy of the JW bible and asked them if I could find one at a Christian Book Store (Ha!). They both looked shocked and cleared their throats and then signaled for the 'Chief' Elder. They told him I would like a copy of the bible, SO he said I could have the one in my hand. Hey! I didn't expect that. I thought they might have a book shop there in the Kingdom Hall. Well, I now have a *New World Translation of the Holy Scriptures* put out by the Watch Tower Bible and Tract Society, 1984 Revision.

The 'Chief' Elder inquired about his message and asked me if I was confused by it and I truthfully said "Yes!" I did comment about the Passing of the elements and did not ask him to explain it, but quickly explained that I have visited lots of churches and different denominations and have seen the elements done in several different manners but never this way. He then said he would like to talk to me sometime and he gave me his address and cell phone number. Now that was a switch. He and no one else asked me for my phone number or address. And I almost got the feeling that this guy is the one 'Confused' and he wants to talk to someone about it. Hmmm! Maybe we can sic the 'Bear' on him. It has bothered me though, that maybe God wants me to call the guy. So, I just turned it over

Hmmm! Who's Speaking?

to God and told HIM that if HE wants me contact this guy, that HE is going to have to give me a sign. I shouldn't have done that, because today, while pulling up info on the web, up pops *Tips on Witnessing to Jehovah's Witnesses*. Well I'm thinking this could just be a coincidence, so I told God that HE's going to have to give me two more signs before I call the 'Chief'.

Oh! I don't think I will be visiting them again. Hey! They didn't have any food for the visitors, and then they wouldn't even let me partake of the bread or wine.

Well Now, more local news....

I went with a team from the Kirk to the Tulsa Juvenile Detention Center on Easter morning. On the spur of the moment I thought I had better check and see if we had enough going. Bill Clark had kept emailing asking for 'Help'. Well we had just the right number to show up. Howard Littlejohn, Jim Holder, Vicky Rogers, Peggy Parks, and myself. Kenny Wamble was there to start us off with the songs and then he left to go do another gig. By the way, Kenny said he had a fantastic turnout Friday night and a great response at the new church that opened up on 11th Street west of Hwy 169. This church is for people who have been in jail or prison, young or old, who haven't been able to find a church where they feel comfortable or welcome at. I think this is 'Fantastic' and I plan on visiting it in the near future.

OK, back to our group on Easter Sunday. I sat back and observed this time, and I tell you, that Jim Holder knew what to say and how to say it to those boys. And Jim was having terrible back pains the whole time he was giving these boys the word about accepting Jesus Christ into their lives. It was so good, that I told Jim that I certainly would not want to follow him. Well, Howard did. And what a job Howard did. His message tied right in with Jim's and between the two of them I figured we would have a whole net full of new fish. Those two were GREAT!

Oh! Hear this. I was sitting on the front row with a couple of the boys during the singing and both of these boys were requesting Kenny to play certain songs and then these boys were singing right along with Kenny without using the song book. They knew all the words. I asked them later where they learned the songs at, and they said they learned them right here in the last two or three weeks. Oh wow! I still have to look at the song book after all these years.

Other Religious Visits

In our small group gatherings at the end, I had 5 boys, one of which had accepted Jesus into his life 4 weeks earlier. You could tell by looking at this kid that his life is entirely different, and he admitted it in front of the other 4. One more boy accepted Jesus into his life in my group this time. Something bothered me however in talking and praying with these guys. Four of them said they are headed to the Rader Center and that they are just here at the Detention Center for a holding period because Rader is filled up. And they told me that while here, it is dead time for them. That means that they do not get any credit for days toward their sentence while in the holding period at the Detention Center. Personally, I do not feel that is right since it is not their fault that Rader is full. Now, you understand these boys might not be giving me the full story, but I do feel someone needs to check into this. If you feel as I do, then see if Jeff or Bill or someone can clarify this.

Hey, that's all the news for now brothers. Keep the Faith. You guys are doing GREAT.

Your KRR, A BIC

Latter Day Saints

LDS on New Haven

Hey Brother Tom & Wayne.... I'm Back and I'm Driving Again.... So, Watch Out World!

The Docs' said I'm doing fantastic and that I will be more fit and in better shape than before. If that is the case, it must mean that I'll be getting into even more trouble than before.

First off, I made a visit Sunday (8/31) at 9 a.m. to The Church of Jesus Christ of Latter-day Saints (Mormon that is). What possessed me to do this?? Well, you'll have to blame John Haley. John told a reliable source that Judge Jeff is a Mormon. And Haley has told me in the past that he has a memory like an elephant and that he is never wrong. So, since this must be true, I decided to visit Judge Jeff's court room on Friday and pray for him. I prayed outside his courtroom (on the 7th Floor at the County Court House) for about 30 minutes. You know, this Judge is surely praying to God about our case and either he hasn't sensed God communicating with him about HIS Will or the Judge needs some encouragement to act upon God's Will. Maybe I should have left a F.R.O.G. (Fully Rely On God) in the courtroom. Anyway, after praying for Judge Jeff, I went to the Presbytery and prayed for them too.

Well, I decided I hadn't gotten into any trouble yet, so why not visit a Mormon Church this coming Sunday and see what God might have plans for me there. The LDS church at 3420 So. New Haven has two Wards (or branches) meeting there on Sundays. The Riverside Ward at 9 a.m. and the New Haven Ward at 11 a.m. I visited the 9 a.m. services, and you'll be pleased to know that I dressed appropriately this time. I noticed on the web that they advised that you dress in your Sunday Best. Even though I was dressed appropriately, they must have realized that I was not a regular. No one greeted me as I entered. As a matter of fact, I had to reach my hand out to someone to get them to shake my hand and say hi.

Like the JW's, the whole church is run by volunteers and no one is paid anything. They usually have 3 speakers each Sunday and, in this case, they had a young teenage girl and a newly married couple speak. The sanctuary would seat about 250 and there were about 150 there. A good

Other Religious Visits

split of all ages was in attendance. There wasn't a nursery service or Sunday school service for the younger ones, so everyone attended the service. Obviously, everyone was used to this, as the crying of babies and talking and climbing around of small children did not seem to faze anyone. Also, of the 150, I dare say that about 1/3rd of them were bored to death during the whole thing as they were either yawning, sleeping, talking, or ignoring the speakers. Of course, the whole service was very routine and I'm sure what the speakers were talking about (the prophets of the LDS) had been heard before time and time again. It was probably the Most Boring church service I have ever been to.

Some things that surprised me were: Considering that at one time the Mormons were considered racists, there were a couple of black ladies there. Also, considering that they believe you go to heaven thru good works and not thru Jesus Salvation, one of the songs was "God Loved Us So He Sent His Son" and one verse in the hymn was 'the one and only way to God was by Jesus'. The Sacraments involved some young men (probably Boy Scouts) passing the bread up and down each row, and then the wine cups. When I got my wine cup, I first thought.... Hey, this is different, it must be white wine. WRONG! It was Tulsa Tap water. What a disappointment that was to me. Then I remembered that the Mormons abstain from gambling, smoking, and **alcohol.** I thought later, surely, they could have served some grape juice. But maybe it was the impression also that they are worried about. Oh! They also did not have an offering which pleased me just fine, since they were acting like I wasn't even there.

For the Mormons to be so happy and friendly when they knock on your door, it totally surprised me how cool they were toward me. They did not recognize any visitors, and obviously, I was the only one. And when I got up to leave, no one inquired of me, no one said thanks for coming, no one looked at me, and no one said Boo to me. As a matter of fact, I had to sit by myself, all alone on an empty pew. That's OK guys; you don't need to get your hankies out. I didn't even cry about it myself. I took it like a man and left that place. When I left, I noticed that I was the only one leaving. I waited about 10 minutes and no one else came out. Now either they were going on to Sunday School classes or they were standing around talking about that strange looking visitor who would come and visit an

LDS church. I am curious now if all LDS churches are this way, so I may have to visit the one in Broken Arrow next.

Well, that's all for now, from your KRR guy,

You Know, I feel that Judge Jeff will finally make his decision on Tuesday, Sept. 9th and that whatever it is, it will be God's Will.

Love you guys, keep up the good work, I'm praying for ya! Your BIC

Other Religious Visits

LDS & LSD: Latter Day Saints & Losing Sanity Disorder

Hey Tom, Wxxxx & Dxx.... it's me, the KKR guy

Well I did it again. You might remember I visited the Riverside Ward (LDS) Mormon Church in Tulsa a few years back and was so taken aback that I thought I should try visiting one in Broken Arrow sometime. This time God directed me at the last moment to check one out. The BSA (Boy Scouts of America) had just revised their membership and decided to allow openly homosexual boys into Scouting. It was not expected to pass until at the last minute the Mormon Church said they would go along with it. I think God wanted me to satisfy my own curiosity as to why they did this. I sent out an earlier email about that.

I called one of the 3 Wards in Broken Arrow to see what time their services were and they had one at 9 and 11 a.m. and another at 1 p.m. It was about 10:30 and so I thought I would hurry and catch the Fair Oaks Ward at 11 a.m. I didn't have time to review notes from the last time I visited an LDS Church. This time I took off with the same clothes I had put on to come to the Kirk, Kakis and a sport shirt. WELL, this time I really stuck out like a sore thumb. Every older male there had on a dark blue or black suit, white shirt and a conservative tie. The younger males, right on down to 4 & 5-year olds, had on dark slacks, a white shirt & a tie, but no suit coat.

The services were almost identical to the Ward Services I attended in Tulsa a few years back. I got there a couple of minutes late and I saw a little 2-year-old girl with a cute smile standing just inside the door and waving. I made some comment to her father that was sitting in the foyer about what a darling little girl she is. No comment. No Smile. No nod. No Welcome. No Hello. So, I went on in to where the services were just starting. They had set up some extra seats in the back of the room because it was Sacrament Sunday and they probably were expecting more. They had about 225 in attendance and I noticed on the bulletin board up front that they had 197 the previous week. The 9 a.m. Ward had 85 the previous week, and the 1 p.m. Ward had 116 the previous week.

Again, there was no denying that I was a visitor since I was not dressed appropriately. And again, no one, not even one person spoke to me the whole time. So, it doesn't seem to matter whether you're dressed appropriately (like last time) or not. If they recognize that you are not one of them, they totally ignore you. As a matter of fact, I think they really wanted to know about who I was and what I was doing there but they didn't want to ask, so I felt like they sent someone out to check my vehicle out. There were 4 men up front and only two of them every spoke. The Bishop said something to one guy (who looked like Security) and I could tell they were looking and talking about me and the guy promptly left, went outside, and probably to check my car out. I sat down near the back between two older men with their LDS attire on. There were 3 empty seats between them, so I sat in the middle seat. They did not say a thing to me and acted like I was not even there. When it came time to sing out of the hymnal they both had one, but there was not one for me. When it became obvious they were not going to share with me, I started looking around. Then one gentleman was kind enough to point to one across the aisle. He didn't say anything and didn't even look at me, he just pointed. I knew all three of the songs that morning, but they caught me off guard once when certain verses were sung by the women only. I quickly caught on though and kept my mouth shut at the appropriate time from then on.

The Sacraments, like last time, were distributed by young high school boys all dressed appropriately and conducting themselves in Military Style. Again, it was whole wheat bread and Tulsa Tap water. Up until this time and during the Sacraments, no one was talking, no one was smiling and it was very formal. Right after the Sacraments, the Bishop thanked everyone for being so respectful during the Sacraments. Then the first speaker (the youth speaker) got up to speak and all of a sudden it was mayhem. All the families (about half the attendees) with 3 or 4 kids each started talking among themselves, little kids started talking and getting out of their seats, some crawling around, some crying and talking loudly. Parents were talking to other parents and appeared to be having a good time, even laughing. And very few seemed to be paying attention to the speaker except for me and it was hard for me to hear with all the other noise and commotion going on. And yet the speaker went right on like nothing was happening. And the same thing happened again when a Brother Mormon spoke. Obviously, everyone was and is accustomed to this except me. It was LSD (Losing Sanity Disorder) for me.

Services ended about 12:15 and everyone got up and again like last time completely ignored me. But like I mentioned in my email I walked over to talk to the young adult Scout Leader and I introduced myself and started a conversation with him. I can imagine how uncomfortable it probably made him and he probably was fully aware that he was going to get bombarded with questions after I left. He was trying to be incognito and crouched down in his chair rather than standing up to talk with me.

Well, do you think I am Losing my Sanity? Why do I keep subjecting myself to visit Churches/Cults like this? Do I have the Losing Sanity Disorder (LSD)? Don't tell me what you think, please.

Your BIC, the KRR guy

LDS (Last Days Salvation)

Hey Tom, Wayne & others…. The KRR guy once more,

Last week's news of Robin Williams' suicide certainly wasn't the kind of news I wanted to hear. I really enjoyed watching his movies and his unbelievable spontaneous responses to everyday questions. He could bring laughter and joy into anyone's day.

Maybe that was the reason God persuaded me to visit some churches on Sunday. Maybe God wanted to remind me how HE can bring laughter and joy into anyone's life who knows HIM.

Anyway, I thought HIS plan was for me to visit Kirk Crossing at 9:30 and then trip on down the road to the LDS Church on West 121st at 11 a.m. This location houses the Wards for Bixby & Jenks and they meet at 9 a.m. and the Sapulpa Ward meets at what I thought was 11 a.m. but found out later it is 1 p.m. I have been wanting to visit another LDS Church since one of their Bishops in Utah recently disguised himself and found out how unfriendly their Church was to visitors. I imagine you recall my two previous reports on visits to one location in Tulsa and one in Broken Arrow. I don't know if news of my reports had reached his desk or not but the article mentioned how no one would speak or even make eye contact with him. Very similar to what I had experienced. No one, absolutely no one (except the cute little 2-year-old girl) spoke a word to me or even acknowledged my presence. I can guess that he wasn't dressed appropriately either.

My visits this time worked out but it wasn't the way I had planned. God evidently had other ideas. When I arrived at the Jenks School for Kirk Crossing, not a vehicle was in site. No sign, no nothing. Were they not meeting because of the big move coming up next week? I thought for a moment and felt God wanted me to go down the road to the Life Church on W. 81st. Now, you have to understand that I had planned out my attire to look appropriate for Kirk Crossing, white dress shirt and brown cargo pants with no tie or coat. I also felt the white shirt would fit in with the LDS Church in a small way. Well the Life Church service at 9 was just finishing up when I arrived there a little before 10. If I waited until their 10:30 service I would be late getting to the LDS Church. So,

Other Religious Visits

after a short visit inside Life Church, where I was overdressed, I skipped on over to the Kirk where you can feel comfortable no matter what you have on. After saying a few hello's, I was leaving when a couple pulled into one of the Visitor spots on the 61st St. side and hailed me down. They were impeccably dressed and the gentleman asked me if the Kirk still had a Traditional Choir. I replied that they have one of the best around and that is why they don't let me sing with them. The couple had visited the Kirk a couple of times about 20 years ago and then they had moved away but they still remembered the choir. The gentleman had just gotten out of the hospital a couple of days earlier and was still recovering from about a 2 week stay at the hospital. He needed some assistance getting up the steep steps and so I helped him up and said the Kirk had better access on the other side and offered to pull the car around for them but they declined. At the top was Good ol' Everett and I quickly filled him in on the visitors. And knowing Everett I'm sure he did everything possible to make them feel welcome and taken care of. You know since I've been sued for ADA inefficiencies recently I am more knowledgeable about ADA requirements and I thought I had better check and see if the Kirk had a sign at the entrance off 61st noting where Handicap parking is. Yup! There's one there, but maybe we need to put flashing lights on it or something.

By now I needed to get going back to the LDS Church on W. 121st, but then God reminded me of another LDS Church I had seen listed at 74th & Knoxville. Well that was right up the street from the Davis' and right around the corner from the Schick's. Now why hadn't they informed me of this? Well, I whipped by there, but guess what? All I could find was a house and no cars were there. Hey, what's going on??

So off to W. 121st St. and Pioneer Drive. I get there just a couple of minutes before 11. One gentleman had just pulled in next to me and he got out and put on his tie and black coat. Oh! Oh! I'm going to stick out like sore thumb again. De-ja vu. Once inside, no one said Boo to me or even looked at me. And here I was walking around up and down some hallways looking for the Sanctuary, opening doors that said Chapel or Hall and interrupting some classes. I actually walked into one room where someone was leading a class and no one even looked up at me. Of course, they were all dressed appropriately. And something else I noticed in walking around was that about 1 in 4 families had a baby in a baby carrier. Did you know that the Mormons have almost double the birth rate of average American families? They are really family oriented.

I finally decided that I had the time mixed up or they had changed it. Anyway, as I was leaving I saw a group of nice looking young family men and God had me open my mouth. I said I was a visitor and commented that obviously, I wasn't dressed appropriately and that this was the 2nd time this day that this had happened to me. I commented that I was overdressed at the first church and now I am underdressed. One kind man finally spoke and said 'Oh No! You're fine' and then he wanted to know what church I had been to where I was overdressed. This is the morning that, Lo & Behold, the Tulsa World had a front-page article by Bill Sherman about Life Church and the tremendous growth they are experiencing. Now I don't know if these young men had seen the article or not but when I told them it was the Life Church down the way where I was overdressed they said 'Oh Yeah'. You see the Mormon Church is experiencing a downturn in growth like so many Traditional Churches right now. The young men then proceeded to tell me their Ward met at 9:00 and the next Ward (Sapulpa) meets at 1 p.m. One young man introduced himself to me and wanted to know why I was visiting there. I explained how I like to visit Churches and how it helps to broaden my view of the different religious groups I come into contact with thru Scouting. He immediately invited me to stay and join him and some others in a committee meeting they are about to have and he would like to introduce me and I would be welcome to participate and make comments and answer some questions if I felt comfortable in so doing. I told him I wanted to get on because I saw another Church I wanted to visit on the way here. You see, going down Highway 75, I noticed several cars parked at the New Kirk Crossing….so that's where they were meeting earlier. As I was walking out, the young father called out my name and came running up and said he hoped I would come back. He would like to talk with me some more and he would introduce me at their Church Service and then wanted me to talk with some of the Lay Leaders and Scout Leaders. Hmmm….. I'll have to check this out with the MAN and see what HE wants me to do.

Then by Kirk Crossing and I see Sean and some others conversing about things that need to be done before the Big Open House next week. I heard that food and snacks will be available so you can bet that I will be there. By the way, it sure is hard to see the Cross from the Highway because it blends in with the trees in the background. I have heard two other people comment about the same thing and they said without seeing the Cross you think it is just another office building. Hmmm! Something to think about. Well another day and the KRR guy just checking things out and letting God bring His joy and happiness into my life before my Last Day of Salvation….A BIC

Hmmm! Who's Speaking?

LDS and 3 4 3

Hey Tom, Wayne & others.... That KRR guy again,

Well after the invitation last week by the young man at the Mormon Church to come back and visit their 9 a.m. Ward Service, I felt God wanted me to go. Unfortunately, the young family man was not in attendance. Either he was sick or had been expelled for inviting me back. I think it may have been something similar to the latter.

Basically, the same treatment I had received b/4 at the LDS Church in Tulsa and the one in Broken Arrow. Of course, I again was not dressed appropriately and I had my Phos Cross on too. There were two other couples there also who were obviously visitors because they were not dressed appropriately and were being ignored too. And one was an African/American couple. Whoa! What brave souls they were.

I was passed a song book this time by the couple I sat down next to and when I commented I would share it with them they pointed out they had the song book on their I-phone anyway. There were about 180 in attendance. It was again Sacrament Sunday and the Sacraments were handled by about a dozen young men dressed appropriately and done again Military style. And again, white bread and tap water. After the Sacraments, a Church Leader came in and sat down right next to me. Hmmm. Plenty of other seats available but he elected to sit right to my left with the other man on my right. I did actually encourage him to sit next to me as I reached over and pulled the song book out of the seat so he could sit there.

They again had two younger people present messages, one female and one male. The male was a recent graduate of Jenks H.S. and I got the impression he has or is about to be out in the Mission Field. Again, it was hard for me to hear from the back of the room with all the little kids doing their thing and parents also talking among themselves. The young man had a timely message about not judging people by their appearance or actions or surroundings. His message was reminiscent of the Utah Bishop who chastised the Mormon Churches for their unfriendliness last November. You can read the Bishops comments by going to your Search Engine and typing in 'Mormon Bishop dresses like a homeless person'. I feel the young man's message was an expansion on this, but it appears

Other Religious Visits

he was the only one who got the Salt Lake City's Bishop's message at this Ward.

After the services, I went up to congratulate the young man on his message. But I was still being observed and members were obviously concerned about what I might say to him. The Ward Bishop came over and stood right behind the young man while I tried to make a few short comments to him. AND, one woman quickly walked right up like I wasn't even in existence, and started talking to him right in the middle of one sentence I was making. Then after she finished, another woman walked up and again did the same thing. I did finish my comment which was a short analogy and the young man wanted to know who I was and thanked me for coming. I did explain that I had been a BSA Chaplain for over 20 years but left them last year when National made a decision I could not go along with. And I also mentioned my connection with the Juvenile Detention Center and the BGEA Emergency Response Association.

My analogy concerned a recent visit to a Popeye's Chicken on Pine at Lewis. I had gone there to grab a bite to eat at 11:55 a.m. The parking lot was trashed out, they did not have any chicken ready (and others were waiting for their orders), they had not brewed the tea yet, the napkin dispenser was empty, the tables and chairs and floor had not been cleaned and only one door was unlocked. I explained to him, that because of that experience I probably would never visit another Popeye's again, thinking that they would all be the same. BUT, because I had previously been to a Popeye's in South Tulsa and one in Broken Arrow (like my similar two experiences with LDS Churches) I knew they were not all the same. I commented to him that is like his comments about judging people and how we need to check things out if they just don't seem right. Hopefully he got the gist of my analogy.

But my visit to the Jenks/Bixby LDS Ward made my visits to the area Mormon Churches 3 4 3. Unfortunately, they all seem to be the same. Hey, maybe the Kirk Crossing might get some Mormon visitors in the future. Who Knows? But I wouldn't Cross your fingers because I feel anything concerning a Cross could turn them off.

Oh! I ran into the Schick's at the KC Celebration later that Sunday and they confirmed that the Mormons have owned a house around the corner from them for several years, but it is not used as a church but they feel it is housing for some of their Mission Teams.

Hey…that's it for now from the KRR guy. Have a Blessed Day… A BIC.

Other Religious Visits

LDS & Forwarding Address
Do you have a forwarding address?

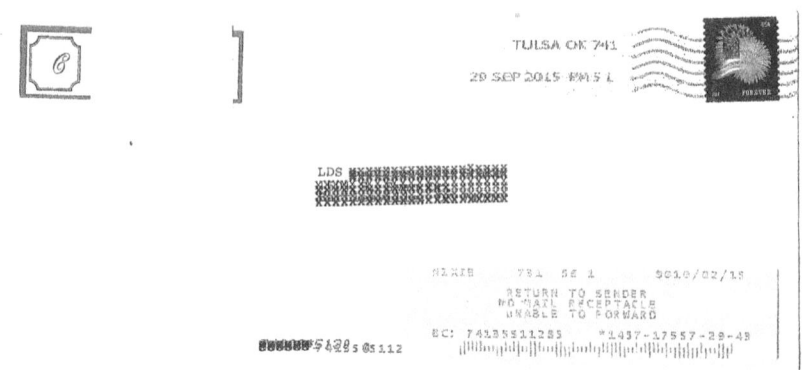

Sunday, December 28, 2014

Hey Tom, Wayne & others….the KRR guy

Another Year gone by and The New Year is approaching and perhaps it is time to ask ourselves "What will be my Forwarding Address?" Am I sure of my Forwarding Address? When you click on the attachment you will see what I received back recently from a letter I had sent to a Mormon Church. I had actually sent them two different letters after two recent visits and they both came back **"Unable to Forward"**. Hmmm…'No Forwarding Address' for this Mormon Church. It kinda makes you wonder?

And they don't have an E-Mail address either so I couldn't connect with them electronically. You know the 'E' stands for 'electronic' but sometimes I like to think of it as 'Eternal'-Mail. That's when God is connecting with us thru His Eternal Mail messages.

Quite often after my Church visits I send a copy of my experiences to the Church to hopefully lift them up and/or to give them some 'Food For Thought'. Since I was unable to e-mail or direct mail this Church I elected to go by and drop off my copy. Well as you can see from the notice from the USPS there was 'No Mail Receptacle' and they were exactly right. There was not a mailbox nor a mail slot. Hmmm! However, I was able to slide my letter underneath the door. You know, I think God was determined for me to find a way to get a message to them.

And also…while there I did notice a large readable sign on their building near the entrance that said "All Visitors Welcome". Hmmm…not from my experience. But maybe there was something in small print that I missed that said "Only if you are a Mormon and are dressed appropriately".

You know, I've had some inquiries about my letters and some of my abbreviations so I thought I would briefly give an explanation. The KRR stands for Kirk Roving Reporter and 'Kirk' in Scottish stands for 'Church' so in essence I consider myself a Church Roving Reporter. I started visiting Churches at a very young age and then got to writing about my visits about 20 years ago when I realized that my home Church Pastors might enjoy hearing about the visits since they are so involved in their own church and never really have the opportunity to go visit other Churches. I was also involved as a Chaplain with the BSA (Boy Scouts of America) about that time and I felt I needed to know more about some of the denominations and religions that the Scouts were connected with that I was coming in contact with thru Chapel Services at Scout Camp. And as a small plug I might mention a book I wrote in 2006 "The Chaplains At Hale Scout Reservation". The book was written basically to encourage others to become Scout Chaplains.

The 'A BIC' stands for either A Brother In Christ or A Believer In Christ which I am, but wasn't always. It wasn't until my early 30's that God finally got thru to me. HE just didn't give up on me and kept trying to get my attention. In High School the YMCA asked me to become a mentor for some 4th & 5th graders. I explained to them that I felt I was agnostic and they should get someone else. But they wouldn't stop and just told me that I would grow out of it. So, I worked with the 'Y' for a couple of years before graduating and going into the Army. In the Army, I joined up to see the world, but I wound up at Ft. Chaffee near Ft. Smith. I had been on a rifle team in High School and at Army Camp I was an Expert Marksman and was told I would probably be trained as a sniper, but lo & behold instead they made me an assistant to the Camp Chaplain. WHAT? From sniper to a Chaplains Aide? Who had that planned out?

After the Army, I headed off to college thinking I could get away from anything religious. I joined a Fraternity and Holy Moly they required you

Other Religious Visits

to attend Church every Sunday. God wasn't going to give up on me and later on HE finally got my attention.

I now am a volunteer Chaplain at the Tulsa Juvenile Detention Center. I'm an annual volunteer for 'Passion' which holds conferences for 18 to 25-year old's, more specifically college students. Passion www.268generation.com is uniting students for a spiritual awakening in this generation reaching utterly millions of students since 1995. And I am also a volunteer Emergency Response Chaplain for the BGEA (Billy Graham Evangelistic Association). They asked me to be a Chaplain after I flunked out of their Samaritans Purse Volunteer workers.

That's a quick synopsis of why & how I became a KRR. And now back to what is important for this New Year. If you or someone you know isn't sure of **Their Forwarding Address** then check out the website www.billygraham.org. And then receive not only a Free Bible from them but also receive a Blessed and Happy New Year.

That's all for now folks.... the KRR guy, A BIC

WAIT JUST A MINUTE...God informed me on Sunday night after writing the above that He wanted more said. God sometimes has a way of getting my attention by physical ways. When I first accepted Christ it was because of a physical touch. And then several times He has awoken me in the night by making my feet feel burning hot. This night, actually at 12:45 a.m., He must have really wanted my attention because He made my whole-body ache so much that I got up, got dressed and got ready to go to the emergency room. I knew I couldn't drive in my condition so I was about to contact my son to drive me to the Hospital. But God sat me down first and wanted more said to the Mormons. I really didn't want to and asked 'Why Me?' But I listened and here is what I feel HE wanted me to say to the Mormons.

I've visited four area Mormon Churches in the past and I have observed them at Boy Scout Camp for several years. They are great family folks. They truly love their kids working with and educating them in a great family way that other religions could take note of. They are also well known for their savvy business abilities. However, they have been misguided by their founder and other Mormon Prophets. Each and every member should thoroughly investigate and check out what they have heard and continue to hear about their religion. They should investigate their bible which in many cases has been reinterpreted and compare it with the one produced by the One True God of Scripture. They should also carefully compare what God has truly said with their 'Book of Mormon' and other Mormon books.

And then after each one has done a thorough investigation, maybe some of them, including their Prophets, Apostles & Bishops should get together and see about forming a new Christian Denomination, and maybe coming up with a new name. Maybe something like 'Family Followers of Jesus Christ' (FFJC).

You know what??? After making notes about the above, I suddenly did not have any more pain and just went back to bed and had a peaceful night's rest. Hmmm!!!

Other Religious Visits

LDS 1 4 4

Hey Tom, Wayne & others…the KRR guy got sent to his 4th visit with an LDS Church,

After the Boy Scouts came out with their new policy I was wondering what the Mormons where going to do and so I felt God directed me to visit the LDS Church in Skiatook. Well I must say I was pleasantly surprised at my reception. You may recall my previous 3 visits to LDS Churches where I wasn't dressed properly and was totally ignored. Quiet a difference at the Branch in Skiatook.

I got there about 11 a.m. on Sunday a couple of weeks back, but lo & behold they had started at 10:30. The door was unlocked so I stepped in and a couple of young mothers with their 4 little ones welcomed me in and said I was late for the Services but they were just starting their testimonies and I could go right in. This is a fairly new building and it will seat 50 people and all the seats were taken. So, one young girl on the back row crawled up in her dad's lap and let me have her seat. As I understand it, a Branch is the same as a Ward, only smaller in membership. A Branch may have 50 to 100 members and a Ward could be up to 600 or 700. And about 10 Wards and Branches make up a Stake. The Stake here is out of Bartlesville.

Hearing the touching testimonies, I realized that Branches and Wards can become just like a large family – sharing things together. It now sunk in on why little children are always running around while an adult may be speaking…it is just like a large family gathering. My attire wasn't quite so out of place here either. One young father had on a sport shirt even. 50 were in attendance and 25 of them were adults and the other 25 were younger family members. One little girl, about 4 years old, who obviously realized I was a visitor, brought me a coloring book, then a Church program, then a pencil, then shared a cookie she was eating with me. Even with the testimonies going on, she wanted me to feel welcome.

About 11:30 things were breaking up and three adults came up to greet me and we talked about the Boy Scouts. I learned that no decisions are made during July because the Utah Headquarters is not meeting. Most likely a decision will be forthcoming in August and it will be to breakaway and form their own organization or join in with TrailLifeUSA. That means that in either case, the Boy Scouts of America will be losing about ½ million members from just this one religious' group.

After our short discussion, I was invited to stay and attend a Bible Study and business meeting but I excused myself and thanked them for their courtesies.

Hey…All Believers should be like that little 4-year-old girl and the world would be a better place to live. Your KRR guy.… A BIC

Other Religious Visits

My Note and My Hope for Mormons....

Sept. 2015

I have had the pleasure to visit 4 area LDS (Latter Day Saint) Churches over the last 3 or 4 years and the privilege to observe some of their Boy Scout Troops at Scout Summer Camp for about 20 years. And for about 15 of those 20 years I served one week as the Summer Camp Chaplain.

I was always impressed with how well their Scout Troops functioned and the number of parents involved even though they never attended any of my Chapel Services. Their Troops would conduct their own Services at their camp sites and mostly their Troops would not intermingle with any other Troops during Merit Badge classes. They kept mainly to themselves. As questions begin to arise as to the direction of how the Boy Scouts of America were going to address issues concerning gay involvement I decided to start visiting Troops sponsored by various denominations and religions to get a feel of what may happen to Boy Scouts as a whole.

Being an inquisitive person, I have always enjoyed visiting other churches or mosques or temples or synagogues. When I visited my first 3 Mormon churches I was impressed with how family oriented and directed they were but then I was also highly surprised at how little attention or recognition they showed a visitor. It was sort of like being at a big family reunion and since no one knew me, they just totally ignored me. I was the uninvited guest. Not one person said hi (except a little 2-year-old girl), no one greeted me at the door or directed me to a seat or thanked me for coming. One location must have been so concerned about who I was that they sent someone out to check out my vehicle. Their Wards and Branches are small in membership to make them more family friendly and so I am sure a stranger's vehicle would be quite noticeable.

But not all 4 of the visits were the same. The last visit I made I felt much more comfortable with and was even invited to stay over for a Bible Study and business meeting. I elected not to stay however since I felt my presence may make them feel uncomfortable. This I know about the Mormons and that is that they do not hold to some of the same New Testament Christian Views that I do. It seems some of their views have been derived by someone's misinterpretation of the Bible and as a result they do not believe in the Trinity nor in Jesus' Free Gift of Salvation and Eternal Life...*1st John 4:1, John 14:6 and 1st Thessalonians 5:21-22.*

My Hope for the Mormons and for our country and really for the whole world is to come to know Jesus as the **Way**, the **Truth** and for **Life** Everlasting *(John 14:6)*. This year the Mormon's have lost 3 of their Twelve Apostles who are the governing body of the church and they will need to be deciding who they want to replace them with. I hope that whoever they decide upon will continue to direct their members to be strongly family oriented and to maintain the same structure of small churches that help contribute to that. However, I also hope that they begin to investigate and open up to the idea that maybe some of their religious views have come from someone's previous misinterpretation of the Bible.

If some become enlightened to the **Way**, the **Truth** and the **Life** and others do not, then maybe a parting of ways should come about just as it has in Scouting and the New TrailLifeUSA and in different Christian denominations and certain other religions.

Our nation and the world are becoming more hostile toward believers and it is more important than ever that all true believers become Good Soldiers of Christ Jesus *(2nd Timothy 2).*

Respectfully,
A BIC

Muslim

Legacy of a Prophet

Hi Tom,

Well, this is your roving Presbyterian Church Reporter again-no, no, no, your roving Church Reporter-no, no, no, your **Roving Religious Reporter** (your **RRR** Man). Yep, I went to a Mosque Saturday night. Actually, it was at the Muslim Peace Academy School at 4620 S. Irvington. Well, what can I say? They advertised a "FREE Dinner and a Movie". The Islamic Society was preparing a Middle Eastern meal before a movie about the life of Muhammad "Legacy of a Prophet". You know me…I'm not one to pass up a FREE Dinner.

Boy Oh Boy, the food was Great, and what a variety of food and the people were really nice. About 30 Muslims and 60 other people were there. I went in and sat down at a table and introduced myself to a man sitting alone. It was obvious he was not a Muslim (he didn't have facial hair). I asked what church he went to and he said Asbury and we talked about Bill Mason and other things going on at Asbury. This guy said he and Mason were born in the same year but he's retired and Bill is still doing a couple of Sunday School Classes and conducting a **lot** of Funeral Services. He asked what church I went to, and get this Tom…The first thing he said when I told him the Kirk was: "Hey they have a Great Scout Troop there. My grandson belonged to that Troop and he became an Eagle Scout under Ken Martin". I'm sorry Tom, he didn't say anything about you, and not even anything about the Church Architecture. And No! I didn't prompt him or say anything about my involvement in Scouting. His grandson was one of the Scouts however that I had go thru the God & Country program back in '97.

Another gentleman joined us shortly and his church was Christ Methodist on South Harvard. He had been busy earlier laying ceramic and vinyl tile in a new building for the youth. Another man joined us a little later and sat down next to me. He was a Muslim. He had a lot of facial hair, a fancy cap, and robe. He's been in Tulsa for about 1 ½ years, coming from San Antonio where his brother is an Allergy Specialists. Prior to that he lived and went to Theology School in Pakistan and got his degree in the Islamic Religion. He told me his name.... but you know Tom, those Arabic names are not easy for me to remember. Anyway, later I found out he is one of the Head Honcho's of the Islamic Society when he went up to the front to answer anyone's questions.

But, back to the movie. Tom, have you ever had one of those calls or mailings where someone offers you a 'Delicious' meal and two FREE nights at a cabin at a place like 'Paradise Hills' in the Heart of the Ozarks? And, all you have to do is listen to a short 1-hour program on the history and amenities of the place. Well, I've taken advantage of those offers 3 or 4 times in my life, and each time I was taken advantage of. Sometimes I was taken advantage of more than other times. Sometimes it was a 'Soft' sale and other times it was a 'Hard' sell, but there was always a sales pitch. The Movie? YES! I got took! What I thought would be about a 1 hr. film on Muhammad turned into a 2 + hour presentation on the benefits of being a Muslim. Oh My! I couldn't believe all the stuff that was in the movie and the playing and twisting of facts. Anyway, they gave me a DVD before I left in case I wanted to view it again. Tom, I don't want it, but I thought you might get something out of it for future reference so I've included it with this report. I know, I know, you can't Thank me enough for my kind generosity. Well, you could invite me to a Free dinner sometime, BUT No! No Thanks! Those FREE? Dinners seem to get me in trouble.

Your Friendly RRR Man,

Other Religious Visits

Letter to Islamic

Sheryl Siddiqui
Islamic Society of Tulsa

Hello Sheryl,

I was one of the several visitors who attended the dinner and movie Saturday night and wish to express my impressions about it. First, I should give you a little history about myself. A white Caucasian, I grew up in the Methodist Church but have been a Presbyterian for about the last 15 years. If you have ever visited a Methodist or Presbyterian Church then you may have some preconceived ideas about the type of person I am. However, unless you are like me and have visited 100's of churches then perhaps you may not understand that not all Methodist, Presbyterian, Baptist, or so many other Christian churches, are the same, even in their own denominations. As a matter of fact, I recently visited two Black Baptist Churches in North Tulsa and they were as different as night and day. One was very open and full of joy and happiness and laughter. There was a Great peace about it, and to me the recognition and feeling of God's presence. The other Church was very formal and authoritative. If you would care to have a more thorough explanation of the differences I recognized, then you may contact me at a later time.

As you can see, I really enjoy visiting churches and other religious faiths. I do not know if God put this desire in me for a purpose or not. But one thing I also normally do is to communicate with the places I visit. Often times just to encourage them, sometimes to give them ideas or thoughts to think about. And sometimes I take what I see and like and pass it on to my church or other churches.

Even though brought up in the Christian Faith, I was not a Faithful Believer or Follower for several years. As a matter of fact, in my High School and College years I considered myself an Agnostic and even expressed that on occasion. But later on, there were some events in my life that God played a part in that transformed me into a person who enjoys life to the very fullest, filled with happiness and joy and peace.

That's enough about me, and now on with my impressions about

Saturday evening. I must say the food that was prepared by your kind members was Fabulous. Some I was familiar with because of a friendship I have established with a Christian Lebanese family who has treated me to some of their native foods. The selection you all presented offered many new and different foods that I had not enjoyed before and they were incredible. I commend those who prepared it all. And **all** the people were gracious and kind.

The film though, I think you and your members could make one that would be more appropriate for showing and distributing than the one presented. If I heard correctly in the film, it mentioned that Muhammad in the Koran said that if you see or hear something that is not good then you should speak up against it. The evening reminded me of years past when I used to receive calls or mailings from a Real Estate Group that would be promoting some property of theirs in some exciting place and if you would just come and see it, they would provide you with 2 Free Days & Nights of accommodations for you and your family and a wonderful evening meal prepared by their finest chefs. And all you had to do was to listen to a short (they usually implied 1 hr.) presentation about the history and amenities of this wonderful opportunity. I took advantage of these offers probably 3 or 4 times in my life, and each time I was taken advantage of. There was always a 'Sales Pitch'. I resented the 'Sales Pitch' as I was capable of making a decision of my own once I was presented the merits of the property. The quote 'Sales Pitch' would sour me on the Real Estate Group and I would have nothing else to do with them. The film "Legacy of a Prophet" soured me, and one person at my table got up and left after 30 minutes, and others may have been perturbed also. I know the Islamic Society is reaching out trying to communicate favorably with Christians, Jews, Hindus and other Faiths since 9/11, and I commend them for that. But, I feel in some cases they may be hindering the understanding and the goal of living together in peace that we all want. If you would want a more in-depth explanation of my concerns with the film, you may contact me.

May Peace and Love Bless You This Week,

Other Religious Visits

7ᵗʰ Century & 21ˢᵗ Century Muslims

Hey Tom…. Hey Wayne and others…. the KRR guy again,

God's been communicating with me again and every time He seems to do something new to get His message across to me. I was going to help out at the Juvenile Detention Center (JDC) Sunday when I got a text from K.T. that it was covered, so I asked God to lead me to a Church on Route 66 to visit. I was thinking God's Shining Light Church but when I got there I was late, so I headed down Route 66 for 3 or 4 blocks and came upon Eastwood Baptist Church. It was a special Sunday for them because the Associate Pastor was leaving after being at the Church for the past 38 years AND they were having a BBQ feast right after Church. I tell you God is looking out for me…Food for the Soul and food for the stomach. Well the message the Associate Pastor gave that day was an inspiring one. Early on in life he lived in sin, even owning and running 3 bars in the Tulsa area and one that featured Go-Go Girls. He told how one day God got his attention and turned his life around. He got married and he and his wife had 7 children and I got the impression they are all helping out and involved in Churches in and around Tulsa.

In a way, his message was along the line I was going to give to the boys at the JDC. I want them to know that no matter what they or anyone has done that God would frown upon, that He/God still loves us and that He wants us to get to know Him on a personal basis. And when we get to know Him as God the Father, God the Son and God the Holy Spirit that we will then begin to know when He is communicating with us. I know personally that He communicates with me almost on a daily basis and sometimes it is utterly amazing how He does it. Maybe you remember some of my experiences such as the Fox at the Cross, the frog in my bedroom, the dove over Moore, the street signs in Colorado, Molly the Donkey, the Bandit Raccoon, the Crowing Rooster and many, many others.

You might remember also my report about a year ago on my visit to the Mosque here in Tulsa. Ever since then I've felt God wanting me to do more. Each morning I pray for them when I put my shoes and socks on. You'll remember that I learned that the Muslims must put on their shoes and socks on their right foot first to please God. Every morning I thank

God for letting me put on my shoes on whatever foot I want to and I pray that the Muslims may someday realize that God is a Forgiving God and that they do not have to earn points to get into Heaven.

The last several issues of the BGEA 'Decision' magazine have had articles on the Muslim religion by Franklin Graham and Billy Graham's daughter Anne and others. Anne describes how millions of Muslims in the world are followers of death and violence and how we need to pray for them (1) Pray the enemy will be exposed, (2) Pray the enemy will be confused, and (3) Pray the enemy will be diffused. She quotes scripture after scripture on how God Exposed, Confused and Diffused the enemy in the past. She specifically mentions 2 Kings 6:8-23 on how to pray for the enemy.

Franklin Graham talks about the only cure for corrupt ideologies and false religions is a personal encounter with the Living God, who *"Wants all people to be saved and to come to a knowledge of the truth"* (1 Timothy 2:4). Only God can transform a murderous terrorist into a servant who is willing to die for the sake of HIS Name. We can remember Saul who became Paul.

Many of the 3.5 Million Muslims in North America claim they are a peaceful religion. If that is so then they should someway disassociate with the radical ones in a very obvious way. Perhaps they should prominently identify their Mosques by maybe identifying them as **21st Century Mosques**. And those Mosques whose members still believe in female circumcision, who believe in stoning and killing their females in the case of sex crimes, who believe in kidnapping and selling young schoolgirls as sex slaves, who consider hijacking and flying planes into buildings killing thousands of innocent people, who cut off the heads of innocent people, who believe the only way to paradise where they get generous amounts of alcohol and dozens of virgins is by being a martyr and killing anyone who is not a Muslim..........then they could be labeled as a **7th Century Mosque**.

But even here with a different tag it will not be a cure all for the peaceful Muslims. When you look at the main-line Presbyterian denomination and the publicity it has been getting over its re-interpreting of the Bible and its allowing of same-sex marriages and gay and lesbian ministers, I dare say that the vast majority of people in America and around the world will connect anyone who says they are a Presbyterian with that belief of

Other Religious Visits

them. Many Presbyterian Churches have broken away from the mainline Presbyterian Church and call themselves Evangelical Presbyterians or Presbyterian Churches of America or Cumberland Presbyterians. However, the majority of people do not realize the difference when there is another name before or after the word Presbyterian. And even the yellow page listings and web listings do not differentiate that well. So, for the peaceful Muslims perhaps they should just look at something entirely different. Maybe they should hear the rooster crowing and just wake up as it says in Mark 13:35-37.

Oh! In case you're wondering how God communicated and got my attention this time, I must say it was a little more painful than just waking me up with Hot feet. I had been telling God for several months I was going to get His message out for the peaceful Muslims and I was Sticking with that thought but I think God was getting tired of waiting and tired of my delays. Lately I thought I should visit the Tulsa University Mosque first. But God must have had other ideas because Sunday night He pushed that Stick right up my rear end and I was in real pain before I finally understood He wanted me to get with it. Now I'm not sure if He just didn't want me to visit the TU Mosque or if He was just tired of my excuses and delays, but the pain went away as soon as I said I would start the very next day.

And if any of you know a Muslim, you might pass this message on to them and then suggest they check out www.BGEA.org and click on 'How to Know Jesus' under Grow Your Faith. And anyone interested in the 'Decision Magazine' they can click on that under News.

And now to my brothers and sisters let us prepare to rejoice in the Celebration of the Resurrection as Paul tells us in 1 Corinthians 15.... your KRR guy...A BIC

Tulsa Mosque: The Happy Mosque

Hey Tom…Wayne…and other BIC's….

Just had a visit to the Tulsa Mosque which I will go into below, but first… do you remember my two visits to two Mormon Churches where I wasn't dressed right or had the wrong color of a suit on? Two visits where I was totally ignored and not one word was spoken to me. Well maybe the Head Honcho in Utah had been hearing reports similar to mine and so he decided to check it out. He decided to visit some Mormon Churches incognito. He dressed down and disguised himself by looking a little unkept (much like what I probably appeared) so no one would recognize him, and lo and behold he was embarrassed to find how unwelcoming the Mormon Churches are. So, he sent out an email and chastised them for their unfriendliness. Hmmm! My! My! My!

Oh! By the way. Do you know that the Kirk has some of the friendliest door greeters I have ever run across? They are fantastic!!! Before you even enter the Kirk, your day is made.

OK, on to the Mosque. God had been nudging me to visit a Mosque. So, I finally got the message and studied up a little on what to expect and how to conduct myself and then waited for God's timing. I planned on attending an evening Friday or Saturday prayer time when they seem to have more attendee's. I was prepared to go between Christmas and New Year's but God evidently had different plans. I wound up going on Friday January 3rd to the after sunset ritual prayer and meeting. This was a couple of days after a Hate Crime had been committed by a man here in Tulsa on a woman who this guy figured must be Muslim because of her appearance. If you remember the news this guy verbally jumped all over this lady because she had parked too close to his car and even intimidated her with a knife and then slashed her tires. I'm thinking 'Well Great' surely God you don't want me to go to the Mosque now do you? They might just be a little upset and unfriendly. So, I was trying to find excuses not to go. A couple of security camera people were to come by my office and check on my cameras and they were to be by around 5 p.m. Well they showed up at 5:30 and didn't leave until about 6:10. The last time I had checked, the last Prayer Call was around 6:00 so I figured it was too late to go. But

Other Religious Visits

God had me double check, and lo & behold the last prayer call now was at 6:35. I checked back on my previous print out on Prayer Times and it said 6 p.m. Hey! What's the Deal? I figured it out later.

Anyway, the Mosque was on my way home so I figured I would drive by and investigate. I get there about 6:20 and there were maybe 8 to 10 cars in the lot. Not very many I thought. A car pulled in right beside me so I thought I would watch and see what entry they went to. No one got out. There was a Taxi cab next to me and I kind of thought that made sense since one see's a lot of Middle Eastern cab drivers. I figured that out later too. I saw a sign posted on what I figured was the main door so I get out to go see what it says. As I go up the steps someone starts honking their car horn and I'm thinking is someone trying to tell me something? The sign read that the Youth Restrooms are being remodeled and are shut down but the Men's and Women's are still open but they are being remodeled some too.

Now I had learned some things that I needed to know about attending a Mosque at Prayer Time, but I was about to learn a whole lot more. And I hope I heard and understood correctly what I am about to tell you. Anyway, I knew I probably should not wear a Cross so I tucked the Cross around my neck under my shirt. I did have on my College Fraternity ring which has a White Cross on it but I figured I could explain that if someone questioned it. And I knew I needed to wash up and to take my shoes off before going to the Prayer Hall.

So, I go in and look for the Men's Restroom and then proceed to go to it. There was a gentleman there already washing up (he's about fortyish). This guy being there was planned by God. God was going to use him and I think God used me too. Anyway, as I was finishing up washing my hands this guy turns and asked me if the soap dispenser was working. I said yes and he replied that sometimes that one doesn't work. He said 'My name is Harom (Aaron)' and I told him what my name was. Aaron and I immediately hit it off and both of us thoroughly felt God planned the whole thing. Aaron could tell immediately that this was my first time to visit at Prayer time. Probably because of the way I washed up. I told him I had been to the Mosque about 3 times in the past but never at Prayer time. I told him I was a Chaplain with the Boy Scouts and that I like to visit other Churches and Religions to get more of a feel where the Boy Scouts

Hmmm! Who's Speaking?

are coming from as far as their faith. Aaron said he was delighted that I had come and that he would show me all around and explain things or answer any questions. Well God had both of us on the same wave link because several times I was thinking about something I wanted to ask and Aaron would answer it before I even asked. Aaron was from Pakistan (where over 96% of the population is Muslim, or over 143 million Muslims and the 2nd most populous Muslim Country in the World). He looked Middle Eastern but talked better English than I do.

First off, I found out I didn't wash up properly. Aaron says you not only wash your hands, but you roll up your sleeves and wash your arms too. And, in his case, you need to rinse off your beard and hair, if you have some. I assume this comes from Muhammad in the Quran as Aaron mentioned that Surgeons have realized the importance of this and that you will see them before surgery washing their hands and arms and then raising their arms up in the air to dry while someone puts the rubber surgery gloves on them. This prevents possible contamination.

On the way to the Prayer Room Aaron pointed out the room where the women will Pray which is separated from the men's Prayer Room. He asked if I knew about taking off our shoes, which I did, but then he went further to explain that they do not want anything to contaminate the Prayer Room because no telling what one may have stepped in or on that day, including dog mess. They do not want anything tracked in on the nice clean plush carpet in the Prayer Room where they will be getting down on their knees with their hands and their heads on the floor.

The Prayer Room was about 5000 square feet and it was totally open and very plain. There were about 10 or 12 chairs along the back wall which Aaron explained are for those who cannot get down or stay down very long on the floor. Aaron asked if I wanted to sit in a chair and I said probably so because I don't know how long I would be on the floor and I might have a hard time getting back up. He said that was fine because he has a bad back and needs to sit in a chair anyway.

He said we will all face the East at Prayer time here in Oklahoma and asked if I knew why? I replied that I thought it was so that they would be Praying toward the Mecca. He then went into more detail about that. Evidently you get more points at Prayer Time if you are facing the right direction. He said sometimes when he is in an airplane it is hard for him

Other Religious Visits

to know which direction he needs to be Praying. I figured if you are in South America you would need to face North & East some.

Aaron then mentioned the importance for Muslims to go to Prayer five times a day and that the first Prayer time starts right at sunrise and then the other times subsequently follow that. Aha! So that was why the time had changed when I checked on it.

Aaron said Prayer Time is announced in predominately Muslim Countries by the use of loud speakers but here in Tulsa they don't do that because they do not want to disturb their non-Muslim neighbors. He said someone will be coming into the room shortly to sound the call to Prayer. Which they did and which I did not understand. So, I had to look it up later.... the person who sounded the call to Prayer is the Muadhan and in English it was:

Allah is Great (repeated 4x)
I bear witness that there is no God except the One God (2x)
I bear witness the Muhammad is the messenger of Allah (2x)
Hurry to the prayer (2x)
Allah is Great (2x)
There is no God except the One God (Allah)

I told Aaron that I had noticed that the Mosque was looking for a full-time Imam and wondered what they were doing in the meantime. He said they were using volunteers for now. The Imam is like a Priest and will read some from the Quran (their Bible) in Arabic and then explain what it says. So, this compared to our Bible Study time or Sermon time.

About this time my cell phone went off and I grabbed it and turned it off and apologized but Aaron said there was no need to apologize. That happens all the time here. And my later observations attested to that. About a dozen or more times I saw someone getting up from the floor and answering their cell phone and just start talking right where they were or maybe walk out the room while talking.

When the Call to Prayer first came at 6:35 there were only maybe 12 or so men and boys in the room. As it got closer to 7 p.m., when the volunteer Imam was to appear, more people begin to show up. When they would first come in they would get down on the floor in their prayer position for

3 to 5 minutes it seemed. A few came in who probably could not get down on the floor so they would go up front and just lean on a wall. After they did this for a few minutes they would get up and then seem to go about their regular routine of visiting with someone. Some came by and said hi to Aaron and me. My dress appearance, casual as usual, blended right in with everyone else. No suits or ties that I could see. While a few might be down in Prayer position, others were up and walking around and talking. Some of the young boys were even running around and talking loudly. A couple of little girls were also present, obviously with their dad or brothers.

While we were waiting for the Imam to appear Aaron kept filling me in on many things. I found out that he is a Taxi-driver and he likes that because it enables him to go to Prayer Time all five times a day. Those Muslims employed in big companies in basically low populated -Muslim countries find it a little intimidating to stop and go to Prayer. Aha! SO! That explains why there are so many middle-eastern taxi drivers! And why seemingly there are some parts of the day when you just can't find a taxi.

By the time the Imam arrived there were a little over 100 in the room and I'd say 90% were middle-eastern. The rest were like me or maybe native-American. I don't recall any Hispanics or African-Americans. I did notice that most of them had a good crop of dark hair. I sort of stood out with my grey hair. About 1/2 had beards and the rest were clean shaven. As the Imam went up to the front, everyone joined up shoulder to shoulder in the front row until it was full from one end to the other, and then a 2nd row begin. Aaron had joined them but he said I was welcome to stay and to hear the Imam. The Imam said something and everyone went down to the floor in Prayer for 4 or 5 minutes. I remained standing along with maybe another one or two I saw. Some little boys were still running around. As they went to Prayer, I went to Prayer with my arms raised up. When the Prayer finished a little 5-year-old boy was standing in front of me and he asked what I was doing. I simply said I was praying to my God just as everyone else was praying to their God. He said Oh! and went on his way. After a bit the Imam asked everyone to sit down and he was now going to explain what he had read from the Quran. Again, a handful went and got a chair while everyone else proceeded to sit down on the floor. Aaron came back and sat down beside me again and said I could stay or leave if I needed to. I asked if this was about the normal crowd and he said yes.

Other Religious Visits

Some stay at home instead of coming, but they do not get as many points if they stay home. He gave the example that they might only get 5 points if they stayed home whereas if you came you would get 10 points. And the points are important down the road because if you don't get enough points you will go to 'Hellfire' instead of Heaven.

Aaron asked what Church I belonged to and I said 'Kirk of the Hills'. He asked isn't that the Presbyterian Church on 61st near Yale? I said Yes! But I personally do not like to say Presbyterian. I explained that when the Presbyterian Division we belong to made the decision to start interpreting the Bible differently we voted to leave. I wanted to totally get away from use of the name Presbyterian because of the confusion it would cause with people unfamiliar with the Denomination, but I was out-voted on that. I commented that it may be similar to the Muslim Religion where they have several different divisions, varieties or sects. Some of these could be more Militant (Islamic Militants), some more compromising (Secularized Muslims), some not so thrilled with the Islamic laws (the Mystics) and who like religious music and dancing. I am not sure what sect of Islam this Mosque fits in, but I know it is not Militant nor Mystic because there was no religious music the whole two hours I was there. Just like in the Christian Religion where we have Baptists, Catholics, Christian Scientists, Episcopalians, Lutherans, Nazarenes and many others, so we find the same divisions with the Muslims. The Christian sects may have some differences of opinion about certain things but do not get into killing each other over those differences except maybe in the case of the Catholics and the Protestants in Ireland. The different Muslim sects in parts of the world do literally fight and kill each other.

I then brought up my concern about Boy Scouts International. I told Aaron that in World Wide International Scouting that about 1/3rd of the Scouts are Muslim, 1/3rd are Catholic and the remaining 1/3rd are all the other denominations and faiths. Aaron was not aware of this and said his children are not into Scouting. I told him about the BSA (Boy Scouts of America) and how they recently elected to allow openly gay and homosexual young boys into the Scout Troops. That was not so much my concern as now the BSA is being pressured to allow openly gay and homosexual Scout Leaders into their ranks. Aaron said 'No Way' and I agreed saying I wonder how this might affect International Scouting and

Hmmm! Who's Speaking?

Muslim parents. Aaron suggested I talk with someone else in the Mosque about this. He mentioned Sister Sheryl Siddiqui of whom I remember visiting the Kirk Scout Troop about 15 years ago to see about her son joining. I talked to her then as the Troop Chaplain and welcomed her to check us out. They came a couple of times but never joined. For what reason, I am not sure. But now, with the BSA changing its' thoughts on 'Being Morally Straight', no Muslim would even think about joining.

Come 8:30 p.m. and the Imam is still talking. Some men have gotten up and left. Some were in the back of the room talking. But if you were up front near the Imam, you were sitting on the floor pretty well at attention and listening to every word. Every now and then some of the kids went running by.

Aaron again asked if I needed to leave, and not knowing how much longer this was going to last, I said I had better get on. So, Aaron got up to see me to the shoe room and to thank me for coming. Now there were about 100 pairs of shoes but I still found mine and just slipped my feet into them. Aaron then commented that they have been taught to always put their right shoe on first because that way it helps prevent them from getting some kind of pain in the side of their left hip. Hmmm! I told him I never paid any attention and asked if he had noticed which foot I put in my shoe first. He jokingly said he didn't pay any attention either.

Aaron was just fantastic and now I'm wondering if he would get any points for being such a great friend. I know that some of my so called 'friends' right now are thinking that Aaron should get a ton of points for having to put up with me.

Two days later, I was talking with about a dozen in trouble High School boys (mainly African-American) and who probably 9 or 10 did not have a dad at home. We started talking about football. We talked about the OU team pulling their upset and getting enough points to win their Bowl Game. Then we talked about OSU and how it looked like they were going to win too, right up until the very last minute. But then they wound up not getting enough points to get the Big Bowl Award. Sometimes life is that way. Some people might think they're going to have enough points to win their way to Heaven but then still worry about what if? Then we talked about being on 'Jesus Team' and there we can have the comfort and

Other Religious Visits

confidence that we will always be winners no matter what the score. For me, what a Blessing that is.

And since we were talking about football, I brought up the name of Tony Dungy who several of them already knew. Tony was featured in a recent BGEA 'Decision' Magazine. He was the first African-American to be a winner in the 'Super Bowl' both as a player (Steelers) and a coach (Colts). He is now involved as an NFL analyst for NBC Sports. He is a fantastic Christian and he and his wife not only had three biological children but now they have fostered, then adopted, six children under 12 years of age. He quit coaching at the top of his career to be used by God to encourage young men to be faithful to their families and in raising their children rather than vacating their homes and responsibilities.

I also told them about finding a Church and that if they do not feel welcome at the first Church they visit, that they should go down the street and try another one. Not all Churches are the same. I told them about my experience with the two Mormon Churches and then went on to explain my visits to about 10 or 12 African-American Churches. The ones I had visited were mostly very open and friendly but there were a couple that were not. If I had only visited the one that treated me like the two Mormon Churches, with not one word being said to me, then I would have gotten the wrong opinion and wrongly assumed that all African-American Churches were the same. I thank God that He sent me to several other gracious and God loving ones.

I also played a song by DeLeon Sheffield (married to a Detroit Tiger player) called 'Come Follow Me' and with a verse that says:

"Why we always gotta judge one another?

Why we always judge a book by its cover?

Weren't we always supposed to love one another?

Like He said?"

DeLeon wants to get the message out to young people in High School to not keep making the same mistakes over and over, but seek God and He'll help you find a different road.

Well, that's it for now from the KRR guy…this report was longer than usual but there was a lot to learn from the 'Happy Mosque'…Your BIC, David Cox

Chapter Sixteen: Trip Experiences

GOD IS ALIVE AND WELL!

Over a Dozen Sightings

Hey Tom,

It's me again. The KRR (Kirk Roving Reporter)! I just got back from my trip to Colorado with my son. I wanted to let you know that GOD IS ALIVE AND WELL! Yup! He sure is! I saw Him. He was busy doing His thing, popping up here and popping up there. You know! Watching out for Andy and me. You know how I can keep Him busy.

Let me tell you how many times He had to pop up for me this time. First off, even though Andy and I are good scouts, we didn't fully do our pre-planning thoroughly. We did take plenty of food, and that is very important. I did check the SUV over pretty well before we left, but there was one small detail I failed to realize the importance of. Now Wayne could have told me this if I had asked him, since he was with the church in Golden, CO for a while. Wayne would have said. **"Be sure and Check your washer fluid!"**

Andy's vacation was Nov. 12th – 18th and he wanted to go snowboarding, so I told him to figure out where he wanted to stay and to make the arrangements. He wanted to snowboard in A-Basin, Keystone, and Breckinridge. So, we made arrangements to stay at a condo in Keystone a couple of months ago. About a week before we left I asked Andy to check on the web and see how many inches of snow they had there. He called me and said he couldn't find any reports on snow amount. So, I suggested

Trip Experiences

that he call Keystone and ask them. He called me back and said they had snow in the upper elevations. What did that mean? He said well, you can take the ski lift up to the top and ski down to where the snow stops. But if you wanted to go home, or go back to the resort areas, you had to take the ski lift down. Well we already had the reservations, so we had to go for it. (#1) Now Tom, I remember telling you I was going and I told several other people who were all asking the same thing.... Is there snow there this time of year? Well, I don't know if too many people were praying for snow for us, or if just one person was praying particularly hard. Anyway, the night we arrived, it started snowing fast and furious. A-Basin got 38" in 3 days. It was a record for the most snow for that early in the season.

(#2) In Denver, before we headed off into the mountains, I pulled off to get some of the local gas for higher elevations. I got turned around and we lost about ½ hour of driving time. I have to think that God did that on purpose, because otherwise we would have been in the wrong place at the wrong time in the mountains. I mean about 10 miles into the mountains on Hwy 70, the snow was really coming down. The radio weather stations were saying that Loveland Pass was Closed and that cars and trucks were crisscrossed and no one can get thru. Thirty minutes earlier and we would have been in the middle of that. The radio was telling everyone to take another route. Even though it meant taking a little longer, we at least made it in to Keystone.

(#3) We got in too late to check-in and get our key, but had been told there would be a box with keys in it if that happened. There was a box there, BUT it had a combination lock on it and we didn't have the combination. Andy looked around and said "Hey! there's some numbers written over here, why don't I try that?" Yup! That worked. This is number three, if you're keeping count.

(#4) The next morning was Sunday morning, and I know that Andy wanted to get up on the slopes bright and early, but he also knows that we find a Church to go to on Sunday no matter what. These Churches have blessed us in some way every time. Yup! It happened again. Saturday night I looked in the yellow pages for a Church to go to that was nearby. Preferably a Contemporary one (Sorry, Tom, but the music keeps me awake). I found a Contemporary Church in Dillon, 6 miles west, that met at 10:30 in the Community Service Center, called the Community

Contemporary Church. We got up early and thought we'd eat breakfast, drop by the Condo check-in office, go grocery shopping (gotta have a lot of food you know), and then go by that Church. We did the first two items and then started looking for a grocery store a little after 9 a.m. By this time, I could sense that Andy was getting antsy, but he didn't say anything. I saw a shopping center on the side of a hill and figured there might be a grocery store there. Going up the incline, I saw something out of the corner of my eye waving in the breeze. Up on the hill was a temporary cloth sign waving that said "One Community Church" Contemporary Service at 9 a.m. It was 9:05. Now Tom, this church was not listed in the Yellow Pages. It is a fairly new church and they are renting space in a new multi-screen movie theatre. They have to meet early so that they can turn it back over for movies at noon. Now get this Tom. A couple of days b/4 we left, David Swezey, a friend thru our Scout Troop and the Landlord of the Mall 31 Cinema, called and discussed maybe leasing the theatre out to some churches. He didn't know if that would be good for the center or not and wanted to know what I thought. Well, I wasn't sure. I didn't know of that. I knew you could find churches in old Wal-Mart buildings and other similar type buildings but had not heard of any in theaters. I'd have to think about that. Well, yup! God led me straight to this one and I got to talk to a couple of the young ladies with the church and asked them how the arrangements were worked out with the theatre.

This church was fairly new, it had about 75 young families in attendance, and a membership, from a roster I noticed, of about 200 families. The service was held in one of the screen areas where there were some nice comfortable seats, stadium style. They had some great contemporary music, then went straight to a movie. Hey! What did you expect Tom? It was a movie house you know. It was a clip from the "Blues Brothers". Now, Tom, for a few minutes I couldn't remember if I was at Church or at a movie theatre. Number (#5) is coming up. I don't know if you ever saw this movie or not, but I hadn't. Anyway, the clip was a scene where the Blues Brothers are visiting an all-black Full Gospel Church. Maybe you remember how I can relate to that. Well, before the clip is over, one of the Blues Brothers sees the 'Light'. And I mean he really saw the 'Light'. Seeing this clip made me think I'd like to see the whole movie sometime. Well, this is (#5). Later that night, back at the condo, after a huge meal (food is important Tom), I'm working on that book and Andy is flipping thru the TV Channels and says "Hey, Dad. Look! They're just starting this movie that we saw this morning. Yup! The "Blues Brothers". I stopped and watched the Whole Thing. Tom, if you haven't seen the movie before, DON'T BOTHER! It was 2 ½ hours long and the only good part was the clip we saw at the movie, err Church, that morning.

The next day, Andy wanted to try out the slopes at Breckinridge, about fifteen miles away. I took a shortcut thru the mountains instead of going the regular route. You know Tom, a short cut doesn't save you a whole lot of time when there's snow all over the mountain road. I took the regular way back to Keystone. About 3 p.m. Andy calls and says he's finished. I told him I'd be there in about 30 minutes. (#6) coming up. I hadn't been listening to any weather reports but I should have expected that there might be trouble ahead when in about two blocks from the condo I came upon a huge dump truck, with a snow plow on the front end, that had just flipped over. One police car had just arrived and I saw another one coming. In retrospect, I'm sure God was trying to tell me something, but I didn't pay any attention. This was #6, but I didn't pay any heed to it, so God had to come to my rescue again very shortly.

It is six miles from Keystone to Dillon. At about mile two, a Blizzard hit. I then turned to the weather station and they were saying "STAY HOME, DO NOT GET OUT! A blizzard is in progress with heavy snow and winds to 60 mph." It was tough to see one car length ahead of you and it got even rougher for me when the windshield wipers started freezing up and could not get the snow off the window. This was a four-lane highway, two headed West and two East with no center medium. It got to where I could absolutely see nothing ahead of me, but you dared not stop or someone would crash into you from the rear. I was sticking my head out the window whenever I could, just hoping I could figure out if I was still on the road. (#7) All of a sudden, some jeep showed up on my right side, about two lanes to my right. I'm thinking, where in the world did that guy come from and what is he doing way over there? I don't even know how I was able to see him, but, it was pretty evident that he was trying to get my attention. He was waving at me and signaling that I come over and get behind him. Tom, I was going west in the lane where cars were going east. I followed this guy as close as I could until he too disappeared. Was

Hmmm! Who's Speaking?

this guy from that church we had visited? Or just someone passing thru? Or could this be one of those times when God sends a mysterious angel and no one can explain it? Sometimes in life we (even Christians) think we are in the right lane, when we're really in the wrong lane. Isn't it nice when someone comes along and guides you back to the right lane. We as Christians should be doing that for others.

I still had no idea how far I was, but I knew I had to get off the highway. (#8) I said "God, I've got to get off this highway, and NOW". You know, God can be pretty quick when He wants too. Bingo!! I see a Green Light. Tom, when God sends you a Green Light, you better go. I immediately turned to my right, assuming that God put a road there. I can barely make out that there is a drive or road on my left after I had turned, but I pull into it and stop. I was going to sit there until the blizzard slowed down some. It slowed down a little after a while. I could then make out a sign right in front of me. It said "Private Drive, No Outlet". Then I looked further and a sign said "Lord Of The Mountain Lutheran Church". Well God made a Believer out of me again. Yes! He is LORD of the Mountain.

I called Andy and told him there was no way I could pick him up. He said he'd catch a bus and come into Dillon. I'm listening to the weather report and they said Hwy 70 is shut down for 70 miles. Andy calls and said he got on a bus but the bus had to get off the highway at Frisco, CO. I said I would come pick him up there, I didn't think it was too far away. I made it into Dillon and go into a grocery store to see how far it was to Frisco. A guy said it is only 5 minutes from here, but the guy said you're not going there now, they've shut down all roads and that Red Cross is opening up shelters for people to stay in. I called Andy back and told him the news. He asked what I was going to do and I said I think I'll go back to the grocery store and spend the night there. Well Tom, listen, where else would you rather be in a Blizzard? Hey, I didn't know how many days these things last. You know, food is important in these situations. Andy asked what he should do, and I said you better stay at the bus station. I know, I know, that sounds mean, but I didn't know how far he would have to go to find a grocery store. But, in about an hour the winds died down and I decided to try and get back to the condo. After another harrowing drive, I make it back and call and let Andy know. Well, I fix a big old pot of Italian Minestrone Soup and eat several bowls. But Tom, I did feel guilty knowing that Andy was still at that bus station and I prayed for him. (#9) Just as I get thru eating Andy calls and says he's on his way. I said the Highway is still closed, and he acknowledged that, but the bus driver was determined to get everybody back so he had put on chains. Andy got back in about an hour, and the first thing he asked was if I had eaten yet. You know, God can sure make you feel really guilty sometimes.

The next three days went fine, but God kept me busy on that book. I had hoped I would have time to ski a couple of days. Maybe God knew if I went skiing that I'd break a leg or something. I did start feeling sorry for myself. I didn't know when I'd get to go back there again, and I'd probably be too old to ski. You know, kind of a pity party. So, I went and ate some more. The last day, Thursday, I took Andy to the Keystone lifts, still in a 'poor me" mood. (#10) I pull up to let him off and I see a couple of Little old ladies in the SUV ahead of me, and I'm thinking how sweet of them to bring their grandkids skiing. Wrong! These gals with their 'blue' hair must have been in their late 70's or early 80's. They proceed to get out of the SUV with their ski clothes and ski boots on. They put on their helmets and grab some skis out of the back end. They swing the skis over their shoulders and head off for the lifts. They were probably nuns. Well, God took my pity party and ruined it.

That night, Andy and I had a lot of food that was going to be thrown out unless we ate it. Yup! We ate it all. We didn't feel too good later, but no food was going to be thrown out.

(#11) We left Keystone bright and early Friday morning and headed east toward Denver on Hwy 70. A few miles into the mountains we see these highway signs that flash different message warnings. These signs were saying "Bright Light Ahead…Slow Traffic". Andy and I are asking, "What in the world are they talking about". Hey, we're from the Bible Belt! Is Jesus coming?? Has Moses come down from the Mountain Top after being with God?? We were anxiously waiting to find out, when we rounded a curve, and WE SAW THE LIGHT. Wow! The morning sun coming around the mountain hitting you in the face, and the sun light bouncing off the snow and ice on the highway, was blinding. It must have been like when the people couldn't look at Moses because he glowed so brightly. I had to immediately put on my sunglasses, but even that did not help a whole lot. The LORD of the Mountain was showing His might and Light again.

We get out of the mountains, thru Denver, and heading toward Kansas. (#12) I start telling Andy about how I feel guilty today, because our Scout Troop was heading to Goodland Boys Home in Hugo, OK later today to fix Thanksgiving dinner for them. I have gone every year since Ken Martin came up with the idea. I had told Ken I couldn't make it this year, and then when I heard later that he couldn't make it either, I really felt bad. Steve Baggett and maybe Beth and their son David, along with some other scouts were going though, so I was sure it would work out. It was just that none of the regulars were going to be there. No sooner had I told Andy this, but a Sign popped up that said turn right to 'Hugo'. It was Hugo, Colorado. Hmmm! God's timing again.

That made me start thinking about some of my trips to Goodland. Tom, I remember one time when Chrissie was there working along with the rest of us. I'd heard you brag about her painting and carpenter abilities, and Tom I will have to agree with you. A time or two when I'd be at Goodland, I'd check on the work I had done and others, and Chrissie's would still be holding up while mine was peeling or fading away. She's really good. Say Tom, if you're at home right now reading this long letter, you might put it down and yell "HEY CHRISSIE!! YOU'RE GOOD AT EVERYTHING YOU DO!". Now, I'm assuming she's off in another room fixing you some food, typing up your notes, painting the hallway, wall papering the bathroom, getting the Christmas decorations down, or something. Now, if she's in the same room with you, maybe you shouldn't yell. You know, we guys don't tell our wives enough how much we appreciate them.

(#13) Whoa! Andy just yelled at me, "Hey Dad, Look, there's Goodland". Yup, sure was, Goodland, Kansas. Not far from Hugo. Hmmm! God's timing again. Now Tom, do you think it would be OK if someone asks me if I went to Hugo and Goodland again this year, I could say Yup! Hey, maybe we should suggest to David Dearinger to check with Goodland, Kansas and Hugo, Colorado about being sister towns. Now, I bet that David doesn't know that an American Indian, by the name of Jim Brown from Goodland, could lay up to 150 bricks a **minute**- as fast as five men could supply him-and he could do it so accurately that no later adjustment to the bricks was needed. Evidence of his work in 1921 is still

Trip Experiences

there on the main street and some side streets. Also, Goodland is the home of America's first patented helicopter. Hey, David better check into this.

Well I can't stop on #13. So, one more, but there were really more sightings, I'm just giving you the biggies. This last one is really unbelievable. Tom, for a year and a half I had a goal of losing 9 pounds. I'd lose 6 and then gain some back. I'd lose some more again and then gain again. I'd be careful of what I was eating, do a daily exercise routine, drink plenty of water, etc., but I could not get that other 3 pounds off. I had just about decided that I was at the weight I should be. (#14) I knew in Colorado that I was not a good boy. I did not exercise, I did not drink enough water, AND, I certainly ate more than I should. On the way home I told Andy that I probably gained 5 or 6 pounds, and he agreed. I wish he wasn't so honest sometimes. We got home late Friday and I did not bother to weigh. The next morning, I got up. I weighed, and the scale showed I had lost weight and was at my goal at last. I got off the scales 2 or 3 times and got back on. I looked to see if the scales needed adjustment. I lifted the scales up and shook them. By the Way, this is the same routine I do when the scales show I weigh too much. You know, sometimes we forget to give God credit when something special happens to us. And sometimes when God does something special for us, its' hard for us to accept or believe it. Now Tom, I don't know how God did it. I don't know what His formula is, but we could make a ton of money on it if He every lets me figure it out.

That's all for now from your KRR…. I pray that you and your family will have a Great Thanksgiving. Eat all you want and then Pray. Let's see if that's the formula.

Your BIC,

BGEA RRT (Billy Graham Evangelistic Association and Rapid Response Team)

Chaplains called on for Emergency Responses

BGEA to Mena, Arkansas

May 2nd, 2009

Hey There, Brothers Tom & Wayne.... Your KRR guy here,

I just got back from Mena. Mena, Arkansas that is. I visited, ate, stayed and **showered** at the Mena Assembly of God Church for a week. Yup, the BGEA contacted me soon after the tornado struck Mena and asked if I could come there right away and help out. First though, they wanted to know how I was feeling. I told them I was due to get my Boy Scout Physical the next day, so they asked me to call them back after the checkup. I checked out OK and so they asked me to come down right away. But they weren't going to let me use the chain saws, or drive the Bob-Cats, or tarp any roofs. Instead, they were going to keep me grounded, as a Chaplain. Boy, those 3' foot chain saws sure looked like fun to play with.

    I got to talk and minister with a lot of people. I was assigned to a chain-saw team out of Ohio and was to talk with the homeowners who had damage or total destruction caused by the tornado. The chain-saw teams were the Front-Line ministers and did such a great job that sometimes I felt like I wasn't really needed.

    Mena has a population of about 5,500 people, and I estimate that there were about 50 churches that served the community and surrounding area. As a result, most of the people were looking on the bright side of everything. I understand that there was even one sign put up for the benefit of FEMA, that said "We Take Care of Ourselves, We don't need FEMA". There are many stories of Hope and Jesus Miracles I could tell you about but I'll only brief you on a couple. Trees, and when I say trees I mean King Size trees (3 feet plus in diameter), were laying all over the place. One family had been wanting to put in a swimming pool for years but had no room for one because of all the trees. Well they commented that now they had room and the hole was already partially dug from where the tree was uprooted. And, you've heard the expression "You can't see the forest for the trees". One lady commented that with all the trees down, that now she can see the view of the Quachita National Forest in the Kiamichi Mountains.

Well, enough of this stuff, but here's something to think about for our new building. **Showers.** There were 30 of us with the BGEA staying at the Church, and they had 2 showers available. What a Blessing that was. And the food! Sorry guys, but I did put on a couple of pounds. All the churches in the area were bringing home made food over for us, and there was a 12-foot table with nothing but desserts on it all day long. And I didn't want to hurt anyone's feelings, so I tried to eat something of everything.

A brief note on more Tulsa local info. I visited God's Shinning Light Church last night and attendance was about twice what it was a year ago. Kenny Wamble is involved in it and they are reaching out to ex-cons and down-and-outers. What a Blessing they are to these people in our community.

Your BIC always, the KRR guy

Hmmm! Who's Speaking?

BGEA to Joplin, Missouri

Joplin and the Big Breezy

Hey Tom, Hey Wayne.... it's me, the KRR guy

I've been to Joplin and back and a couple of guys have wanted me to report to the Kirk about the whole thing. Surely, they don't want to hear the whole story. Way, Way too much to say. Anyway, the BGEA, contacted me and wanted to know if I could make it there on short notice and stay a week. I told them I could make it the week of June 5th, knowing I could still go to Goodland just b/4 going to Joplin. However, they had an emergency come up and wanted to know if I could come up right away, by June 1st. The best I could do was to go up on the 3rd and stay thru the 11th.

I joined up with 5 other Chaplains. Two from Illinois, one from Houston, one from St. Louis, and one from Siloam Springs, Arkansas. Mainly Missionaries or Ministers. We were there to assist the Samaritans Purse volunteers. All of us put in long days, about 15 hours per day for the whole time, but God gave each of us the energy to make it thru.

The damage caused by an EF5 Tornado has to be seen to understand the immensity of the power of nature. The news was correct is saying the damage caused by the EF5 was 6 ½ miles long by ½ to ¾ quarters of a mile wide. The media did not explain though that this Tornado was an EF2 or EF3 for a short distance before and after the EF5 part. So, there was additional destruction before and after the 6 ½ miles, making the damage almost 13 miles altogether. Most Tornados seem to have major destruction of about 20% with peripheral damage of 80%. Well this one was just the reverse...80% major and 20% peripheral. You could go blocks and blocks and see nothing standing, only bare trees where the bark had been stripped away. No leaves, no branches. And yet on the edge of the storm, you could look across the street from where there was nothing left and see trees again and homes with only some roof damage. 154 lives were lost and yet the consensus is that it easily could have been 10 times that number. God played such an important role in saving so many lives. You heard over and over of the miracles He performed. May 22nd was Graduation Day for the Joplin High School and, a few weeks before, with so many

Trip Experiences

Graduates and their families to participate, the school board decided to move the Graduation to the Southwest Missouri State College campus. The College was spared any damage, but the High School was destroyed with the gymnasium roof totally collapsing where the ceremonies were to have been held. Literally hundreds of lives could have been lost there.

St. Johns Hospital, 9 stories high and about a block long, destroyed. The building is still there, but every window on all four sides are gone. The whole building was literally twisted anywhere from 4 to 11 inches on the foundation. The building will have to be imploded and built again, but the talk now is to rebuild somewhere else. And again, the Freeman Hospital, just two blocks away to the South, hardly touched at all. I talked with a guy in his early 50's who was in the hospital at the time recovering from surgery. He was in a room with another man and the last thing he remembered was the other guy being sucked out the window. The next thing this guy remembered, when he came too, he was in a hospital in Springfield, Missouri. He admitted that he hadn't had time for Christ in years past, but he has turned his life over to Jesus now. I and a couple of other Chaplains were asked to be present and be of support on Pay Day at a destroyed Nursing Home. This Home was part of a chain, but Headquarters had decided not to rebuild and the 60 or so employees would be told on Pay Day that they would no longer have jobs. I noticed one lady, with an 8-year-old boy, having difficulty, so I went up and talked with her. She said she had lost her car, lost her home, and now has lost her job. Before I could offer some words of encouragement, her 8-year-old boy spoke up and said…" Yes, but mom, remember, we're going to get a New car and **it's going to have a GPS in it**". That brought a smile to her face and to mine. Often times it's the youngsters that find the hope and the positive side of our problems.

The people in Joplin are finding hope and they are looking to the future. Sure, some have lost everything and yet have found a job elsewhere. They will be moving on to other areas, but they too are looking to the future. The volunteers with the BGEA had shown up from all over everywhere. I met some from as far away as Washington State and New York, and all are such a blessing and inspiration to the people of Joplin. They are the Real Ministers and they are the ones that really show the Love of Jesus Christ to their brothers and sisters in time of need.

Hmmm! Who's Speaking?

Some of the people in Joplin have always been helping others and it was obvious that some of them were having difficulty asking for help for themselves now. One lady approached me and asked me to call on her pastor. She said the church had been totally destroyed as well as the parsonage and that the pastor really needed some help but he was faking that he didn't need it. A couple of us paid him a visit (a Baptist Minister) and sure enough he said he could handle it. We left him a card and phone number so that just in case he could use some volunteer help he could call. The next day he called and asked for help. What a difference it made in him when all those volunteers showed up. His whole attitude changed and he started talking about when he got his new church rebuilt and all the brand-new homes that would be built right around him, and all the new young families that would be moving in, and all the new members the church would be getting. He just needed to be reminded that there is a time when care givers may need to be care receivers. Both are a blessing and both are needed.

Well I got back just in time to get ready to take off for a week as Chaplain at Scout Camp. I could say a lot about Scout Camp too, but I'll only mention a couple of highlights. Chapel averaged around 350 to 450 attendees out of 860 campers. Well, I took my first Confessional this time. A Catholic Scout came up to me one day after Chapel and wanted to Confess. I explained to him that I wasn't a Priest and offered some other alternatives, but he wouldn't take no for an answer. Then a Jewish Scout approached me on another day and wanted to know if he could have one of the Phos Crosses I passed out. And one of the Scout Masters informed me that the three Muslim boys in his troop, who originally said they didn't want to go to Chapel, came after all. Hey! As a good Scout I try to be respectful of all religions and yet I try to get my point about the Cross, across too.

Here's hoping you had a Great 4th…. and now are prepared to go forth and preach the Good News.

Your' BIC

Trip Experiences

Joplin and the Boogie Woogie Rocks Nursing Home

Have you ever felt like God was calling or asking you to do something for Him and you resisted or talked to yourself and said something like…'God! You've got to be kidding" or "You're not talking to me, surely!" Or maybe you're saying "I don' think I'm hearing you correctly God!"

Let's read in Scripture about times when God was asking other people to do things for Him…

In Exodus 3:10-12 God is telling Moses that Moses is to lead His people out of Egypt…" *Now go, for I am sending you to Pharaoh. You will lead my people out of Egypt."* And Moses replies…" *But who am I to appear before Pharaoh? How can you expect me to lead the Israelites out of Egypt?"* Then God told him….."*I will be with you…."*

In Romans 12:6 it says…" *God has given each of us the ability to do certain things well."* Here Paul is saying to the Christians in Rome and to all believers, don't ever under estimate yourself, use your God given gifts to spread the Good News and to serve others.

And in Jonah 1:1-3…" *The LORD gave this message to Jonah: Get up and go to the great city of Nineveh! Announce my judgment against it because I have seen how wicked its people are."* But Jonah got up and went in the opposite direction in order to get away from the LORD…. Jonah didn't feel comfortable with the Ninevites and didn't want to minister to them about God.

Like Jonah, sometimes we want to turn and run away from God, rather than to obey Him. Jonah finally went and gave God's message to the people of Nineveh and what a profound difference it made in their lives. We too should not just put our focus on people we feel comfortable with. God loves us all – including people not in our Special Group, or our background, or our race, or even our Christian faith.

Now, let me tell you 'How the Boogie Woogie Rocked the Nursing Home in Joplin, Missouri'.

For those of you who may be too young to be familiar with the term 'Boogie Woogie', it is simply a music style that is known as the "Father of Rock & Roll". It was very popular in the late 30's and early 40's and Northeast Texas (Marshall, Texas to be exact) was its 'Birthplace'. Its popularity began to fade in the 50's. So, if you are in your 80's & 90's, the

Boogie Woogie music brings back some very fond and happy memories of when you were in your 20's.

When in Joplin recently, shortly after the EF-5 tornado hit there on May 22nd, 2011, I and a couple of other chaplains with the BGEA Samaritan's Purse Relief Teams, were asked to visit a Nursing Home. This particular Nursing Home had not been damaged by the tornado, but some residents had been sent there from another Nursing Home that had been destroyed, and we were asked to call on them to see how they were doing.

I was driving, along with Tom, an American Missionary to Russia for about the last 15 years, and Chip, a Baptist Minister with a Church in Arkansas. On the short drive to the Nursing Home, Tom proceeded to talk about how he just doesn't feel comfortable in Nursing Homes. He doesn't feel like that's his gift. He just doesn't seem to communicate or interact with them very well. Tom went on about this for about 2 or 3 minutes, just before we arrived and were pulling in to our destination. Tom apologized and asked if Chip and I would mind going on in while he just stayed in the van. I parked in a shady spot under the drive entrance canopy, since it was a rather warm day, and Chip and I got out and headed for the Nursing Home entrance door while Tom stayed in the van. On the way in, Chip said to me...."You know, Tom never should have said what he did." I asked what he meant by that and Chip said..." If God wants Tom in here – God will get him in here whether he wants to come in or not."

As Chip and I go in, I stopped in the foyer, or the lobby area, as there were 12 or 15 residents there sitting in their wheel chairs. Chip headed down a long hallway after inquiring about someone. I became engrossed in conversation with some of the residents in the lobby when shortly I see Tom with a couple of bags in his hands following a lady with several bags in her hands. Tom looked at me briefly and gave me that look like - "OK, OK I'm in here, but not for long." Tom then proceeded to follow the lady toward another long hallway. On the way out of the lobby I'm sure Tom saw the little old man in a wheelchair that was situated at the end of an upright piano next to a wall. The gentleman had his head down and was just staring at the keyboard, completely emotionless.

Pretty soon, I see Tom coming back up the hallway obviously in a hurry to get out of there. NOW, let me make myself perfectly clear.... I did not know Tom very well and I know everyone else in the Nursing Home

Trip Experiences

knew even less about him. I didn't know if Tom could sing, or dance, or play a piano. But God knew Tom. God knows all about Tom. Well, just as Tom got back to the lobby, he looked over and saw that little old man next to the piano. Tom politely asked the gentleman what he was doing. Well, the old man lifted his head up – looked right into Tom's face, and said…"I'm waiting for you to play the piano!"

Well, Well, Well – Guess What? Tom can play the piano and he can play the piano very well. Tom sat down on the piano bench, with his back to everyone in the place. Tom asked the old man if he had any requests, and then Tom played three great songs. Then the old man must have requested the 'Boogie Woogie'.

I am so thankful that God had put me in the back of the room so that I could see what was about to happen. One lady, obviously in her mid-90's, was being wheeled into the lobby by a staff person. The poor lady looked completely physically and mentally incapacitated. BUT, just as soon as Tom started playing the 'Boogie Woogie', this lady started coming to life. Her head started bobbing, her arms started shaking and her legs started moving. As I looked around the room – she wasn't the only one coming to life – everyone was doing the same thing, those in their walkers, those in rocking chairs and those in their wheelchairs. Tom, with his back to everyone, was completely oblivious to what was going on in that room.

As Tom finished up, he thanked the old man, shook his hand and said he needed to get on his way. He proceeded to go back outside to wait for Chip and me. He was totally unaware of how God had used him in such a powerful way. Once I got outside, the first thing I asked Tom was…. What caused him to come into the Nursing Home. Tom said it got hot in the van, so he got out and sat down on a concrete bench. A lady drove up and started unloading several bags, so Tom asked if he could help her and the next thing he knew he was inside the Nursing Home. I then proceeded to tell him how God had used him to lift up and brighten up everyone's day. Obviously the 'Boogie Woogie' not only reminded them of their youth, but it also reminded them of the joy to come when they join their Heavenly Father [Revelation 21:1-6].

How about you? Are you ready for that glorious day when your new life begins and the old life is left behind? If you're not sure you're ready, then I invite you to check out the web site at www.BGEA.org and then click on 'How to Know Jesus'.

And if you're already ready for that new life, have you shared it with anyone lately? Are you thinking…I just don't feel comfortable doing that. Then I invite you to turn to God. He's right there and He's willing and able to help you. A BIC

For additional information on Boogie Woogie:
    www.bowofo.org (the Boogie Woogie Foundation)
    www.cdbaby.com …some Gospel Songs by Jimmy Maddox like:
    'This Train is Bound for Glory'
    'Can't Nobody Do Me Like Jesus'
    'This Little Light of Mine'
    www.youtube.com …type in Bill Gaither Vocal Band and the song:
    'I catch 'Em, God cleans 'Em' for a video presentation

Trip Experiences

BGEA to Moore, Oklahoma

The Dove Over Moore

After the tornado struck Moore on Monday, May 20th and then hit South Oklahoma City on May 29th, I was contacted by Al New with the BGEA RRT (Billy Graham Evangelistic Association -Rapid Response Team). Al sent out an email on June 17th saying that the BGEA had decided to extend their stay for two more weeks and was looking for additional Chaplains. Al contacted me on June 18th about helping out from June 23rd to June 30th. I had previously worked with Al in the Mena, Arkansas tornado in 2009 and the Joplin, Missouri tornado in 2011.

The following information compares some of the tornado information in those areas I visited.

AREA	DATE	EF RATING	MPH	WIDTH/ DISTANCE/ TIME	FATALITIES
MENA	04/09/2009	3	165	—	3
JOPLIN	05/22/2011	5	275	1.0/22.1mi/38min	158
SHAWNEE	05/19/2013	4	230	—	2
MOORE	05/20/2013	5	275	1.3/17mi/50min	24
EL RENO	05/31/2013	5	295	2.6*/16.2mi/ —	18

*widest on record

FYI: EF5's normally average only 1 out of 1000 tornadoes.

A few stories of where one saw God's involvement and presence in this deployment...

I had scheduled myself to be Chaplain for Boy Scout Camp the same week of this deployment but then backed out, with remorse, in late May when Boy Scouts of America (BSA National) voted to change the 103-year-old rules and direction of BSA. Evidently God had other plans for me that I was unaware of at the time.

Hmmm! Who's Speaking?

In visiting the Memorial Site at Plaza Towers Elementary School where seven children died I heard the story about **Chris**. He was 9 years old and left his safe place to go and console and protect his little friend across the hall whom he had heard crying and shouting. **Chris**' friend survived with his help and **Chris** is now in a better place with God. And now God is using **Chris** to save even more by bringing them to know God in a more personal way.

In visiting a site where a Samaritans Purse team was cleaning a field of debris, the homeowner talked about her 3 donkeys. Not far from her was a 110-horse farm and they had 100 of their horses killed or put down because of injuries. All this homeowner had were 3 donkeys and it was too late to find a safe place for them. Just before going into a tornado shelter herself, she saw the 3 donkeys underneath 3 trees in the pasture. Obviously, the Donkeys realized they needed protection from hail or whatever else was about to happen. Donkeys are very cautious and will do what they need to do for self-preservation. After the tornado had blown over, the homeowner came out of her shelter to see her mobile home and the barn destroyed. Also, the 3 trees were heavily damaged, BUT the 3 donkeys were OK. Hmmm! Did the cross symbol on the back of the donkeys have something to do with that? In the Old Testament, Zachariah 9:9, Prophecy tells about the Messiah, or King, will come riding on a Donkey. Then in the New Testament, Matthew 21:4-7, Jesus fulfilled that Prophecy when He entered Jerusalem riding on a donkey.

Now to the Mourning Dove. It is not often that you may see a Dove and particularly in a recent tornado path. Doves are seed eaters and will be seen maybe in areas around fields. I had seen a few crows, starlings and sparrows during the week, but not a single Dove. Then the astonishing finish to the week came on the last day of the week. It was Saturday afternoon around 2:30 p.m. I and another Chaplain were sent out to pray off a team of 25-30 Samaritan Purse volunteers. It was the last work order for them and they would be leaving there to clean up and head back to their homes in other parts of Oklahoma or even other states. The volunteers had just finished clearing and cleaning a home lot that was just a block from the Plaza Towers Elementary School. You could easily see where the school used to be as there were now no homes to block the view. And there were really not even any trees, except for one lonely tree on this home owner's lot. The tree had been spared and new leaves were sprouting out on the lower branches as a result of recent rains and the fact that the tornado had come thru 5 weeks prior now. The upper branches were still quite visible as the moisture had not reached to the top limbs yet. All the grass in this area had also been ripped from the ground, so only dirt was visible.

As Chaplains we were to thank the volunteers for all they had done and Pray for a safe journey home for them. The volunteers hardly ever get to see the homeowners they have so graciously and lovingly helped out. The volunteers normally have a Bible they have all signed and written messages in to present to the homeowners, but most of the time it is up to the Chaplains to track the homeowners down and present the Bible to them. So, as Chaplains, we get to hear and see the expressions of joy and gratitude from the homeowners for the volunteers. I was explaining this to the volunteers and telling them how much the homeowner appreciated them and how much God loved them too for what they had done. As we circled up to pray, one of the Samaritan volunteers standing right next to me exclaimed "Look, Look, a Dove is landing on the upper branches of that tree." Sure enough, a single Mourning Dove landed on an open branch and proceeded to look right at the volunteers. As everyone Oohed and Aahed I proceeded on with our Prayer. The Dove remained perched on the branch and remained there until just about everyone had taken a picture and then it quickly and quietly flew off toward the school.

Now if you will, let me say something more about the significance of this Mourning Dove. You will notice that it is called a 'Mourning' Dove and not a 'Morning' Dove. Mourning is defined as an expression of grief or as the period during which a death is mourned. Hmmm? And then in Scripture, doves are said to be the most important bird mentioned. For one thing they are one of the first birds mentioned in the Bible. The dove is mentioned in Genesis 8:6-11 as Noah sent forth a dove to see if the storm was over and if calmness and peace had returned. And in the Gospels… Matthew, Mark, Luke & John we are reminded of Jesus Baptism by John the Baptist and how God came from Heaven "like a dove" and lighted on the shoulder of the Lord Jesus – the visible evidence of the Holy Spirit. Hmmm! Was God 'speaking' to all these volunteers? Just ask them.

David Cox, A BIC… May Peace be with you for now and always

Oh, I might add that my Chaplain partner, Harry, the Baptist Minister from Florida, saved the day for the Billy Graham Association one day. We were pulling in to a 7-11 Convenience store to pick up some ice for the volunteers and all the parking spaces were filled in front. However, I noticed a parking space or two in front of the store right next door to the 7-11. As I started to pull into a space, Harry hollers, "You can't park here!" And he was absolutely right. It was a Liquor Store. So, we drove further down to a vacant damaged car wash and parked. You see, our vehicle was emblazoned with two magnetic signs that proudly proclaimed the Billy Graham Evangelistic Association. As sure as we had parked there, the Devil would have sent someone with the media to take a picture. When we mentioned the incident to the other Chaplains we took quite a ribbing. And then, low & behold, a couple of days later as I pulled into a damaged self-storage lot so we could get information on our next call, the owner came running out with a camera in her hand. I jumped out to see what the matter was and she asked if she could take a picture of the vehicle. As it turned out she and her parents are great supporters of Billy Graham and she just wanted a picture so she could show her parents and friends of the time a Billy Graham vehicle parked on her lot.

Well, well, well. You never know when the Lord might be guiding you in the right direction.

Trip Experiences

BGEA to Houston, Texas

Houston & Harvey

Sept. 2017

Hey Wayne, Dan and others…. the KRR guy out and about

Well God got me to Houston and back safe & sound but He had to convince me first. The BGEA Chaplain Rapid Response Team (RRT) contacted me by email when Hurricane Harvey appeared to be heading for a direct hit on Corpus Christi. In the past, since I drive, I have informed the RRT that I would cover any disasters within a 500-mile limit of Tulsa, so I have been to three tornado disasters in Arkansas, Missouri and Oklahoma in the last few years. However, when I pulled up Corpus, it was 675 miles from my house so I was going to waive the call this time. Well, as you know, Harvey changed course and was going to make its main hit in Houston. The RRT called me on Thursday, Aug. 31st at 2:45 p.m. and asked if I could be in Houston the very next day.

I told them OK and they told me the address to go to. I and others were being put up at the New Downtown Campus Church for First Baptist Church of Houston. This was a new branch of the main church serving College Students and mostly younger families that was still in the remodeling stage. It was just a few blocks from the home church. Hmmm! 1st Baptist Church of Downtown Houston? I had just visited the 1st Baptist Church of Downtown Tulsa a couple of weeks prior (about 40 years in the making). Was God preparing me? Well, I pull up the address of the Houston Church and put in my Tulsa home address to see what the mileage was. Hmmm! 498 miles from my house to where I would be staying. OK! God! OK! I'm going.

Destruction from EF4&5 Tornadoes happen quickly and the damage is usually 1 to 2 miles wide and 10 to 20 miles long. As Emergency Response Chaplains, you don't have to go far to find food, shelter, gas and other essentials. Damage from Category 4&5 Hurricanes may occur over several days and be 400-500 miles in circumference. As Chaplains in Tornado areas you call on 5 to 10 people a day who have lost their homes or been affected in some way. In Hurricane catastrophes, in the early stages, you are calling on thousands of people being put up in temporary shelters. In Houston, instead of 4 to 6 Chaplains in Tornado areas, 30 to 40 were needed. We reached 43 Chaplains in a couple of days after I arrived. About 1/3rd were from the Carolina's and 1/3rd from Florida and others from California, Ohio, Virginia, Arizona, Missouri and me from Oklahoma. Well, in a few days we lost all the Chaplains from Florida because of the news of the Irma Hurricane heading towards Florida. And the Chaplains from the Carolina's were a little anxious too. In Houston the Chaplains were disbursed to 4 different locations, the George Brown Convention Center sheltering 6,000, the NRG Center sheltering 5,000 and two smaller locations.

The Chaplains are given an orientation meeting before embarking and the first instruction is to be Flexible. That is important because as Chaplains for the BGEA we never knew from day to day or hour to hour if we were going to be allowed into a shelter or whether we could bring in any Bibles. Normally Red Cross made the decisions and it was dependent upon who happened to be in charge that day or at that time.

Many of the affected people in Texas, and now Florida too, have gotten a sudden realization of the importance of knowing Jesus Christ in a more personal way. And many of those who didn't know Jesus before, are now wanting to know more about Him. I came upon one young man who approached me who had obviously been badly beaten up (Black eye, Broken nose, cuts & bruises). I asked him what had happened and he said he had accepted Jesus Christ into his life a couple of days earlier and he was out spreading the Good News to others when a homeless street person wanted him to shut up and beat him up so bad before the Police got involved that an Ambulance had to take him to the hospital. But he was out of the Hospital already "Thanks to God" he said and he was so excited about his New Life that he was going right back this day and start telling other people about Jesus.

And today, I attended a going away party for a great Christian couple (the Hords) from the Kirk who are moving to Florida to be closer to family. Well God had the timing perfect. They found a location in Florida recently. They've missed the stress of Hurricane Irma and their new home hasn't been damaged and as they are great Disciples for Christ they are

Trip Experiences

greatly needed in Florida right now. May God Bless them on their new Harvest in Florida.

Hey, Brothers In Christ, things are happening right now…. Hurricanes, Earthquakes and no telling what's next… Is God trying to get some people's attention?? Maybe we should read Mark 13 where Jesus tells us about the future. Hmmm! Something to think about and something to have others to think about too.

Until next time…your BIC…. the KRR guy

P.S. You can go to www.billygraham.org and check out the News and the Photos on the Chaplains Ministry in Texas and you might even see me under the 20 Images. And if you have an interest in being an Emergency Response Chaplain with the BGEA you can check that out too on their website

God's Way Is The One Way Always

Hey Tom, Wayne, Dan & Shawn…. the KRR guy again,

My son Andy & I took off for a short trip to Colorado the first of this month. Andy loves Colorado and has been entertaining the idea of getting a job in Denver and moving there. So, we took off to enjoy ourselves and check it out with God in control. I had been praying for God's direction for Andy and that God might show him the way. Lots of beautiful God created sites along the way and fun things to do. We wanted to do White Water Rafting down the Royal Gorge and God planned the perfect time for that. Little did we know at the time that the only way to see the Royal Gorge was thru the Gorge itself on a $6,000 special made rubber raft made for 4 rafters and a guide.

We had been on Level 1 and 2 raft rides before and now were seeking more adventure on Level 3 & 4 raft rides where the rapids are much faster and exciting. This special raft incurred much more paddling and you had to sit on the edge of the raft so that you could reach into the rapids deeper with your paddles. There were no security straps to hold you in and if you fell out there were specific instructions on how to save yourself. A level 5 rafting has been discontinued because according to our guide, guides just do not like the risk and it takes too much out of them physically and emotionally. We got completely drenched along the way, but thankfully it was not from falling in.

The reason why this is the only way for vacationers to view the Royal Gorge is because of a forest fire last fall. The fire destroyed 48 of the 50 buildings that adjoined the Royal Gorge Bridge, shut down the Cog Railway down into the Gorge and the Arial Tram that went across the Gorge. Now, even the White-Water Rafting has some additional risks it didn't have before because the roots of the trees that were burned on the top and sides of the Gorge are now rotting out. This causes soil, rocks and even boulders to become loose and to tumble down into the river.

Andy had been informed of a Church we should visit in Denver, the Orchard Road Christian Center (ORCC), so we searched it out on Sunday morning. Now you have to understand that sometimes it is difficult to find places in parts of Colorado because of sign ordinances. I do not know if it is a city, county or district regulation but in Denver obviously, you cannot post a sign on a billboard or on top of a building. It appears that signs cannot obstruct a view nor be overly large. The big bold Golden Arches of McDonalds are a no, no. As a matter of fact, I did not even see a cross above a Church or a highway sign designating a Hospital.

We did find the Church finally, with some difficulty. It certainly did not look like a Church from the exterior, just another office building. It was interesting because it was Mission Sunday at ORCC and I got to talk to some Missionary's that had tables set up in the lobby. The service itself did not turn Andy or me on and Andy said if he moves to Denver he would search out another Church. I was still praying for God's guidance for Andy. Pastor Reece did have a good message that day and it included the story about a 1960 Nairobi Mission team. At the time, Nairobi was having problems with highway looters robbing and killing people. This Mission Team had been out in the countryside ministering to people and was heading back into town for the night when their car broke down. They were going to have to spend the night in the car until morning so they prayed for safety and went to sleep. Everything went fine and they got a good night's rest. A couple of days later they were holding a Revival in the town and as they were winding up a local native came up to accept Jesus Christ into his life. He informed the leaders that a couple of days earlier he was among about ½ dozen men who had seen them on the highway outside of town and that they were going to rob and kill them. As they approached the car they saw 13 armed men around the car protecting those in the car. This new Believer then said he realized that these people were special and that their God was protecting them.

Well that was interesting but here is the rest of the story. When the Mission Team got back home to America their Pastor asked them how the trip went and if they had any problems. When they brought up the story about the one young man coming to Christ, the Pastor got inquisitive about the timing and then added more to the story. On that particular night, the Pastor said God woke him up and told him the Mission Team was in trouble and to immediately start praying for them and to call in some others from Church to pray with him. All in all, 12 men showed up and with them and the Pastor, all 13 of them Prayed throughout the night for the team. Hmmm! How about that!

But on with my story now. Andy has some connections with Owens & Minor (a hospital supplier) and some hospitals in Denver because of his work at St. Johns Hospital here in Tulsa. So, after Church services we headed off to find where Owens & Minor was located. We found it and then decided to check out the immediate area as far as a place to live. We discovered that if he decided to live in the vicinity that he would need to greatly increase his ability to speak Spanish. Driving thru the area we came upon a street that was named 'Andrew Avenue'. Hmmm! Was this a message from God? Then, just a few blocks away Andy exclaimed 'Look' a street named 'Tulsa'. Whoa! I was driving so I told Andy to take a picture of that. Now I am really thinking, 'God is this where you want Andy?'

I really didn't have time to analyze or check out that sign until we got back to Tulsa. I found where Andy had sent that picture back by way of Facebook and one of his friends had commented about it. They had responded that Tulsa is the Way, it is One Way and All Ways. I now looked closer at the sign. Hmmm! Was God's message saying…'Andy', 'Tulsa is the Way, It is **the Only Way**, and For Always?' Andy and I sat down and discussed this some. The odds of us running onto a sign that said 'Andrew' in that short drive around might be 1 in 10,000. Then when you add in the sign that says not only 'Tulsa Way' but also 'One Way' and 'STOP (Looking) All Ways', then the odds might be as high as 1 in 100 million. Hmmm! Doesn't God make life interesting and exciting?

***And something which caught my attention from the Presbyterian Lay Committee at www.layman.org was the article about the '**Arkansas tornado victim's message of hope that goes viral**'. Just type that into your search engine. And then click on and read what her friend Jessica Soward said about her friend 'The Cheerleader' of Vilonia, Arkansas **on Soward's personal blog**. Vilonia was hit by an EF2 tornado on 4/25/2011 and then just 3 years later, almost to the day, with an EF4 tornado on 4/27/2014. Then, if you would, look at about the 4th response by a Melissa Fisher where God communicated with her via a text message on her cell phone.

Trip Experiences

Hey Everybody…..'Always be joyful. Never stop praying' 1st Thessalonians 5:16-17.

David Cox, your BIC

Chapter Seventeen: Music

Victory and Israel Houghton

Israel in Tulsa, Israel Houghton that is

Hey Tom…. Hey Wayne…. the KRR guy here,

Sorry guys, I couldn't attend your classes Wednesday night because I went to see Israel. He and 'New Breed' brought their national tour to Victory Christian Center. I and about 3,500 others were 'Jumpin' and 'Thumpin' and Praising God for a couple of hours. About 1/3 were College Kids and the rest were older. Some even older than me. About half were blacks and half were whites and a few were half & half, including Israel. He told his 'Story', which was a message in itself. His white, drug addicted mom got pregnant at age 17. Her mom and others were encouraging her to get an abortion but she had enough sense not to do that. But, since she was on drugs, the State (Calif.) told her she was not fit to be a mother and they would take the baby when it was born. It so stressed her out that she decided to kill herself. But as she was walking down the street a lady on the other side of the street came over and said: "God just told me to come over to you and to tell you that He Loves You". Israel said this was the first time his mom had ever heard this and that she accepted Jesus Christ in her heart right then and there and immediately changed her life. For the last 10 years Israel has been telling this story everywhere he went in hopes that if the lady who talked to his mom was still alive that he and his mom could find her. WELL! A lady called a few months ago and said it might have been her if this happened in Oceanside, CA. Well to make a long story short, It Was. And they showed a video of the reunion that happened this summer.

Oh! Kenny Wamble and I were chewing on breakfast last week and somehow the discussion came up on how Kenny started coming to the Kirk. He said if it hadn't been for Weldon Saylor he wouldn't be at the Kirk. He and Sheri were looking for a new church to join and they had visited the Kirk a couple of times, but no one acknowledged them. Everyone seemed to have their own swarm of friends. But they decided to give the Kirk one more try. Well, Weldon came up to them and started a great conversation and even invited Kenny to Wednesday morning Bible Study. He and Sheri have been coming ever since. *Hmmmm! It sounds like we could use some more Weldon Saylors in our Church.*

Well, I had better sign off for now…Have a Great Week guys…Your KRR guy

Jesus Culture

Hey my Brothers and Sisters of Christ....

I want to pass on a little information I have learned about a Worship Group I first heard at Passion 2013 in January. The group is Jesus Culture, originally out of the Bethel Church youth ministry in Redding, California. They formed in 1999 and came out with some albums in 2006 and then really came on the scene with a live album from Chicago in November 2011. Kim Walker-Smith, one of the Worship Leaders, has just come out with a new album tied in with their 'Still Believe' Tour in the Western U.S. They are touching the lives of thousands upon thousands of the New Generation in the U.S. and around the world.

The New Generation that I encountered in Atlanta at Passion 2013 (over 60,000) are really connecting with them. The purpose of Jesus Culture is 'to ignite revival in the nations of the earth and to lead young people to experience the radical love of God'. They also offer some on line courses for New Generation ministry leaders to help them introduce and challenge the New Generation to a revival culture and to challenge them to dramatically have an influence in the world around them. For more on this go to www.jesusculture.com and click on 'Emerge'. They are presently preparing to move to Sacramento because there is a passion for revival with the Churches there and they will be helping with 'A Billion Soul Harvest'.

You can see the group performing live by going to Jesus Culture-Holy-YouTube or one titled Passion 2013 – Jesus Culture Kim Walker 'Holy Spirit' YouTube. And check out Kim's song, "Did You Feel The Mountains Tremble".

Your BIC

Lyrics for my song- GOOD NEWS

The following are the lyrics written by David Cox with God's help for his granddaughter Ashlynn. I am not a song writer by any means, but one evening God put this on me and I scribbled it down on a yellow legal pad in about 2 hours....

GOOD NEWS (North, East, West, or South)
Oh God- I look to You
For guidance and direction
Oh God- You are my compass
When I've turned the wrong way
You can turn me around
You bring me Good NEWS (North, East, West or South)
(Scripture: Mark 1:14-15.... Jesus went to Galilee to preach God's Good News. "At last the time has come!" He announced, "The Kingdom of God is near! Turn from your sins and believe this Good News!)

Don't let forces like material things
And idols and greed lead me astray
(Scripture: Galatians 1:6-7... I am shocked that you are turning away so soon from God, who in his love and mercy called you to share the eternal life he gives through Christ. You are already following a different way that pretends to be the Good News but is not the Good News at all. You are being fooled by those who twist and change the truth concerning Christ.)

You are the way, the way, the way
There is no other way
You are the way, the way, the way
There is no other way
(repeat)

Draw me close to You
Steer me in the right direction
Help me when I go the wrong way
Don't let me waste another day.

Another day away from You.
Your way is always the right way

You are my God forever and ever
And You will be my guide until I die.
(Scripture: Psalm 48:14…For that is what God is like. He is our God forever and ever, and He will be our guide until we die.)
You are the way, the way, the way
There is no other way
You are the way, the way, the way
There is no other way
(repeat)

Even though I feel
I'm going straight
I need to listen to You- God
When You say go this away.
I should put my trust in You
Even if You send me off another way
(Scripture: Psalm 25:4…Show me the path where I should walk, O God; point out the right road for me to follow. Acts 8:26… As for Phillip, an angel of the Lord said to him, "Go south down the desert road that runs from Jerusalem to Gaza.")

Rap Song For Tom

Hey Tom,

I hear thru the Grapevine that you're needing some extra prayers and some encouragement about the long-awaited surgery. Well I'm praying, but I also came up with this Rap Song that I am sure will encourage you, even more so, to want to get out of town.

    Hey, Hey, This Raps for Tom

    Hot Feet, Hot Feet, Jesus woke me up
    You're gonna get better, so don't you fretter
    Wake up, Wake up, God's taken up your case
    Get up, Get up, Better get ready
    The phone's gonna ring, and then you'll start to sing.
    Hot Feet, Hot Feet, Jesus woke me up

    Now surgery ain't funny, and it costs a lot of money
    But the Church is here, and we're all a praying for ya.
    So, you better get ready when they up and call ya.
    Take that pain and that cane and throw'm in the gutter
    Hot Feet, Hot Feet, Jesus woke me up.
    Jesus says there's more for you to do
    So, you're gonna get better
    Get a smile on your face cause Jesus says He Loves ya
    Eat the right food, cause the doctor says you need to.

    No more Milky Ways or Universe Bars
    Put your hands up, Put your hands up
    And touch the Atmosphere
    Get up, Get up, Better get ready
    The phone's gonna ring, and then you'll start to sing.
    Hot Feet, Hot Feet, Jesus woke me up.

Hmmm! Who's Speaking?

I am not going to sign this note so you will not know who sent it to you. I am afraid if the word got out that I am a Rap artist, that I would be inundated with requests for appearances, and truthfully Tom I just don't have the time. And whatever you do, do not tell that KRR guy, because I hear he goes around blabbing on everybody and everything.

U2 Can Know JC

Hey, Wayne, Dan, and others….

Well, Well, Well…. Guess who just came to town? Yup! U2. Hey! I love these guys. They are so sneaky. Maybe that's another reason why I like them. Do you remember Francis Gary Powers and the U-2? The US Secret Spy Plane. This plane was to provide critical intelligence to decision-makers. Hmmm!

I've studied a couple of books about these guys in years past. One book 'WALK ON- The Spiritual Journey of U2' is by Steve Stockman. Steve is a Presbyterian pastor and has his own radio show on BBC Radio Ulster. He is also the Presbyterian Chaplain at Queen's University. The other book 'Get Up Off Your Knees' is a collection of sermons based on U2's work. It also provides a six-week program (6 one-hour classes) on pursuing God with us.

Here is some stuff I learned about them (www.U2.com). They were formed in 1976 in Dublin, Ireland. They originally started out as a Christian band (with a different name) but quickly realized they did not want to be labeled that because the church started telling them what and how to play. U2 wanted to reach an audience that liked Pop Rock, Pop Punk, and Rock & Roll. And they wanted to reach an audience that was not particularly Christian but might hear coded or Secret Christian messages. Even the name of the band 'U2' most likely came from the US U-2 Secret plane. The song 'Beautiful Day' on one of their more recent albums 'U2- All That You Can't Leave Behind' was when they started beginning to be a little more bold with their messages. They even have a message on the front cover of this CD that probably 99% of the buyers would not catch. If you look closely at the cover you will see the band in an airport terminal and you can even see a terminal directional sign in the background (J 33-3). Well, if you look up Jeremiah 33:3 in your bible, you will find…. *"Ask Me (the Lord) and I will tell you some remarkable secrets about what is going to happen."* You can find more information about the album cover and the airport shown by going to www.feelnumb.com.

When U2 fans are interviewed it's interesting to hear them explain why they are such loyal fans. Many say their songs and lyrics are uplifting and fill you up with so much hope. Hmmmm? Could it be that U2 is telling them about God?

Chapter Eighteen: JDC-Juvenile Detention Center

The Boogie Woogie Strikes Again!

Hey Tom...Hey Wayne...guess what? More news from the KRR guy... and the JDC visit

I'm sure you've heard the phrase 'Leave Well Enough Alone'. This simply implies that doing more will not improve it.

How many times do we want to do a little more or just say a little more, when we are already sufficient or have already made our point.

Scripture refers to this in 1st Timothy 1:6 where in the NIV Paul says...*Some have wandered away from there and turned to meaningless talk.* And the NAS says...*For some men, straying from these things, have turned to fruitless discussion.*

Recently, on a Sunday morning, I visited the Tulsa Juvenile Detention Center. I was the Worship Leader that morning and God had put it on me to talk about Boogie Woogie. Why? I had no idea until later.

I started off with my usual American 'Signing' language which showed the boys that 'God Loves You' and then mentioned how they would be amazed at how many ways God can communicate with us. I then asked the 12 boys (and notice the number 12), if any of them knew what 'Boogie Woogie' was. I received 12 pair of eyes looking at me like 'What in the world is this guy talking about?' It was what I expected, so I went into my explanation of Boogie Woogie. I told them that it was considered the 'Father' of Rock & Roll music and that it originated in East Texas in the late 30's and early 40's and faded from the scene in the 50's. It was also known as 'Fast Western' and it was a type of Gospel that the Black lumber jacks came up with. These lumber jacks would hop on a train and travel from one logging camp to another and they must have picked up on the rhythm of the train sounds and incorporated it into their music.

Now I had recorded a couple of Boogie Woogie songs off the web so that I could play them for the boys. I had listened to both songs on my Boom Box earlier that morning to be sure they were in working order. The first song I had I was also able to find the lyrics, so I printed them off for the boys to read. It was called 'I Catch 'em, God Cleans 'em". I went over the lyrics with the boys before I played the song and explained to them what the writer/composer was talking about. The lyrics and the music can be found on your Search Engine by typing in "I Catch 'em, God Cleans 'em by the Gaither Vocal Band" The song starts off with…

> *I was drivin' round down south Louisiana*
> *Stopped in a town called Galliano*
> *Saw a sign on a church that said 'fish fry tonight'*
> *A little old Cajun preacher was preachin'*
> *Reminded me of an old camp meetin'*
> *It brought St. Matthew four nineteen to life.*

I then explained about how you can see this guy driving thru Louisiana and seeing a sign saying 'Free Fish Fry' tonight. So, he stops to get some good ol' South Louisiana cookin' and it brought back some memories. One was Matthew 4:19 where Jesus is calling out his **12** disciples, some of whom were fishermen by trade. Jesus said: *"Come, be my disciples, and I will show you how to fish for people!"*

Then this guy tells about the 'preacher man' and what he says. The guy then goes on to say what happened to him and how the 'preacher man' got his attention. He said the preacher was short on religion….meaning the preacher didn't go on and on about Hell Fire and Brimstone and how he should be livin'. Instead the preacher was long on grace. Otherwise, saying over and over how Jesus Loves us and Died for us and washed away all our sin. Then the guy says the next thing he knows, he's accepting Jesus Christ into his life.

I then played the song for them on my Boom Box. As that song finished up, I slipped in the 2nd disc to play another Boogie Woogie song.

BUT, even though everything showed it was playing,.. NOTHING was coming out. I tried everything I could for the next minute or so, BUT I could not get any sound out of it. SO, I gave up and went on into my short message about the BOOGIE WOOGIE THAT ROCKED THE NURSING HOME in Joplin, MO.*

After that, it was time for me to wrap my part up. I closed off in Prayer and then the next thing I know, God was putting words in my mouth and I said if there's anyone here today that wants to Join Up and be on Jesus Team like the guy in the song, then I'll hang around in the back of the room for a few minutes. Well, Lo & Behold, three of the boys came to the back and accepted Jesus Christ into their lives. Well, Well, Well, three more 'Fishers' of men. And later, when I checked the 2nd disc out to see why it didn't play? It worked perfectly. Hmmmm! Do you think God had a hand in that? Do you think He was saying "STOP! You've caught 'em, Let Me do the rest". You know, sometimes we can go 'overboard'. We need to stop once we've got 'em in the boat and let GOD handle 'em from there.

How about you? Have you jumped in the boat yet? If not, then I invite you to check out the web site at www.BGEA.org and then click on 'How to Know Jesus'.

And if you've already been cleaned, then it may be time for you to 'go fishin' for men. Jesus will show you the way.

To hear the song above, go to www.youtube.com... and type in the Gaither Vocal Band and the song: 'I catch 'Em, God Cleans 'Em.

And if you have an interest in touching the lives of young men, then go to www.savingourboys.org and hear what Sam Mehaffie has to say.

And to learn more about how to disciple men, then go to www.battlezoneministries.org.

JDC- Juvenile Detention Center

The JDC 's at the JDC

The Jesus Disciples Crew at the Juvenile Detention Center

Hey Tom, Hey Wayne…. the KRR guy,

Ben was filling me in on what happened last Sunday at the JDC. Randy & Willie were confronted right off the bat with a young man who flatly stated 'He used to believe in Jesus, but he doesn't anymore'. Now, I wasn't there but evidently God used this young man to stir things up. And God must have provided Randy & Willie the wisdom and words to help this young man out. And not only was that young man helped, but I understand every boy there that morning had tears in their eyes before Randy & Willie left.

The week before this we had a JDC crew meeting at the Kirk and I got to meet for the first time KT, a young married man in his late 20's or early 30's. I was really impressed with his testimony and he is going to be a great asset to the team. He is going to team up with me and I think I'll just let him take over. He will be able to really connect with the guys. This guy sings rap and he found Jesus Christ while he was in a Detention Center himself. He's a member of Church on the Move (Willie George's church). I'll fill you in some more down the road as God uses KT to communicate with the boys at JDC.

Now, even more current news about one of the Kirk Youth teams out with the Kirk Karpenters yesterday. The team I was with built a ramp for a man named Phillip around 4th & Memorial. What a fantastic group of boys and one girl (she happened to be your Granddaughter Tom). Phillip attends Memorial Methodist Church and his neighbor next door has attended Will Rogers Methodist Church for over 40 years. I had a great conversation with both of these gentlemen and have visited both of their churches and knew of some common friends and members of their churches. BUT, where God really stepped in was when a couple of young boys appeared on the scene a couple of houses up the street. As I found out later, they used to live across the street but they had moved to another part of town and were just by with their dad to pick up a few things still in their old house. When I saw them, I thought I'd approach them about a Phos

Hmmm! Who's Speaking?

Cross. I asked Zak if he'd like one of his team to go with me. Well, Hayden Anderson was standing right there and Zak asked him if he'd go along.

Now, I had no idea that Hayden was a Life Scout, but I should have guessed because he is such a great guy. Anyway, as I get started talking to the two brothers (one 13 and the other 8) about the Phos Cross, the older one interrupts and asked me if I was the Chaplain at Scout Camp Tom Hale. What in the world? I'm only there one week out of the year. And most of the Scouts there are from Texas or other parts of Oklahoma. And now Hayden joins in the conversation because he's a Boy Scout too and all of a sudden, I lost control. All three of these guys are talking Scouting and they knew some mutual friends at Kirk. They were sharing Scouting experiences and everything else. Now, what are the odds of Hayden and me running into a couple of boys, who just happened to show up on this day, at that exact time, at that project, in that part of Tulsa, who were outdoors, who we saw, who happened to be Scouts, who happened to see me once before dressed entirely differently, who knew mutual friends, etc., etc. What? Maybe 5 million to 1? Maybe 10 million to 1? WHO planned all this out? WHO put this all together? I think you know WHO? Hayden said he knew.

Oh Yes! And you know WHO is still stirring things up with the young people in the world. At Passion 2012 at the Georgia Dome in Atlanta. Passion contracted for 42,000 seats. They had to turn some 18 to 25-year old's away. SOLD OUT. They squeezed in 44,000. And they were hoping for Contributions, to help stamp out Slavery, of $1 mil. Well, they got $3.1 mil. That was contributions that averaged over $70 per attendee.

And, Winter Jam 2012 in Tulsa at the BOK Center. Packed out at 17,000 and they had to turn some away. WHOA! Someone we know is on the GO! And my ears are still ringing. Ten great Rockin' Worship Bands were there. I'd say #1 was 'Skillet'. I noticed a young teenager in front of me who seemed amazed, but not with it. With the 9 groups that performed b/4 Skillet, this teenager was just sitting there looking around, while it looked like 16,999 others were jumping up & down, waving their arms, flashing their cell phones and whatever. Then, when Skillet came on, this guy came ALIVE! He was jumping up & down, he knew the words and lyrics to every song and he was singing them out at the top of his lungs, and recording the whole thing on his cell phone. I tell you, you never know what kind of Christian music might turn some of these teenagers on, but thank goodness there is something out there for every one of them.

Hey, you guys have a Blessed Day.... I'll keep on truckin' and listening to the ringing in my ears. Your KRR guy, A BIC

In God We Trust

Hey Tom, Wayne & others…the KRR guy again,

Sunday the 7th was my day to be the Worship Leader at the Tulsa Juvenile Detention Center. A few days before that I had thought about what Worship music and message I would present. However, God had something else in mind. I do not like to repeat something but maybe in about six months so that some of the youth might not hear the same thing twice. But God had other plans…He wanted to use Lecrae Moore and his song 'Divine Intervention' and tie it in with the message of GOD'S BANK which I had just used a couple of months prior. I kind of questioned God but He got thru to me that He had some new things to add to the old message.

Sure enough, Friday evening on Channel 6 News there was the story about the guy in Claremore who almost got stuck taking 9 Fake $100 Bills. Maybe you saw the news? Anyway, the guy was advertising his 1998 Ford Expedition and someone called about it, so the guy hurried home to show it. The prospective buyer showed up and hardly looked the car over and said he would buy it with cash. He gave the seller 9/ $100 Bills and was ready to drive off. The seller, who said he knew nothing about $100 Bills, said he would go in and get the key to the car. God decided to use this guy to get the buyers attention. The guy first thought the Bills felt a little funny as he went into his house. He asked his wife what she thought and she said the color doesn't look right to her and then this guy noticed that all 9 had the same serial number. So, he had his wife call Rogers County Sheriff Scott Walton to come check these guys out and he would try to detain them for a little bit. Well you know the rest of the story.

Anyway, I then pointed out to the boys that the FBI trains their people to be able to spot Fake $100 Bills instantly by setting them down during a session and having them look over a Real $100 Bill for several hours. Then in the next session they give them Real & Fake $100 Bills and want to see how quickly they can separate the two. I then held up a Bible and explained to them how important it is to know the Real Bible so that they can tell when someone is a Real Christian and talking to them about the Real Bible. I explained that there are Fake Religions and Fake Christians

JDC- Juvenile Detention Center

all around us and we need to be prepared to know the difference. Jesus knows the difference as in Matthew 7:21-23.

Now Verse 3 in the song 'Divine Intervention' by Lecrae says:

> *They say in God we trust*
> *But what's the bigger sin*
> *That we don't trust in Him*
> *But trust the stuff on which it's written* (money)

Well God Inspired me to print out the back of our US Currency where it is printed IN GOD WE TRUST to show the boys. Sunday morning, just before Chapel at the JDC, I went by my office to print off some copies of the back of a $5, $10, $20 & $100 Bill all on one page. I placed them on my printer, hit 'color' and then hit 'copy'. Lo & Behold only the top half of the $5 bill printed where it showed IN GOD WE TRUST. I checked to see if my paper feeder was OK and tried again & again & again. Hmmm! Maybe it's the 'Color' so I put a colorful magazine on the printer to see what would happen. Hey! It printed out OK. Hmmm! Maybe the printer can't pick up the color on the money so I'll just print it out in B&W. Same thing...only the top half of the $5 Bill where it shows IN GOD WE TRUST. I was running out of time so I managed to print out the top half of each bill where it shows IN GOD WE TRUST and then assembled them on one page, made copies, and hurried down to the JDC.

Ben and Randy were there too and I explained to them and the boys about my copier not copying the back of the bills where it says IN GOD WE TRUST. I tried all sorts of things and it just wouldn't let me print the money. I then mentioned that new technology and the new 'Bills' must send a signal to where you can't print money. I then jokingly said that in the near future I wouldn't be surprised if technology might even send a signal to the Government and the FBI telling them that someone at this computer at this specific address is trying to print some fake money and go arrest them. Everyone got a laugh out of that.

WELL!! Here's the rest of the story. After I left I went back to my office because I had some more questions about the printer and the bills. I wanted to see if God had a hand it that and if He would only let the printer print the part of the Bill that said IN GOD WE TRUST. Then I got inquisitive

Hmmm! Who's Speaking?

about the Latin meaning of the motto on the back of the $1 Bill…the 'Annuit Coeptis Novus Ordo Seclorum' and went to my search engine.

BINGO!! A Government Notice popped up and wiped out what I was pulling up. The Government notice looked official and it stated that they had detected some illegal use of my computer and they had shut it down. WHAT??? The notice then did go on to say that they would allow me to use the computer if I paid a Penalty of $300. I could click on one of four companies they had posted and send them my payment by credit card and then they would allow me back on my computer in 15 to 20 minutes. I remember two of the companies were Office Depot and I think Staples. BUT, then I started noticing some miss-spelt words in the Government Notice and realized that this was some sort of a scam probably coming from someone in Russia. I clicked a few more buttons and got the notice off and back to where I started. Well what I jokingly mentioned at the JDC about printers in the future being able to contact the FBI about illegal printing?? I think maybe the future is already here? Now some of you may be Tech-savvy and already knew about all this but it was all Greek or Latin to me and I'm just glad that God got me thru it all and I know for sure to put MY TRUST IN GOD.

Those of you who are venturesome might want to look up that Latin Motto and see what it means and then see if the government or someone in Russia is checking on you too.

The KRR guy…A BIC

The Attitude Indicator

Hey Tom, Wayne and others….the KRR guy again

I did my monthly visit to the JDC (Juvenile Detention Center) with YFC (Youth For Christ) in Tulsa this last Sunday. I was prepared to give my message and play a couple of worship songs that tied in with the message but I did not realize what else God had planned.

After I arrived with my bag with my Boom Box and CD's, Tom Cox shows up along with Sandon Jordan who were going to lead the Chapel Services in Section A. Neither one of them had a boom box or musical instrument or any CD's, but Tom did have a little red cylinder about the size of a pint jar. Curiosity got the best of me and I asked Tom what that little round thing was. He told me its' a wireless speaker that ties in to your iPhone. He informed me that this is the new technology. You don't need a big boom box or a bunch of CDs'. You just plug this little speaker into your iPhone and pick the songs you want to play. He plugged this little bitty thing into his phone, turned up the volume and lo and behold it about BLEW me out of the room. WHOA! Here I was about to give a message about airplane technology that came about in the late 1920's and early 30's and here was new amazing technology for 2015.

I and Alex Montero partnered up for Section B where it's all boys (ages 13 to 18) who are in the jail for a little more serious type of crime than those in Section A. As the boys are being brought in (and they voluntarily decide) the last boy is dragging behind and one of the staffers says something to him and the boy must have said something back that wasn't complimentary so the staffer says "you know, you better watch your 'Attitude'". Well, Well, Well. That was what my message was going to be about that day. See Copy Attached.

THE ATTITUDE INDICATOR
JDC 7/5/2015

Message: Anyone here today ever flown in a plane? Anyone here who has never flown? Anyone here who has actually flown a plane?

Let me give you a little information about flying planes. The very first aviators or pilots did not have any instruments to help them fly like the planes do today. In the late 20's and early 30's the aviators flew by what was called **"the seat of their pants"**. (Demonstrate and ask the boys to participate so they can see what this feels like). Your rear end has the most contact with the plane and it can tell you if your pitch is not level with the horizon or if your roll is not right. The Pitch refers to whether the nose of the plane is pointing upwards or downwards. The Roll refers to whether the wings of the plane are banked to the left or to the right, or if they are parallel to the horizon. So, what is meant to "fly by the seat of your pants?" The more the pilots flew the better they became at using their senses or intuition. They depended upon what they could see out of the open cockpit of their plane and what their seat was telling them.

As planes got bigger and faster and begin to fly at night, and into clouds, the pilots realized that they could not trust their senses. So, instruments were developed to help the pilot fly a true course. And one of these instruments was the **Attitude Indicator**. This indicator helps the pilot keep the plane on a level course. It shows the Pitch and Roll of the plane in respect to a horizon shown on the dial.

In our lives we sometimes indicate to others what our attitude is. Maybe we've heard our parents or others tell us that we need to adjust our attitude. How can we get help to adjust our attitude?? Whenever we sense or feel our attitude is not right, we need to focus on God and ask Him to help adjust us when we're up or down or tilted out of shape. He will then help us to get back in line and oriented with Him.

How is your attitude? Are you parallel with God? Do you want to learn more about Aviation Attitude? Then study some airplane flight books and go listen to some flying instructors.

Do you want to learn more about your Personal Attitude? Then study this book (the Bible) and go listen to some Preachers and Teachers. Check out 1st Corinthians 10:33 where Paul talks about having a 'Serving Attitude' and Philippians 4:8-9 where Paul talks about keeping your focus on God.

Today's Prayer.... You know God there may be some of us here this morning that are going to need help with our attitude today or sometime this week. Those of us who have become to know You, will sense when You're telling us to adjust our attitude. There may be some here who don't know You (God) that well yet, so we pray that this day, or sometime this week, that they will seek to know You more.

Reminder Item: Toss a small glider plane and explain how Gravity brings it down. Explain that this small plane will not last forever. It might get lost or broken or thrown away. But, I hope that whenever you see or hear a real plane, that sometimes it will remind you of this short message and that maybe you will pause and check your attitude and see if it's lined up with God. Also, maybe a plane will remind you, if you haven't already, that it's time to check God out and invite Him into your life.

Associated Music: Shawn McDonald "Gravity", Brett Yonker "The Way" or David Crowder "Lift Your Head Weary Sinner."

Illusions, Illustrations, Images

Summer 2013

Title: Illusions, Illustrations & Images (What's the Difference?) Re-done version of Boy Scout Chapel Message of Summer 2010)

Opening Prayer:

What is the difference between illusions & illustrations & images? Well, I went to my dictionary to find out. What was interesting was that all three root words were on the same page in my dictionary, one after another.

Illusion was defined as: 'Misleading visual images or false perceptions of what one sees.'

Illustration was defined as: 'Using drawings, diagrams, pictures or images to help clarify or make something easier to understand.'

Image was defined as: 'A reproduction of the form of a person or thing.'

So! Can an illusion of an image be used as an illustration? The answer is Yes!

Scripture: OT Exodus 3:2-4...*Suddenly, an angel of the LORD appeared to Moses as a blazing fire in a bush. Moses was amazed because the bush was engulfed in flames, but it wasn't burning up? "Amazing! Moses said to himself. "Why isn't that bush burning up? I must go over and see this." When the LORD saw that he had caught Moses' attention, God called to him from the bush, "Moses! Moses!"*

OT Proverbs 8:17..." *I love all who love me. Those who search for me will surely find me."*

NT Colossians 1:15... (Paul wrote this) He said: *"Christ is the visible image of the invisible God."*

Message:

In the Scripture, we just heard, God spoke to Moses from an illusion of a burning bush and it amazed Moses and aroused his curiosity. We too must realize that God may use unexpected sources or signs or illustrations when he wants to communicate with us too. It could be people, thoughts, illusions, experiences, or even something else that He uses. But like Moses, we too must be willing to investigate, and be open to God's surprises and illustrations.

Several years ago, I attended a program on how to be more positive. The speaker passed out a black & white picture like one of those I've passed out to you. (Holding up the 'Old Woman' picture) ask the guys/gals what they see. Some of you will only see an image of an 'Old Woman' or 'Witch'. Some of you will see an attractive young lady. If you only see one image, then try to broaden your view so that you can see both images. It's sort of like looking at a glass of juice and seeing it as either half empty or half full.

Don't just focus in on some negative thing in your life, like being here in JDC, but look for the good things. Can this experience here make a better person of me? Maybe, just maybe, while you're here you'll even accept Jesus Christ into your life. Or maybe you've accepted Him into your life, but not seriously before.

Another black & white picture shows a wine glass. Can you see another image in this picture too? Two people face to face?

Now, I would like for all of you to take the black and white picture that looks like just a jumbled mess. We're going to make something beautiful out of it. Follow my instructions and let's see what we can do. I want you to focus on the picture for about 30 seconds with the arrow pointing up. And I want you to look and concentrate on the 4 small dots in the center of the picture. They run up & down. I will start counting shortly, and then after I count, I want you to look up at the ceiling or a white wall. Focus on a particular area. Then in a second or two you should first see a circle of light appearing. Then, maybe after blinking once or twice you will start to see an image. OK! Is everybody ready? Start looking at the four dots while I count. (After 30 seconds, have them look up to the ceiling or a white wall).

Now, many of you saw this <u>illusion</u> become an <u>image</u> that <u>illustrates</u> the most important person to know in your life. Yes! That person is Jesus Christ. Take this illusion with you and show it to someone who didn't make it to Chapel today. Or take it home and show it to your parents and friends and explain to them how it works and about the message today.

Reminder item: copies of illusions

Hmmm! Who's Speaking?

Associated music: Beautiful Day by U2. Point out the CD cover with the picture of the airport terminal. J33:3..." Ask Me (the Lord) and I will tell you some remarkable secrets about what is going to happen"

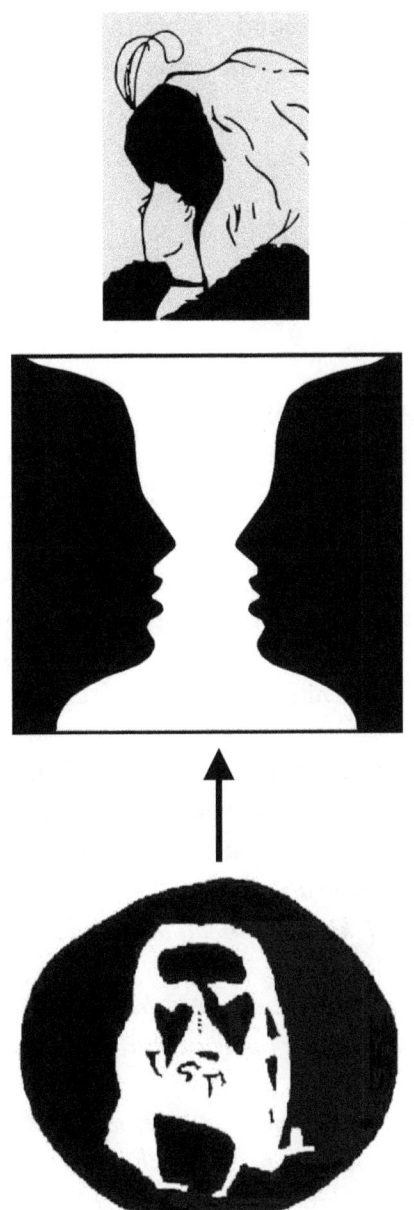

FOR OTHER ILLUSIONS GO TO WWW.BRAINDEN.COM

Geese & Geezer
(What's the Difference?)

Opening: You know they sound almost the same and the spelling is similar. In the spelling of the word geese, you simply change the 's' to a 'z' and add an 'r'.

Geese
Change 's' to 'z'
Geeze
And add an 'r'
Geezer

So, what is the difference? Well geese live 20 to 25 years while a geezer usually is someone that lives around 4 times longer (80 to 100). But there is also a Big Difference in the meaning. A Geezer is defined as an 'A cranky or cantankerous old man who doesn't get along with anybody and doesn't care if anybody needs help or not'. Now Geese…....They are just about the exact opposite and that's what we're going to learn about this morning.

Opening Prayer & Scriptures

Scripture: OT Genesis 6:19-20…God is giving instructions to Noah about the Ark and what to put on the Ark…*Bring a pair of every kind of animal- a male and a female- into the boat with you to keep them alive during the flood. Pairs of each kind of bird and each kind of animal, large and small alike…...*"

OT Genesis 7:3…*There must be a male and female in each pair to ensure that every kind of living creature will survive the flood.*

OT Job 12:7-8…*Ask the animals, and they will teach you; or the birds of the air and they will tell you, or let the fish in the sea inform you. Speak to the earth, and it will instruct you. Let the fish of the sea speak to you.*

Hmmm! Who's Speaking?

Message:

In the Scriptures we just heard, God is telling us things we should know and learn, from things He has created.

Recently someone sent me some information about geese. I already knew some interesting things about geese, but obviously, this person had spent a lot more time than I had really researching information on geese. And here is what I found out.

The "V" formation that geese fly in? Well God had a good reason for including this in their natural instinct and something for us to learn. Each bird creates an uplift for the following bird when it flaps its wings. Well this uplift helps the whole flock by enabling the birds to increase their flying range by an estimated minimum 71%. Instead of 60 miles, they could fly over 100 miles. When a bird gets out of the formation it can feel the drag of flying alone, so it quickly gets back into formation. God is pointing out that like geese, when people share a common direction and a sense of togetherness, they too will find the going easier and quicker.

When the lead bird gets tired, it rotates back and another bird moves to the point position. We too should realize that our success depends on working as a team, taking turns doing the hard tasks and sharing leadership.

You have probably heard the familiar sound of geese honking. Well the geese in the rear are 'honking' so as to encourage those up front. And the lead geese will 'honk' occasionally so that those in the rear can tell when they may be falling too far behind. So, the point is… we too should remember to be encouraging to others when it is needed, by what we say and how we say it.

Now occasionally a bird gets weak or even wounded and when this happens, two other geese will drop out of formation to help it and provide protection. They will stay with that one until it can fly again or it dies. Then they take off again with another passing flock or catch up with their own flock. God asks us too, to be of assistance to our friends in time of need.

Here is something important to remember too. Geese will pair up and mate for life. One gander (the male) with each goose (the female). But, in case one is killed, then the other may go and find a new mate so that their species will continue to survive. God too, asks us to pair up as male and female, like the birds & animals & fish of the sea so we too will survive.

And one final thought. Geese will feed in groups as many of you may have seen. If you have observed this, you probably saw at least one of the geese scouting out for trouble and watching out for the others, ready to warn them of any approaching danger. Well you know, God is always doing this for us.

Chapter Nineteen: Passion

Passion 2013

www.268generation.com

Isaiah 26:8 *LORD, we love to obey your laws; our heart's desire is to glorify your name.*

Hey Tom, Hey Wayne…. And others

Hey, I don't know about you, but I sure am worried about our country's direction right now. And I hear and see where Franklin and his dad Billy Graham are worried too. In the October issue of 'DECISION' (www.billygraham.org/decision), the BGEA monthly magazine, the front cover portrayed ACCEPTING GOD being overshadowed by REJECTING GOD. When you have, political parties Booing God and not wanting God's name mentioned at all in their platform, it worries me and God. In Romans 1:28…" *When they refused to acknowledge God, He abandoned them to their evil minds and let them do things that should never be done*". When you get a political party or candidates Okaying abortions, it worries me and God. Because God says in Jeremiah 1:5 *"Before I formed you in the womb I knew you, before you were born I set you apart to speak for Me to the nations."* When you get rejecters of God saying it's OK to have unnatural marriages, it worries me and God. In Romans 1:26-27 it says *"That is why God abandoned them to their shameful desires. Even the women turned against the natural way to have sex and instead indulged in sex with each other. And the men, instead of having normal sexual relationships with women, burned with lust for each other.* And in Romans 1:32…" *And, worse yet, they encourage others to do them, too."* Oh My! I have to ask myself, 'Has God given up on us?"

Passion

BUT, you know what? God is making a move right now and He's making it with the sharpest and the brightest generation. Yes! It's the New Jesus Generation of the 21st Century. He wasn't involved with the 'Hippies in the Sixties' or the 'Jesus Freaks in the 70's'. BUT GOD is making a change with those who are 18 to 25 years old right now. These are mostly college students or college age young people. God started making His move in 1997 in Austin, Texas. I got involved with the 268generation in 2003 as a volunteer in Sherman, Texas and was so impressed and got so lifted up, that I have been involved with them at least once a year ever since. I'll be going to the Georgia Dome in Atlanta Jan. 1st thru 4th. Last year Passion 2012 committed to 42,000 seats in the Dome. They had to turn thousands of students away. These 'On Fire for Jesus' students came from every state and even dozens of foreign countries. This new year 2013, Jan 1st thru 4th, Passion has committed to all 73,500 seats in the Dome and I hear it is filling up fast.

After gathering in the Dome for great worship leaders and great speakers, the attendees then break down into smaller venues in surrounding buildings and hear more great speakers that address different issues that an attendee may have a special interest in. They then break down into small groups within that venue and pray and discuss among themselves what they can do to make a change in this world.

AND, what a change they are making. These young people are not embarrassed or ashamed of their love for God, for Jesus, for the Holy Spirit. When they get back home they are sharing their love with their friends and classmates. They get involved with all sorts of worthwhile causes. You will see them carrying their Bibles and wearing items that express their love. You will see them on their knees or with their hands held high in Praise of God. And not only will you see them doing this at their church, but you may even see them in the middle of a football field, on their knees, in front of a crowded Professional game and on National TV.

These young people are wanting to make a Change, to make a Change for Jesus Christ. ***And you can help them. The College Minister at the Kirk, Scott French, says some of these students need some *CHANGE* to enable them to get to go. If you have some loose *Change*, say a buck or two or even more, contact Scott and let him know. And do not think they may get too much *Change*, because if that happens they just pass it on to a worthy cause. Last year Passion's request for donations to Help End World Slavery was a goal of $1 million (an average of about $25 per attendee), well these students brought in $3.1 mil (about $75 per attendee).

I might mention something that happened a few years ago at a Passion gathering that Passion learned to never do again. That was the year that Passion asked the students to bring coats and shoes to donate to the needy. Well, well, well, I saw it myself…those students started taking off their own coats and shoes and shirts and…, well as I said Passion learned to be a little more careful in what they ask for.

Check with Scott at the Kirk or check with your Churches College Ministry or your College University and see about helping or if they are aware or involved.

If you start getting down with the way the World seems to be going, then I invite you to visit <u>www.268generation</u> or just type in Passion 2013 in your Search Engine. Seeing and hearing what God is doing with this New Generation is inspiring and up lifting. And if you want to get choked up about what is happening, then type in 'Passion 2012 Glimpse Video' and click on the 'you tube' 12-minute version or the 4-minute shortened version on 'A Summary of What It's All About'. A BIC

Author & son @ Passion on a Ranch outside of Sherman, Texas

Passion and The Toothbrush

Toothbrush closes down world's busiest airport

January 13, 2013

Hey Tom, Hey Wayne…. It's me, the KRR guy again,

Just back from Passion 2013 at the Georgia Dome in Atlanta. Yup! My 10th exciting year with a Passion Conference and as a Volunteer Security Door Holder. I wasn't alone. There were over 60,000 attendees geared to 18 to 25-year-old College Students. Students from over 2,000 universities from all 50 States and 51 Foreign countries this time. There were about 3,000 Volunteers and about 30 of us were on the Security Team. And hey, Scott was there with about 1 ½ Dozen of the Kirk's Brightest and Sharpest College folks.

Each year I think they can't make the Passion conference any bigger or better and yet they do. I talked with a couple of our guys from the Kirk who attended last year and this year and they both commented on how they were impressed that this year they were able to feed 60,000 plus in the Georgia Dome in only 20 minutes. Listen, you know how important food is to me too. You don't think I am influencing these guys, do you?? But Spiritually, these 60,000+ New Generation young people are beginning to make an Impact. God is using each and every one of them to Glorify Him.

And our Kirk attendees made a name for themselves with the volunteers too. And it was a Positive + impression. With 60,000 plus lining up to get into the Georgia Dome on the first day, guess who got there hours early so they could be the first ones in line? Yup! Our Kirk group. A couple of the volunteers, when they asked me where I was from and I said Oklahoma, they replied well there must be a whole lot of you from Oklahoma because they're all over the place and in the very front of the line to get into the Dome.

And me? This time I was assigned to the Dome for the whole time. 14 to 16-hour days standing up, walking around in Section B, keeping an eye on things. I did get about 5 hrs. sleep each night which was more than some others got. One volunteer came up and advised me that there

Hmmm! Who's Speaking?

was a Double Decker bus full of protestors parked a couple of blocks away. I contacted the appropriate person, who I am sure contacted the police, who I am sure handled the situation appropriately. I can imagine that the protestors were cautioned that some 60,000+ students on Fire for Jesus Christ might converge on them sharing their love of Jesus with them.

And the Toothbrush? Well, the downtown hotels were booked up by the time I signed up, so I had booked a hotel near the airport and rode the Sky train daily to the Atlanta Airport and caught the MARTA train into the Dome each day. The last day, about 7:35 a.m. as I arrived at the Airport, the Airport Security stopped me from entering the airport. I told them I just wanted to go in and catch the MARTA, but they said the MARTA had been stopped and it couldn't come into the Airport area. They were contacting the bus line to give rides to everyone to the next MARTA stop up the line. As I was talking with the Security, I see the Atlanta Bomb Squad truck and Police pulling in. Uh Oh! A bomb threat? During Passion, all of Atlanta Security is advised to be Alert and Cautious to possible threats, even though Passion does its best to keep the Conferences as low key as possible.

It wasn't until the next day, after I had gotten back to Tulsa, that I pulled up the information as to what had happened at the World's Busiest Airport. You know, I think you could fit 20 or 30 Tulsa Airports into the Atlanta Airport. Anyway, someone had gone and left a bag in the airport unattended and the bag contained a battery powered toothbrush that was on and going tick-tick, tick-tick, tick-tick. Now, we'll probably never know if it was one of the Passion attendee's that left it there unwittingly while they went to the restroom or if it was someone who was intent on creating a disturbance. But, in either case, it shut down the airport for 40 minutes, created a problem for thousands of people, and delayed and threw off air traffic.

And maybe it was someone who was upset with Louie Giglio, one of the founders of Passion & the 268 Generation. As you may have heard, Obama had invited Louie to give the Benediction at the Presidential Inauguration on Jan. 21st, and some protestors objected because Louie is a True Follower of Jesus Christ. The protestors had found something Louie had said in a Sermon about 20 years ago about homosexuality being a sin as described in the Bible. *This is specifically addressed many times in the Bible…i.e.: Romans 1:26-27; 1 Corinthians 5:9-13; 6:9-20; 1 Timothy 1:9-10.*

I respect Louie for withdrawing from that invitation. Louie loves God and God loves everyone. And God wants us to love Him in return by living the way He wants us to live. Tom, you probably remember when I lost my oldest son almost 25 years ago to complications caused by AIDS thru homosexuality. I loved my son very much and it distresses me when I see people going down the wrong path in life. In my son's case, it was a High School teacher who led him astray at a vulnerable age. Too many people today are leading are finest young people astray. At the Juvenile Detention Center, where I volunteer some, I see young men who have been influenced in the wrong way by movies, videos, gangs, and even family members. Some of them are told about and even promised False Rewards for what they do. I commend people like Louie and others who are doing their best to bring those who have taken the wrong path and to bring them to a loving relationship with God. Getting to know Jesus as our one and only True God helps each and every one of us to live a life in His Glory.

Oh! One last thing. God communicated with me about the 3rd day in an unusual way. That afternoon, the attendees left the Dome about 4 to go out and eat somewhere. The Dome volunteers could take a break then for about 1 ½ hours and go to a special club room in the Dome and sit down and put your feet up and grab a snack. My feet were so sore by then I could hardly walk. Since the Club room was on the opposite end of the Dome, I decided to sit down in one of the 72,500 Dome seats and put my feet up. I looked around and I couldn't see anyone else in the whole Dome sitting down. There were a couple of hundred techs on the floor field getting the lights and sound prepared for the next session so I just relaxed and was about to dose off when all of a sudden there was a loud Boom! Boom! It shook the whole floor and even my seat. What in the world? Well it was Lacrae the Worship Rapper getting warmed up for the next session. Lacrae is one the of more popular Worship leaders right now. I sat there and enjoyed Lacrae and looked around and felt like someone really important because he was performing just for me. No one else in sight and then a bright red light came on and shined right in my face. I wondered for a moment if this might be something like arriving in Heaven. And then, when I got up to go back to my station, I felt better than I had since the first day and my feet were as light as feathers. Hummm! Now Who could have caused that???

This year the attendees contributed over $3.3 million to 22 or 23 different organizations that are helping some 27 million people that are caught up in slavery and sexual traffic. And if anyone is interested in contributing or checking this all out you can go to www.268generation.com/passion2013.

Also, you can go to www.catholic.com and type in Homosexuality which has some interesting Biblical information.

Hey, Hey, Hey…. Your BIC, the KRR guy, getting the New Year started off right

PASSION 2016

Hey Tom, Wayne and others…the KRR again at Houston,

Well, Well, Well, my 12th Passion Event to help out since 2003 when it was held on a Ranch outside of Sherman, Texas on Memorial Day weekend. I've been to one each year since then as I was so impacted with that one. If you remember that far back that was the one where all the 20,000 or so 18 to 25-year-old mainly College Students camped out in tents and a terrible storm blew in and knocked down about 90% of the 7,000 or so tents. Obviously the 10% of the tents that had remained in place were put up by Boy Scouts. A couple of girls had pitched a tent up on a rolling hillside right beneath the only tree around and when lightning struck they were hurt and had to be taken into Sherman to the hospital. Needless to say, that was the last time that Passion was held outdoors.

That event locked me into volunteering at least once a year when it was to be held in the U.S. John Piper, a featured preacher speaker, talked about his experience at that event which he wrote about at www.desiringgod.org/articles/what-happened-at-oneday03 Piper tells that 3,700 students requested more information about mission agencies and 782 said their bags are packed and they are ready to go into the mission field. And 1,469 wanted more information about going to seminary. He mentioned one very touching testimony from a young 24-year-old student from Florida (Jonathan) who had a wedding date set for the day before the event and then he and his bride were taking off for a honeymoon to Hawaii. Three weeks before the wedding his wife-to-be had heard about Passion '03 and asked about stopping in Sherman the first day before going on to Hawaii. They were blown away by God both literally and spiritually and immediately cancelled their honeymoon trip to Hawaii and then and there committed their lives to foreign missions.

Passion now has so many attendees from every state and dozens of countries that they have a hard time finding an indoor facility large enough to handle the event. This year they had over 1,600 colleges & universities represented. Also, this year they had to hold the event simultaneously in three different venues…two in Atlanta and the one in Houston. Football games and other events happening right around New Year's eliminate many of their choices. However next year, 2017, they will be back in the Georgia Dome in Atlanta that will hold over 70,000. When I was there in 2013 they had over 62,000 in attendance. Since their inception, they have reached over 20 million students.

I always look forward to helping out because it gives me so much hope for the future of the world. And after a year of negative things I hear and see in the news everyday this lifts me up and gets me off to a positive start. If any of you would like to get lifted up too…then check out Passion and see about volunteering at www.268generation.com. *Isaiah 26:8…" LORD, we love to obey your laws; our heart's desire is to glorify your name".*

I hope everyone's New Year is starting off on a positive note. It has for me…

Your BIC, the KRR guy, David Cox

Passion 2017 YES! Or Passion 2017 NO!

January 7, 2017

Hey Wayne, Dan and others…. The KRR guy out and about,

Well I had made flight and hotel reservations to attend Passion 2017 at the Georgia Dome in Atlanta for 1/1/17 to 1/4/17 and was looking forward to it as usual. I have been attending every Passion Event held since 2003 somewhere in the U.S. A few days before leaving though my cell phone disappeared. I spent a whole half day looking all over for it, checking everyplace I had been in the last 24 hours. I checked everywhere & everything 3 or 4 times, clothing, cars, office, inside, outside…. but no phone and I needed that phone for Passion since I'm on the Security Team. I was thinking was it the Devil trying to keep me from going or was it God saying 'Not This Time'. After praying for God's direction, I finally cancelled my reservations but I asked God to let me know some way that this was His plan and not the Devil's.

After cancelling late Thursday, I got up the next day planning on buying a new phone. I go by QT first and pick up a coffee and a paper and drive over to my office to park and read the paper. For the first time, ever in about 40 years I parked facing 31st St. and a couple of car spaces away from a car I was trying to sell for my granddaughter. Well God must have directed me to look at the parked car and I noticed where the tires looked like they could use some air, so after reading the paper I go get in it and take it to QT to get aired up. I was afraid I might have aired them up too much so I open the car door again to see if I could find attached information about the proper amount of air in the tires. Well guess what I see in the process? Yup! Right before my eyes is my cell phone. OK God you're making me feel better already. Anything else You can do?

Well since I wasn't leaving town that gave me the opportunity to help with the Chapel Service for the boys at the JDC (Juvenile Detention Center) on Sunday, Jan. 1st.

When I arrived Sunday at the JDC, lo & behold no one else was there to lead the Chapel Service. The staff was surprised to see me because they figured no one would show up on New Year's Day, but they hurriedly informed the boys and all 23 boys elected to show up plus 3 of the staff.

I explained to the boys that I hadn't planned on being there that day, but that God had different plans. I played some worship music from Passion and told them how God can communicate with you in ways you never expect. I told them about how I should have died 8 years ago, at the Chapel at a Boy Scout Camp but God had decided…Not Yet.

When I had arrived at that Scout Camp in July 2008 and walked up the hill to the Chapel, I discovered that the Chapel had not been de-weeded. Hmmm! Weeds in a Chapel does not sound appropriate so I went back down the hill and mentioned it to the staff. They said they were too busy checking in 750 or so scouts for camp and couldn't do anything about it right away. I told them not to worry, just get me a weed eater and I'd take care of it. One staffer got me a weed eater and filled it with gas and said that was enough gas to probably do two or three times the area needed to be de-weeded. I go back up the hill and had ½ of the Chapel de-weeded when I got a terrific pain in my chest and could hardly stand up. So, I sat down and asked God if He was trying to communicate with me. Soon I felt good enough to stand up and finish the de-weeding. But when I tried starting the weed eater…. with 4, 5 or 6 attempts and no starting….I checked out the gas and Lo & Behold it was Empty. So, I sat down again and asked God if He was telling me the Weed Eater was literally out of Gas and that I was physically out of Gas. I still wanted to do my Chapel services for the week, so I told God if He would help me get thru the week at camp I would promise to go see my doctor just as soon as I got back to Tulsa. Well, God did His part, as usual, but I didn't do my part. I was feeling so good after camp that I decided I could put off going to see my doc. God had to get my attention again in a couple of weeks.

Now before I went to Scout Camp I had given blood 3 or 4 weeks prior and my blood pressure was 124/64 and a pulse rate at 64. And then a few days before leaving for camp I had to have a Scout physical checkup by my doctor and again everything looked great. When I finally go back to my doc after camp and explained to him what had happened at camp, he immediately set me up with an appointment with a cardiologist the next day at one of the local hospitals. Well the doc there did some different kinds of tests and took some x-rays. He came back to see me in about an hour and right up front told me I should have died at Scout Camp. What? He could tell by my expression that I had my doubts so he took me into the next room and showed me the x-rays and explained that my hearts 3 main coronary arteries were 99%, 99% and 90% blocked. I should be dead. He informed me he had admitted me to the hospital and had contacted a Heart Surgeon, I didn't know, at this hospital to do a triple by-pass the next morning. Now I still wasn't so sure I wanted this to happen and I knew a Heart Surgeon, Dr. Whiteneck, from my church who I would prefer to do the surgery. When I mentioned his name, my Cardiologist agreed that Whiteneck was a great doctor but he does his surgery at another hospital in Tulsa. I said well I'll call him and set up an appointment. But the Cardiologist said I could not drive and so he will call an ambulance to take me there. I thought hmmm...well OK. But then he said one more thing that finally convinced me.... he said now before you go get in the ambulance I need you to sign a piece of paper. I said what's that about? He said it is a liability thing so that in case you die in the ambulance on the way there, that no one could hold him or the hospital liable. Well the Doc, with God's help, finally got my attention. A few weeks after the successful triple by-pass I sent the Doc a note explaining everything and how God had played an important role. The Doc sent me a nice note back. He thanked me very much and explained how he feels that he is God's instrument in his practice of medicine. He reflected on some things that have happened in his life and how he is looking forward to that time of his own death and having God explain to him how HE has used him in his own life.

After telling the boys about this, God had prepared me for something else. Just before I left the house that morning, for some reason I picked up a book, 'Touching Heaven' by another Heart Surgeon, Dr. Crandall out of Palm Beach, FL. I showed the book to the boys and explained that a lot of heart doctors become true believers because of things that happen that just cannot be explained except that God played a hand in it. I told them about one story in the book where Dr. Crandall had a patient on the surgery table and the electricity went out. Everybody was freaking out trying to find some emergency power. Dr. Crandall even crawled underneath the surgery table. The patient had flat-lined and after several minutes Dr. Crandall gave up and said the patient was dead and to prepare him for the morticians to pick up. As Dr. Crandall prepared to leave the guy sat up and started talking. He asked Dr. Crandall what he was doing under the table and why the nurses were running around all over the place. Hmmm! The guy was physically dead, but his Holy Spirit was seeing everything going on.

Now Dr. Crandall and my Tulsa Doc also have something else in common. Dr. Crandall lost a young son to leukemia too. You might want to check out Dr. Crandall www.chaunceycrandall.com. He's written 3 or 4 books. The one I had read was 'Touching Heaven' which just came out.

As I was closing out my time with the boys at the JDC I mentioned that if anyone wanted to talk to me before I left about getting to know God better then come on up. As I was packing up one of the staff said one of the boys wanted to talk with me. I invited the boy up and he immediately asked me when I got to know Jesus and how it happened. I asked him what his name was, Jose, and told him the first thing he needs to do is to invite Jesus into his life and so I led him into a Salvation Prayer and then told him to start learning as much as he can about Jesus thru the BIBLE (Basic Instructions Before Leaving Earth), church or other Believers. He promised me he would.

2nd Corinthians 6:2… For God says. *"At just the right time, I hear you. On the day of salvation, I will help you."*

Then another young man came up to me who I had recognized from a month or two back when he had come up to me and asked for prayers. This time the young man asked me if I could leave the book 'Touching Heaven' with him so that he could read it. I turned to one of the staff and he said it would be OK. The staffer even implied he and others would like to read it too.

Well, Well, Well……God, I think I know now why You told me 'Not this time for Passion'. But then I was soon to find out more.

Very early Sunday morning (Jan. 1st) around 2:30 a.m. God woke me up by putting a phone number in my head 918-369-XXXX. Three times in about 3 minutes He hit me with that number. Now from previous experience I knew I would not be able to go back to sleep unless I wrote this down. So, I grabbed a piece of scratch paper and wrote the number on it. It was on a note I had written Scrubbing Bubbles & Lysol. Some items I needed to remember to pick up to clean some toilets. Hmmm…. later it dawned on me that sometimes we need things like these to clean things up and then other times we need God to clean things up. Anyway, once I arose that morning I got to thinking that could be my old phone number when I lived in Bixby. The 369 implied the Bixby area and I had recently moved from there. Now I don't know if you are like me but I never call myself and for the life of me I couldn't remember if that was my old phone number or not. I'm thinking God must have put my old phone number in my head for some reason. So, I stopped by my office on the way to JDC to look up my old phone number. You know what? It wasn't my old phone number after all. Now What God?

After leaving the JDC I head back to my office to try and figure out why God put that phone number in my head. I go to Reverse Phone number on the web and lo & behold it pulls up an address just 2 blocks from where I used to live. Now I'm thinking for some reason God must want me to communicate with whoever has that phone number & address and let them know He is there for them. I didn't feel like He wanted me to call them at that phone number but to personally contact them, so I head off for the address. When I arrived at the address and rang the doorbell a couple of Asians answered and I asked them if this was the Rxxx's residence. They said No! That they had bought the place about 2 years ago, and they did not know their name or where they went.

OK God. Is that the end of it? Just then I noticed a young father and his little daughter right across the street getting some things out of the car so I go over and asked the father if he knew anything about the people who used to live across the street and explained that I felt God was using me to try and contact them. The young father replied you know God sometimes has used him too. He told me the lady's husband had died about two years ago, and he thought she had moved to Broken Arrow. He suggested I go back to the Search and type in her name now and not the phone number. Which I did, but I had to wait until the next day, Monday, Jan. 2nd.

And now the search pulls up an address in Broken Arrow all right at a Retirement Center, so off I go that afternoon. When I arrived, I went in to the front desk and explained why I was there and if Mrs. Rxxx was there. The gentleman there said she had been there but she moved about a year ago, and didn't know where she went. Then something clicked and he said I think she moved to another Retirement Center near Woodland Hills off of 71st. So, off I go again, with no address but a general idea where it was. It was getting late in the afternoon and I figured it would be dinner time pretty soon in a Retirement Center so I had better hurry. Well God had to lead me there with His GPS (God's Positioning System) because it was not where I had pictured it, and He got me there quickly.

I pull into the parking lot and go inside and there is no one at the front desk. There were four nice ladies sitting in the foyer and after a couple of minutes one of them asked me if they could help because the front desk person will not be back for a while. So, I simply said I was interested in knowing if a Mrs. Rxxx was a resident there. The lady talking to me said, Yes! And she's sitting right here next to me. Whoa!

I quickly explained to Mrs. Rxxx that I didn't know her at all but that for some reason God wanted me to let her know that He's there for her. I quickly explained how I finally located her and how I had lived just a couple of blocks from her at one time on 114th St. in Bixby. She quickly filled me in on some things that her friends were not aware of. For one thing, she doesn't have that phone # anymore. And then she asked if I was connected with the minister who lives on 114th St. who called on her right after her husband died. I said No! I wasn't aware of that. I'm a Chaplain and I'm just doing probably the same thing the minister did…letting her know that God is with her-always.

OK! I now know why God had said…'Not This Time' about Passion. He had other plans. But then He added a little more satisfaction. When I pulled up Passion 2017 on the web to see how things went. Lo & Behold… God let me know that He didn't need this guy from Oklahoma because He had someone else from Oklahoma who was Much, Much Better Known to the 55,000 plus attendees from over 1,900 Universities and 90 foreign countries. Yup! Not publicized at all, but Oklahoma's own Carrie Underwood was a surprise attendee & she performed her Award-Winning Country Christian song "Something in the Water" (The River of Life) with the David Crowder band. Whoa!!

Hey, Hey, Hey, The KRR guy out and about, trying to figure out what God's got to Say!

Hey, Keep the Faith…your BIC

And hey, if you like to read…you might check out a book by David Cox 'The Chaplains at Hale Scout Reservation'

Chapter Twenty: Scouting

God's Bank

I just got back from Boy Scout Camp and I had one of those God Things happen at Chapel early one morning. As Chaplain for the week I had planned on the message on Tuesday to be 'GOD'S WHIRLWIND'. The day before, something had reminded me of a little something extra to add to the message that I had run across about 10 years ago and it came back to me. I couldn't remember the whole thing, but I remembered enough to go ahead and try it. And since I felt God had brought it to my attention that I had better bring it up. I hold two early morning outdoor Chapel services each day at camp.

This particular morning, before I started the main message, I pulled out a fresh $20 Bill and asked the audience (about 150 Scouts & Leaders) if anyone would like this $20 Bill. I suspect that every hand went up. So, then I showed them that I was going to crumble and wad the bill all up. I then held it up and asked if there was anyone now who would want the $20 Bill. Again, every hand went up. I then said wait just a moment and I threw the $20 Bill down on the dirt & rock & grass, stepped on it and twisted it into the dirt. I then picked it up and asked if anyone now would like this dirty, crumbly $20 Bill. Again, every hand went up. One young Scout, on the front row, was jumping up and down waving his hand shouting that he wanted it. So, I asked him why he would want this nasty looking $20 Bill. He gave me just the answer I was hoping for. He said…" It still has value". Ahh Ha! He was exactly right. It still had value and worth. You could even take it to a bank and they would exchange it for a brand new $20 Bill.

I then went on to explain to them, that in our lives we too can get

Hmmm! Who's Speaking?

beaten up. We too can say something, go places and do things that we are not proud of. We can sin and get ourselves all dirty too. BUT, God still values us too. God still wants us. God still knows our worth. All He wants is for us to come to Him. And when we do, then GOD'S BANK will renew us and we will be a New person.

After this I went on to my message of the day and closed it out with this little tidbit… I told them how I had read recently how the FBI trains their people to recognize a fake $100 Bill. The trainees are given a Real $100 Bill and they are told to look it over very closely. They are told to study that $100 Bill over and over. So, they spend hours and hours checking it out, feeling it, smelling it, looking it over and over. Then later, when they are given other $100 Bills, some real, some fake, they can immediately recognize those that are not real. I then held up a Bible and asked them… "Do we need to study this book over and over?" Well, if we do, then we too can tell when someone is trying to lead us astray with something that is not real. And then too, we can tell when God is speaking to us.

The first Chapel ended then and I started preparing for the 2nd Chapel in a few minutes. I thought I had better check to see if I had another clean $20 Bill and I didn't, but just then a couple of young Scouts showed up and sat down in the front row. One of the Scouts caught my attention and said "Chaplain, it looks like there is some money laying on the ground over there." So, I step over to where he was pointing…. And Lo & Behold!! THERE IT WAS! Not a $1 Bill, not a $5 Bill, not a $10 Bill, BUT a nice clean $20 BILL. WHOA! From God's Bank? Right out of the sky? Smack dab in the very front of the Chapel? NOW I have been going to this camp for the last 12 years or so and I have never seen any money lying around on the ground. Why now? Why right after the message about the $20 Bill?? Why in the Chapel? And the bill was tri-folded…..Father, Son & Holy Spirit? Was God speaking to me? I think so!

Now I did take the $20 Bill to the Scout Office to the 'Lost & Found'. Some Scout may have needed that $20 Bill to buy some things in the Trading Post. I never did check to see if anyone claimed it. I had hoped they would and that I could tell him how God had used him in a Special way at Chapel.

In Luke 15…. Jesus talks about the Lost Sheep, the Lost Coin and the Lost Son. Luke 15:32 *"We had to celebrate this happy day. For your brother was dead and has come back to life! He was lost, but now he is found!"*

Hey! How about you? Do you feel lost? Do you need to be renewed? Maybe you need to check out GOD'S BANK. Or maybe you know of someone who feels of no value or is waiting to be found. If so, then check out the web site www.BGEA.org and then click on 'How to Know Jesus'.

BAM! BAM! Going for the Gold! BAM! BAM!

As Chaplain of the week for the Tom Hale Boy Scout Camp recently, I had the opportunity to go around and visit the various campsites and to fill in the Scout Leaders about a 20-year-old Eagle Scout who is **going for the gold** in London on July 30th. Jon Michael McGrath II is from Tulsa and joined up with Boy Scout Troop 1 when he was 11 years old. Troop 1 is one of the oldest Troops in the Nation. It was formed on May 10th, 1910 just 3 months' after the Boy Scouts of America was founded on February 8th, 1910. It has been meeting at the First Presbyterian Church in Tulsa since early 1911 and everyone is invited to visit its Historic Scout Room built in 1925. See them at www.troop1tulsa.com.

Information I had read and heard, about Jon Michael, describes him as first picking up a shotgun while at Camp Tom Hale in 2003. I was fortunate to be at Camp Hale in 2010 when Bud Kunze was there too. Bud was the Scout Commissioner the same week I was there and I learned Bud's version of the story about Jon Michael. Bud is affiliated with Troop 26 in Tulsa and their Troop was at Camp that week. Troop 26 was formed in 1954 in Tulsa. They meet at Good Shepherd Lutheran Church and they see that as many of their Scouts as possible become Eagle Scouts. They have over 60% of them making Eagle whereas the National Average is 4%. See them at www.troop26.org. Bud is an inspiration for everyone. Still actively involved in Scouting at the good old age of 85 in 2010.

Bud filled me in on Jon Michael and what happened in the summer of 2003. Bud was the Scout Commissioner that week and was helping out at the Shotgun Range during Free Time. When Jon Michael showed up Bud tried to discourage him from shooting because of his size. He was only 11 years old. He was stocky, but too short. Bud explained that they didn't have any shotguns that were short enough for him. Jon Michael said he wanted to shoot because he was curious about it and something was nudging him to try it out. As the story builds, you will understand WHO was doing the nudging. It was the MAN! Jon Michael told Bud that he had never shot a gun before and that his family really wasn't into hunting and he just wanted to try it out. Bud said he still kept trying to discourage the young Scout and told him to come back next year. Then Jon Michael said he had already bought 10 shells. So, Bud finally relented, went and found the shortest shotgun there was, which still wasn't the right size. Bud gave the Scout a few basic instructions and let him go onto the range. Bud fully expected Jon Michael to miss all 10 clay birds. To Bud's surprise, Jon Michael hit all 10. So now Bud was curious. Was it just luck or did this Scout have a God given gift?

As the Scout came walking back, Bud asked him if he would like to shoot 40 more shells. Bud said Jon Michael got all excited about shooting some more, so Bud gave him some money to go buy 40 more shells. Well, Well, Well! Guess what? Jon Michael shot 48 out of 50. A new record for someone this young and using a shotgun that was too big besides. Bud then told the Scout Staff member on the Range to go over the Shotgun Merit Badge information and to award Jon the Merit Badge.

Bud went on to contact Jon's parents, since when Jon got home his parents might not realize what an accomplishment their son had done. And maybe the parents really never encouraged him about shooting. Bud explained to them about their son's God given gift and encouraged them to get him involved in Shooting Sports. Well, they did, and in 4 short months they had him entered in a World Skeet Championship in San Antonio competing with gunners four times his age and he won his first gold medal. From there Jon Michael has won all sorts of medals nationally and Inter-nationally. He holds the Junior World Record of 397 of 400. And in January of 2005 he was recognized as the youngest All-American Athlete of any sport at age 12. He became a resident athlete at the U.S. Olympic Training Center in Colorado Springs and will be representing the U.S. and his Cherokee Tribe in London at the Olympic Games in Skeet Shooting. I understand the Skeet Shooting is on July 30th, 2012.

With all the tournaments around the country and around the world that he was involved in, it also speaks highly of Jon Michael that he was also able to earn the Boy Scout Eagle rank before turning 18.

Not only is Scouting proud of Jon Michael, but I also wanted to point out at summer camp of all the opportunities for other young boys and men to perhaps find a talent or gift from God that they were not aware of. There are over 50 different Merit Badges at Camp Tom Hale. From Archeology to Woodcarving, including the 3-R's...Reptiles, Robotics & Rowing.

www.halescoutreservation.org. And not only did Jon Michael discover his God given gift, but many others over the years have discovered a talent that they can use in their profession, occupation or hobby while at Camp Tom Hale. What a great opportunity for these young men to discover early on what their gift is. Many of us can go thru our whole life without knowing or understanding what gift or gifts that God has given us. And when that God given gift is discovered, then what does God want us to do with it? He wants us to Glorify Him by telling others about Him.

God's gifts to us are given freely. He gives them to us voluntarily, at no cost. Why does He give us these gifts? Because He loves us – each and every one. And His Greatest gift of all was His Son. And His Son says in Luke 11:13 *"If you people know how to give good gifts to your children, how much more will your Heavenly Father give the Holy Spirit to those who ask Him."*

Maybe some of us will never find some of the gifts that God has for us, BUT we can be sure of the Gift of Eternal Life. Jesus tells us in John 4:14 *"But the water I **give** them takes away thirst altogether. It becomes a perpetual spring within them, **giving** them eternal life."*

Have you received this Gift yet? You might want to check out www.peacewithGod.net, a BGEA presentation. Or you can check out www.BGEA.org.

The Sequel (QT & Muffins)

Some things are not what they seem.... The Sequel

Last year I gave a message at Scout Camp about Blueberry muffins and donuts. Well since then God has provided a sequel and here is the message I passed on this year at Scout Camp.

How many of you here like Blueberries? What about donuts? Well, I like them both and I'm going to talk more about them in just a minute, but first let's get into our Scripture verses.

Scripture: OT Proverbs 14:12...*There is a path before each person* **that seems right,** *but it ends in death.*

On Mountain hikes – you can get thirsty and come across a sparkling, cool, clear mountain stream. You think, aahh, I'll quench my thirst here. But the stream may be full of deadly poison. Some things are not what they seem.

NT 1st Thessalonians 5:21...*You should* **test everything** *that is said, and hold on to what is good.*

Even some religious practices may have endorsement or approval by others – but you need to really study the matter and check the Scriptures. It could turn out to be wrong. Some things are not what they seem.

Hmmm! Who's Speaking?

Message:

A year ago, I gave a message about Blueberry muffins and donuts and how I was totally thrown for a loop when I found out from my favorite QuikTrip (QT) Convenience store that I was better off eating 5 donuts instead of one blueberry muffin. Hey, raw blueberries have great nutritional value. Eating them will help your Night Vision and they will help your learning capacity and motor skills. Now I don't know about the rest of you, but I can certainly use some help in those areas. Well you can imagine my surprise when QuikTrip printed off the nutritional values of the blueberry muffin and a glazed donut and I found out I could eat **5** donuts and have less Saturated Fat than one blueberry muffin. And because my arteries have a tendency to clog up, I have to watch the amount of saturated fat I eat.

Well, I stopped eating blueberry muffins, BUT just this spring QuikTrip came out with a brand- new product. They showed a picture of a beautiful Maple Pecan Croissant on one of their big sidewalk signs just before you walk into their store. You know, one of those crescent shaped light and flaky rolls, and it is topped with maple sauce and fresh native pecans. And you know pecans are an original high-energy natural food. Hey, that's got to be healthy for you and it would taste good too. The first two times I went to QuikTrip, they were Sold Out. They said they were so popular that they couldn't keep them in stock. The third time in I lucked out, they had 4 left. I quickly grabbed one and went to the checkout counter. Again, I wanted to see how much better off I was eating this Maple Pecan Croissant than one of those glazed donuts. So, I asked them to print me off a copy of the nutritional value of the Croissant. BUT, this time when they handed it to me, I thought I would just put it in my pocket and not look at it until I finished eating my croissant. I didn't want to take the risk of something spoiling the enjoyment of eating that Croissant. I went out to my car and proceeded to eat that Maple Pecan Croissant. OH! Boy! Was it Good. Light & fluffy & crisp and with just the right amount of maple and tasty native pecans. After enjoying my Croissant, I got out the printed piece of paper showing the nutritional value, fully expecting it to be much better for me than one of those Blueberry muffins and maybe even better than a donut. WHOA! WHAT! THAT CAN'T BE? WAS SOMEONE PULLING MY LEG?

It was worse than the Blueberry Muffin. As a matter of fact, I could have eaten 3 Blueberry Muffins OR even **15** Donuts and had less Saturated Fat than that one Maple Pecan Croissant. A donut had 3% of my daily amount of Saturated Fat, the Blueberry Muffin had 15%, and the Croissant had 45% of my daily allowance. Yep! I could have eaten 15 donuts and not have been any worse off as far as my daily amount of Saturated Fat. WHOA! SOME THINGS ARE NOT WHAT THEY SEEM.

And recently, I came across some information about a religious cult group called Scientology. I was reading some information about the founder that is up on their web site. It said that the founder is on record as being the youngest Eagle Scout ever. Knowing a little about this church group, I questioned that, so I contacted the National Eagle Scout Association. Lo & Behold, it is not as it implies. True, he is the youngest, BUT he earned it back in 1923. At that time, the requirements to make Eagle Scout were not nearly as difficult as they are today. He attained the Rank of Eagle in less than a year because of the fewer requirements and merit badges needed back then. The Eagle Scouts here today can attest to the fact that now it may take 3 or 4 years to attain the rank of Eagle.

So, in closing today, I want to encourage each of you to listen to the Scripture advice in Thessalonians and don't scoff or reject a person when they are telling the truth, BUT, instead, carefully check out what people say, accepting what is true and rejecting what is not true. When it is about religion, you need to check the Bible. When it may be other things, you can go to some web sites like: www.truthorfiction.com, www.snopes.com or www.scientifiamerican.com.

Hey! Where are you right now in your life? Do you need to check in and see what your religious value is? If so, then I suggest you check out www.BGEA.org and click on 'How to Know Jesus'. And if you've already comfortable with your religious value, then have you shared it with others? Do you need some help in doing that? Then check out www.SearchforJesus.net, a Billy Graham guide for volunteers to minister to others by the internet.

E-Mail to A Scoutmaster

Subject: Camp Tom Hale Chaplain

Thursday, June 21st

Hello Mr. Scoutmaster,

I was the Chaplain at Camp Tom Hale the week of June 10th. I do not remember talking to you, but I did visit your campsite one afternoon to leave some information about P.R.A.Y. and their 4-segment Patch Program to create interest in scouts to complete or think about doing the "Duty to God" or "God and Country" religious program. I hope someone in your Troop may have an interest in taking this program and running with it.

The main reason for this email is however, to relay something that God laid on my heart last night. God got my attention last night, or early this morning I should say, at about 1:30 a.m. He has awakened me a few of other times like this in the last couple of years, and it is very apparent that He wants my attention and He wants me to do something. He made me so uncomfortable and feverish that it woke me up. The first thing, and about the only thing, that I recall is a circle with some numbers in the center of it. I laid there hurting for several minutes and trying to understand what the numbers stood for. I finally had to get out of bed and on my knees and pray. While praying, I recalled your troop number which were the same numbers God had informed me of and I felt that maybe God was wanting me to pass a message on to you. I don't know if there is a problem in the Troop right now, or if someone in the Troop is having a problem, but God wants you to know that He LOVES each and every one of you. I feel He wants me to encourage you and to let you know that He is standing alongside you. Everything will work out all right because He is in control.

If there is a problem or someone is hurting, then ask others on your Scout Committee to turn it over to God in their prayers. You and your Troop will be in my prayers too, until God directs me otherwise.

Your Brother in Christ and fellow scouter.
David Cox

Scouting

Almost immediately, I received a reply from the Scoutmaster stating he appreciated my concern, encouragement and prayers as the Troop is working through addressing some serious issues that came up during Scout Camp.

Chapter Twenty-One: Trail Life USA

Trail Life Climbing

Hey Tom, Wayne & others.... the KRR guy out and about and filling you in,

As you may be aware I dropped out of Boy Scouts a couple of years ago when I could see that National Headquarters was no longer taking the narrow path. This was after I had been a Scout Chaplain for 15 years and had even written a book for other Boy Scout Chaplains (The Chaplains at Hale Scout Reservation). I got excited when I found out that other people in the Headquarters and around the country were getting together to form a New Organization www.TrailLifeUSA.com. I felt this new organization would be the new alternative to Boy Scouts and an organization built upon the same original principles of Boy Scouting. I knew that Scouting's first caving in of publicly allowing young men who openly professed to be gay into Scouting would only be the first step to future changes. Actually, Boy Scouts had always allowed young men into Scouting who may have felt they were gay but just did not go around professing it and flaunting it. Scout Leaders may have even tried to guide them back to the narrow path.

From previous experiences, I knew that it would be just a matter of time, maybe 3 or 4 years, before Scouting would be pressured into making more conciliations. So, in a sense I was surprised when really in just a little over a year, since Trail Life got organized and was prepared to accept Troops of young men, that along came Scouting's new cave in. The new cave in does not satisfy the gay agenda however. So, most likely next year Scouting will cave in again.

Check out Trail Life on their web site and then pass the word. There are now Troops situated in 49 States. There are 25 in Oklahoma and 3 here in Tulsa. One troop is sponsored by a Catholic Church, one by a Baptist Church and one by a Non-Denominational Church.

Also, you may want to hear or read an interview with the chairman of the board of Trail Life USA on the 'here & now' public radio web site that was heard on July 28th, 2015. It was about religious groups that are upset over the recent Boy Scouts' decision.

If you are concerned about our future, then please pass this on…. the KRR guy, A BIC

Chapter Twenty-Two: Miscellaneous

The Phos Cross

Jesus said to the people "I am the light of the world. If you follow me, you won't be stumbling thru the darkness..." John 8:12

There is a song that is out now that is one of the oldest (if not the oldest) hymns known. The hymn in Greek is called 'Phos Hilaron' which means joyful light. Hilaron = joyful or hilarious/ Phos = light

This song is over 2000 years old. First records of it date to 4 A.D. It was sung in the evening at the tomb of Jesus in Jerusalem as a permanently lit candle was brought from the tomb. The hymn symbolized the Light of Jesus and the Joy of His Resurrection.

I have a cross that I wear that is called a Phos Cross. This is because it has the capacity to Glow or give light in the dark. Inside this Cross is phosphorous, and when you hold it close to a light it will glow. The longer you hold it near the light, and the closer you get it to the light – the brighter and longer it will glow.

DID YOU KNOW...

That our body has phosphorous in it too? It is one of the six key elements that make up our body. If you weigh 100 pounds, then you'll have a whole pound of phosphorous in you. Our supply of phosphorous comes from things we eat. Look at a milk carton or a box of cereal or even potato chips for instance and you'll see that phosphorous is one of the ingredients. Dieticians know of some of the benefits of phosphorous but they can't really explain what the main purpose it plays in our body, But Maybe, just

Miscellaneous

Maybe, God knows what the main purpose for it is. Maybe you've heard people say of someone: "that person has a special glow about them".

In Exodus 34:29 – When Moses spoke to God up on Mount Sinai and wrote the Ten Commandments... **His face glowed after spending time with God.** And in Exodus 34:34-35 whenever Moses went to speak with God, **the people would see his face aglow.**

Do you suppose? Do you suppose? That while my cross gets its strength and source of power from light...that maybe you and I get our strength and our glow from being close to our Father/Son and Holy Spirit and spending time and staying close to Him as much as we can? If so, then we will glow and we can be a light for others, and people will know that we have been with God.

There is an interesting story about a Carnival Glow Cross by the Comedian TV star Tim Conway that can be found at www.guidepostsclassics/TheCarnivalCross and go to Tim Conway on Answered Prayer.

Whooooa! Whaaaaat A Weeeeek!

Earthquakes

Hey.... Where were you when the **BIG ONE HIT?** Let me report in on some Earth-Shaking News.

After the 4.8 quake on Saturday, Nov. 5th, @ 2:13 a.m. it was soon time for me to get up anyway and head out with the Kirk Karpenters Mission team. This team goes out about every weekend from my church to build a ramp for someone with a physical handicap. This time it was a mobile home park on King Street. I had hernia surgery a week or so prior and had forgotten that my doctor, Dr. John King, had given me instructions not to lift anything over 20 lbs. for the next 3 weeks.

It was not until I got to the site on **King** Street that something clicked about what Dr. **King** had told me. When I mentioned to our team leader, Richard, he immediately requested that I become a bystander rather than a participant. Something about the fact that the Church insurance wouldn't cover hernia surgery for volunteers. With my limited carpenter abilities, being asked to be a bystander was really not that earth shaking to me anyway.

The 4.8 quake that morning was not to be the last of the earth shaking that day. The really big one, the 5.6, hit about 10:15 p.m. I was watching the late news, after the Alabama vs. LSU overtime game and just as the news came on and the Newscaster started to talk about the earthquake at 2:13, my TV and house started to shake. My first thought was, WOW! This new modern technology is something else. I don't even need to go the 3-D movies anymore where you can get the effects with the seats shaking. I can get the same effect right in the comfort of my home now. Then it dawned on me that this wasn't déjà vu, it wasn't an illusion, it was happening again.

How appropriate this all was, because the next morning I was to do the worship service for the boys at the Tulsa Juvenile Detention Center. My music and message were to be a repeat of one I had done for the Boy Scouts b/4 at summer camp called 'Illusion, Illustration & Image'. Do you think God might have had something to do with this?? Attached is a copy of that message that I used for the Boy Scouts.

This time I was able to add a couple of other Scriptures: Revelation 6:12 *"I watched as the Lamb broke the sixth seal, and there was a great earthquake…",* and Revelation 8:5 *"Then the angel filled the incense burner with the fire from the altar and threw it down upon the earth; and thunder crashed, lightning flashed, and there was a terrible earthquake."*

I ask you, when was the last time you can remember when Oklahoma had earthquakes, tornados, flooding, lightning, thunder, and high damaging winds all on the same day? Yup! We were still having aftershocks of the big one, when on the 7th of November there were also tornados, baseball size hail, wind gusts up to 92 mph and flooding. WHOA! Is God trying to get our attention? Does He have a message for us?

Well, all of this happening certainly spooked my awareness, especially with Halloween just preceding all of it. Oklahoma certainly is getting impacted lately by things mentioned in Revelations. Did Sir Isaac Newton really have something figured out? What did he mean when he said (about 400 years ago) that the world will experience a big change directed by God around 2060? Are we as Christians, and especially Oklahomans, supposed to go out and share the Good News about Jesus Christ? That is what we as Christians are commanded to do, but do we need to start doing it with a little more urgency?

Is this all just an Illusion? Or is God using these things as an Illustration of His Great Image? Check the illusions you can find on your search engine and type in Optical or Visual Illusions.

And if you're all Shaken Up and wondering what the Real message is, then go check out the web site at www.BGEA.org and then click on 'How to Know Jesus'. And if you already know what the message is, then get busy and start telling others.

God and the Psychiatrist

Hey Tom…. Hey Wayne, the KRR guy again,

You know, my dictionary talks about psychical as 'being some type of perception that is not explainable by any known natural laws'. So, to me that means God must be the only One who can explain it. Let me tell you what happened last week and then you can tell me what you think.

On Tuesday, about noon, I was standing in the checkout line at SAM'S with some CFL bulbs and paper towels for the Mall. While waiting, my thoughts turned to the gigantic slice of hot Pizza you can get for a buck & a half at SAM'S. Now, I full well know that pizza should not be a regular supplement of my daily or weekly food intake. But, temptation was nudging me. Quickly though, I figured God must be coming to my rescue when I glanced over and noticed that the pizza line was about 12 people deep. I didn't have the time to wait in line that long for something I shouldn't eat anyway. BUT, as I finished checking out…. Temptation got the best of me.

As I joined in the line, I heard someone call my name. A lady, who was sitting at a table waiting for her husband to get some pizza, caught my attention. She was the Secretary/Receptionist for a psychiatrist who had been a tenant of mine for the last 6 or 7 years. He had lost his wife a couple of years ago and then decided to retire about six months ago. I had not seen the secretary or the psychiatrist in the last six months. The lady came running up to me and gave me a big old hug like she hadn't seen me in years and years. Now, I knew her a little better than the psychiatrist because she was the one who always brought the rent check or contacted me when there was a plumbing, electrical or some other maintenance problem.

We exchanged greetings and got caught up to date on what was going on in our lives. After that, I noticed that the lady behind me in the pizza line had kept pushing my cart forward to where I was now the 3rd in line. So, I excused myself and got back in line and got my pizza. Hey! Maybe God was saying it was OK for me to have pizza this time after all.

After I finished my pizza, I went by to say goodbye to the lady and her husband. As I was about to go, she asked me if I would go by and see Dr.

Miscellaneous

F. She told me that he has Parkinson's and is starting to have difficulty in getting around and has moved into a retirement home where he has some help. Now, I didn't know Dr. F that well and I had heard that he was living at Grand Lake or in OK City with his son's family. I asked where he is living and she told me he is in Tulsa at Montereau. I asked 'is that the retirement home on 71st? She said 'Yes' and said that it would mean so much to Dr. F if I went by to see him. Now I rarely go down 71st St., but occasionally I do go down Sheridan, so I told her when I was in the vicinity I would try and make it a point to go visit him.

You know, I have never been to Montereau and wasn't even sure how you get in to it. As I left SAM'S I was telling myself that I need to remember what she asked me to do, and in the next 10 days or so, or in the next few weeks or a month or so, when I was in that area I should check in on Dr. F.

OK! Here we go! I get back to my office in about 10 minutes. As soon I get there, one of my co-workers (Carl from the Kirk) buzzes me and says he has a customer who wants one of the electric fireplace stoves but they do not have any way of transporting it. Carl says they would like it today, ASAP. I told Carl, my day was pretty well booked up, but we did need to sell that stove. So, I asked him if they lived close by. I heard Carl ask them and they said at 6800 So. Granite. That did not ring a bell with me, but then Carl told me that they said it is near 71st & Sheridan, just a few miles away. Then Carl said it is where Montereau is. MONTEREAU? "What? God are you kidding me? It's only been 10 minutes! "I tell Carl what has happened and we get the stove ready to go and then Carl helps me load it up.

It is a heavy dude and I'm wondering how I'm going to be able to unload it and get it up to Room X13. I get to Montereau a little before 2 and drive around the place and cannot find a 6800 S. Granite. As I stop at a STOP sign I see a white Pickup across the way with a Security Guard. I flag the guy down and told him what address I was looking for. He starts telling me how to get there and then asked why I wanted to know. I told him I was making a delivery for some folks there. He then asked me who. He knew them and knew exactly where they lived, and told me to just turn around and follow him. When we get there, the guy comes back

Hmmm! Who's Speaking?

to my SUV and asked if I needed any help in getting it in the building. What a Blessing.

Once we get it inside, the guy tells me to take the elevator up to the 4th floor, take two lefts, and Room X<u>31</u> will be on my left. I'm thinking Room X13 but I'm not going to correct this guy. I mean how can he know where everybody lives out there? Must be 400, 500 or maybe even more residents. So, as I walk by X31 (and there are not any names on any of the doors there) I head on down the long hallway looking for X13. Whoa! After 3 or 4 long hallways, I find X13. I ring the doorbell, but no one is home. Oh My? Did the people forget or did I just beat them getting there? As I go back down the 3 or 4 long hallways, I decided to stop at X31. I ring the bell and Lo & Behold the lady answers the door and says "Wow! You're already here". I set the stove up for her and tell her how God had used her and her husband to get me to Montereau to see Dr. F. She told me they will look him up.

Well, this psychical thing is just beginning. As I leave I realize now that I had better be sure and go see Dr. F or you know WHO will be awfully upset with me. I was now going to need to find out where Dr. F. lived. As I was driving around, I saw another white Pick-up that was a landscaping truck. I flagged down the driver and asked him if he knew where one would go to find out where someone lived. The guy told me to pull into the first driveway on my left and go inside to the Information Desk. Now Dr. F has only been there for a couple of weeks but they knew immediately what room he was in and how to get there. Go down a long hallway on my left to the elevator. Just as I was approaching the elevator I saw a pool table with 4 or 5 guys playing pool. Wait, a minute, I think I recognize one of them. Yup! B. Bates from Wednesday's Kirk Bible Study. He was just about to knock in an easy shot, so I waited to say something after he finished the shot. WHAT? Bates missed the easy shot? So, I commented to all within hearing…" Bates! Are you trying to 'snooker' everybody?" Bates was surprised to see me there. A Ha! Maybe this was the reason God wanted me there at this exact moment. Hmmm! Only God knows.

Dr. F was also surprised to see me. You know, many psychiatrists are not very outgoing. They know how to listen. They know what questions to ask. Like "How did that make you feel? When did you first start feeling that way? What do you think caused that? Why is that so? Etc." I feel that Dr. F is going to have difficulty in mixing in with the rest of the retirees at Montereau and so I talked and prayed with him about that. I left him, feeling that maybe I had benefited him some with God's help.

I left there and was driving back toward my office, when Carl calls me again on my cell phone and asks "Are you still there?" I said where? Carl said at Montereau. I said no, I'm on my way back to the office. Well, get this! Carl said he just had a call from a guy who wants me to go by and check on his mom's clock at Montereau. WHAT? "God did I mess up?" "YOU want me to go back right now?" "Can I wait until tomorrow?"

You know? I decided to wait, but I think God wasn't too happy about that. You see, the next morning, when I call the guys mom to set up a time, she tells me that I've already been there. That she's already seen me. WHAT? Well it turns out she and her son wanted me to fix the clock because they had originally bought the clock from me. BUT, unbeknownst to her, her son had called me, and she had mistakenly called my competitor, who quickly jumped at the opportunity. So, now I'm thinking OK God, I learned my lesson.

Oh! Before all this happened, I was having breakfast with Pastor Dan and some other Wednesday a.m. Bible Study guys and Dan informed me that you (Tom) and Shano have started a Bible Study at Montereau on Thursdays. I think God wanted me to pass this info on to Dr. F.

Late Wednesday afternoon, some Curio cabinets arrived and one was a Special Order and the lady wanted it as soon as it came in. I called her Thursday morning to set up a time and to verify the address on E. 88th St. She wanted it around 10 a.m., BUT the address was wrong. They wanted it delivered to their new address at 6800 S. Granite. WHAT? Yup! They had just moved into Phase 2 at Montereau. OK! OK! God. So, you still want me to get back out to Montereau, but You do not want me to put it off. Now this curio is a Really Big Old Dude, and heavy too, so I had to call in someone to help me out. We get there at 10 a.m. and by now I'm getting to know my way around out there pretty well. We get the cabinet to their unit and I proceed to tell them how God had used them too in all of this. And they tell me they will look up Dr. F too.

I needed to get my helper back to his work though, so I didn't have time to go see Dr. F. I was sure God would understand. NOPE! As soon as I get back to the office, I get a call from a guy who wanted me to pick his Grandfather clock up for service. He lived six blocks from Montereau. WHOA! OK, OK, after I pick the guys clock up I'll go by and visit Dr. F.

Well now it was getting pretty close to lunchtime when I get to Montereau and when the receptionist calls Dr. F's room, he doesn't answer. She suggested that I go see if he is in the dining room. I check with the Maître de' and she knew Dr. F and yes, he was eating at a table all by himself. As I walk in I see tables full of people and then Dr. F sitting at a small table all by himself. I sit down and have a short conversation with him and I asked him if he played pool because he might enjoy playing some pool with some guys I saw there a couple of days ago and I told him to watch out for the pool shark. I also told him about the Bible study that the Kirk has on Thursdays and invited him to check it out. As I get up to leave, I hear someone call out my name and lo & behold it was the Pool Shark and his wife. They were lunching together just one table away. I talked to B. Bates and pointed out Dr. F to him. Now, what are the odds of me running into Mr. B the only two times I have ever visited Montereau? I think God has a plan for Mr. B. I don't think God care's whether Mr. B is a Pool Shark or not. At least Mr. B will not try and get out of going to Montereau and God probably feels Mr. B can get Dr. F to the Bible Study on Thursdays. Now, if you agree with me, and we all feel God has a plan for Mr. B, then we should all encourage the Pool Shark (excuse me I mean – Mr. B) to do as God guides and directs him.

As Always…. A BIC, the KRR guy

God's Whirlwind

Intro: How many of you are familiar with a Whirlwind? They have Major Whirlwinds which includes tornadoes and they form above the ground and come down. The Minor Whirlwinds are much smaller and of less intensity and they start spinning on the ground and go up. Some are called dust devils and debris devils because they can circle up leaves and litter and lift them up to great heights.

> Scripture: OT Exodus 3: 2-4.... *Suddenly, an angel of the LORD appeared to him as a blazing fire in a bush. Moses was amazed because the bush was engulfed in flames, but it didn't burn up. "Amazing!" Moses said to himself. "Why isn't that bush burning up? I must go over to see this." When the LORD saw that he had caught Moses' attention, God called to him from the bush, "Moses! Moses!"*

God may use unexpected sources when communicating to us too. It could be people, thoughts, experiences...even whirlwinds. We must be willing to check it out and be open to God's surprises.

The Whirlwind

Where my office is located, on the street level, I can see people out my window coming and going on my south lot. I'm hardly ever watching though because I'm concentrating on something else. But a few weeks ago, I saw 3 guys, stock boys, with the furniture tenant next door, taking some trash, cardboard and Styrofoam, out to the trash containers which they do several times a day. This time though, God wanted my attention. As the guys were about half way to the trash with a big cardboard box, God created a whirlwind that caused some Styrofoam in the box to come flying straight out and circling up into the sky. That stuff was circling up about 30 or 40 feet into the air. It couldn't help but catch my attention and I started to go out and help them, when God kind of informed me to just watch. Well these guys were really getting excited and looking around. Finally, they decided to take the box back up to their backdoor. BUT, it was taking a lot of effort to pull this box. I questioned..." The box is only

Hmmm! Who's Speaking?

cardboard and only has Styrofoam or other cardboard inside it, so why does it appear to be so heavy?" Only moments after this, God reminded me that I had been wanting an empty box to put some electrical items in to take and donate to the Habitat for Humanity Store and this would be a good time to find one. So, I go out and start looking in the cardboard trash container to see if I can find the right size box. And Lo and Behold, while doing my 'dumpster diving', I find not one but three brand new boxes that still had yellow straps around them. They were unassembled book shelf kits. Hmmm! It didn't take long to figure out what was going on. So, I go into the furniture store where the 3 guys are and the manager and a couple of sales people and I told the manager that I was getting ready to take some items and donate them to the Habitat store and I was wondering if it was OK to take the 3 Brand New Book shelves that they were throwing away out in the trash and donate them too. The manager looked a little puzzled at first and asked me to describe the boxes. It then didn't take the manager very long to figure out what was going on either, so he kindly said, "No! Somebody else wants those and they are probably coming by later to get them". Well, guess what? The next day there were 3 new stock boys who were all excited about their new job.

You know, God knew what was about to happen and He wanted something done about it.

Do you remember in Exodus 3, verse 16 …God told Moses to go and tell others what he saw and heard at the burning bush? Has God spoken to you of late? Maybe He has and you just didn't realize it. Perhaps you need to get to know Him better.

Our God is a God who acts and speaks to us in different ways. One of the best ways to tell others about Him is to tell what He has done and how He has spoken to us.

Recently I read how the FBI trains their people to recognize a fake $100 Bill. The trainees are given a Real $100 Bill and they are told to look it over very closely. They are told to study that $100 Bill over and over. So, they spend hours and hours checking it out and looking it over. Then later, when they are given other $100 Bills, some real, some fake, they can immediately recognize those that are not real.

Do we need to study, this book, the Bible over and over? Should we check it out very closely? Well, if we do, then we too can tell when someone

Miscellaneous

is trying to lead us astray with something that is not real. And then too, we can tell when God is speaking to us.

AND THEN when God speaks to you…. PASS IT ON.

Hey! How is your life going right now? Do you feel like you're in a whirlwind, going around and around? Maybe you need to check God out. If so, then I invite you to check out the web site www.BGEA.org and then click on 'How to Know Jesus'

Stranger Payback

The first Sunday in November found me at the Tulsa Juvenile Detention Center playing some music with a message for about 20 boys who were locked up for some pretty serious crimes or actions. I added a message about the 'Kirk Ramp' and was preparing to leave when Ben and Don came in. Don is a retired Presbyterian minister and it was his first time at the Detention Center. I told the boys that if God was nudging them today to accept Jesus Christ into their lives, to get with Ben or Don before they left.

I hadn't heard Don talk before, so I decided to stay until about 10:30 to hear what he had to say. Don has an intriguing deep, gravelly voice and a manner in his presentation that captured the boy's attention. As Don was talking, one boy leaned over and whispered to me and wanted to know how old Don was. These boys are all under the age of 18. Once they reach 18, they are transferred to the jail with the older adults.

A little after 10:30 I picked up my sack of stuff and quietly exited from the rear of the room. I wanted to attend my home church that morning and it takes about 20 minutes to get there. When I arrived, I reached to get my Bible and lo & behold it wasn't with me. Surely, I hadn't left it at the JDC? After searching another time or two I realized I must have left it there. Oh Great! Another 20 minutes back there and then another 20 minutes to get back. I thought, well I'll call Ben and ask him to pick my Bible up. But No! I would probably interrupt Ben right in the middle of his message. I was really starting to get upset now. I thought maybe I could go back later in the day, But No, I had a pen in my Bible and you can't leave anything there that the boys can use as a weapon or tool. Not even paper clips or papers with staples. As I started heading back I thought what if Ben and Don happen to see my Bible and they pick it up and are bringing it back while I'm heading in the opposite direction. Well, I am now really frustrated and upset, so I decided to just turn it all over to God, and I told Him that He must have a reason for me having to go back and I will just leave it all up to Him. My frustration and anger quickly left when I turned it all over to the Man.

As I arrive there the 2nd time and get checked thru the five locked doors, I see that Ben is just wrapping it up. Ben was asking a few questions

Miscellaneous

about the boys in order to complete a survey. Ben had just asked how many of the boys had a father at home. Twenty boys, about 1/3rd Black, 1/3rd Hispanic & 1/3rd White and not one hand went up.

This is normally pretty typical. Fathers are in Jail, dead, living someplace else, or just totally unknown.

Well I spotted my Bible on top of some other books on a book rack. I pick it up and start to leave with Ben and Don, when one sharp looking Hispanic boy comes up to me with tears in his eyes and wanted to talk with me privately. You hardly ever see one of these boys with tears in their eyes and they sure don't want any of the other boys to see them that way. This young man's name was Ricardo and he was blind in his left eye. I suggested a place around a corner and kind of out of view. I first off asked him if he had ever accepted Jesus Christ into his life. He immediately told me he had, BUT he has been praying to God and God either doesn't hear him or isn't answering him. Ricardo said he wants to kill himself. As we sat down, I asked him what was going on in his life. He started telling me about his little two-year-old girl and his ex-girlfriend who wasn't letting him see his daughter. Now remember, this young man is 17 or younger and already has a two-year-old daughter. (Ben told me later that there was another boy in there that day that had two kids already.)

As I listened to this young man and could see the hurt in his heart I had to call on God to tell me what to say. I remembered what Don had told the boys right off that was encouraging to them, and that was in Jeremiah 1:5 where God says *He knew you before He formed you in the womb of your mother, before you were born He set you apart and appointed you as my spokesman to the world."* And then it dawned on me why God sent me back to the JDC. I explained to Ricardo that God is already answering you. I told him I had already left the place, when God up and sent me back, a 'Stranger', just so he and I could talk. I encouraged Ricardo to continue to learn more about God and the more he knows about Him the more he will realize when God is communicating with him. I told him I don't know why he is in jail right now but later on he might understand God's plan. Maybe God wanted him out of the way right now so HE can communicate with the girl friend. I closed with a Prayer and then again reminded Ricardo to continue to get closer to God and to put his trust in Him. Ricardo thanked me for being there and I told him to Thank

Hmmm! Who's Speaking?

God. I could tell he was sincere and was feeling better right then, but I didn't want to leave there without telling Security to keep an eye on him because he was talking suicide. It later dawned on me that when Ben asked the boys there about their fathers, that some of the boys, and most likely Ricardo, had probably made a promise to never be like their dad was to them. And now, Ricardo's ex-girlfriend is keeping him away from his little girl, which he most likely promised to never abandon and to not be like his dad was to him.

No wonder he might feel so down right now.

PART TWO…. Pay Back Time about two weeks later…

Saturday before Thanksgiving. I had told my family that I would deep fry a turkey for Thanksgiving and in order for it to get thawed in time to deep fry I had to get busy. Well, the more I thought about it the more frustrated I got. I had checked and I was going to have to get another box of Peanut Oil and some more propane. And last year it was cold outside and it took forever for the oil to heat up and I had to continually go outside and check on it before and during the cooking. And then also last year I had to cook the turkey out on my front driveway. I used to fry the turkey on the back patio, but I was now sharing my backyard with my neighbors two inquisitive Great Danes. Great dogs and great to have them protecting my house too but I couldn't afford to have them get hurt or to accidently burn my house down.

Well grudgingly I decided to give it a shot this year and buy what I needed. And to beat the crowds at Wal Mart I go in early Saturday morning, 6:45 a.m. to be exact. As I get there, there are already several cars on the lot and in the store. Hey? What's going on? I quickly figured it out. You see, Hostess had just announced that they had shut down. No more 'Twinkies'. Hostess Deliveries are early in the mornings and serious 'Twinkie' lovers or prospective e-bay sellers were already lining up at the check outs. I proceed over to the meat section where no one is at except for one professional looking man with no 'Twinkies' or anything else yet in his cart.

I spotted 3 end aisles with turkeys. I needed a turkey no larger than 13 lbs. to fit in my pot. As I dug thru the first section, they were all 15 lbs.

Miscellaneous

or larger. I moved to the next section of 'Butterball' turkeys and they were giant turkeys, 20 lbs. or better. As I went to the 3rd section, and grumbling the whole time, the gentleman came up and started a conversation. NOW, how many times have you had a professional looking man come up to you in a Walmart and start a conversation??? I never have before! The guy starts off with a comment…" I don't want you to think I'm following you, but you seem to know what you are looking for". I explained to him that I was trying to find a turkey 13 lbs. or less so that I could fry it in my deep fat fryer. Well, this 'Stranger' said he was on the same mission to, but he was looking for about a 14-lb. turkey. He had bought a new Electric deep fat fryer last year and it would take up to a 14 lb. Turkey. And the Great thing about his new Electric turkey fryer was that he didn't have to mess with the Peanut Oil any more. WOW! I thanked him for his information, found my 13 lb. turkey and headed off to find the Peanut Oil. WHOA! The first aisle right after the turkeys? Guess what? A stack of Electric Turkey Fryers, and they were 'On Sale'. Two types. One where you used water instead of oil, but you still used it outdoors. The other one you used only 2 gallons of oil instead of 3, BUT the important message I read was that you could use it in the house on top of the kitchen counter. As I was putting one into my basket, the 'Stranger' was coming by and I gave him a thumb up and he said 'You will really like it'. AND I DID.

I left Walmart with a much-improved attitude. On Thanksgiving morning as I fried my turkey inside the house on my kitchen cabinet I Thanked God. No more grumbling about turkey frying. No more frustration. No more griping. Just enjoying the frying. 30 minutes and we were done. Then it dawned on me. Who was that 'Stranger'? Where did he come from? Did Some One send him? I think I know the answer.

Like the young Hispanic man, how many times do we fail to understand or realize when and how God is communicating with us. We shouldn't be a 'stranger' to God. We need to know Him more. He wants to be our friend.

A BIC

Does God Still Speak to His People?

E-mail Ministry

This is a great message found at www.emailministry.org that was published on May 16th, 2014. It is a story about a young man who had just been to a Wednesday night Bible Study and the Pastor had shared about listening to God and obeying the Lord's voice. And then that same night, shortly after the Bible Study the young man experienced God communicating with him and directing him and at first the young man thought the whole thing was crazy but at the end realizing how God had used him to answer a total stranger's prayers.

The Perfect Mistake

Email Ministry

This message can also be found at www.emailministry.org that was published on January 23rd, 2015. This true story is about a member of a small church in Chicago in the Great Depression years who mistakenly let his new glasses fall into a box heading for an orphanage in China. The member was quite upset and even complained to God. A few months later he realized how God had used his glasses to answer a Missionary's prayers. So, there may be times when we shouldn't complain about things about a new detour or missing a Green Light…. Because God may have saved us from a speeding ticket or even our life from a deadly car accident.

Tom's Retirement Celebration

Hi Guys,

Tom Grey is retiring at the Kirk because of some health issues and I had planned to send him a letter. The Kirk then wanted me to tell the story at Tom's Retirement Celebration at the Renaissance Hotel. Also attached is a letter that I gave to Tom that was a letter I had sent to son's buddy (Ed) back in 1988. Here is basically what I told the audience about Tom....

I had found a picture of Tom in the 1987 Southside Rotary Directory when he became a member and they posted that up on the screen when I started. At that time, I was attending First Methodist Church in downtown Tulsa and really didn't know Tom and he didn't know me. It was probably lucky for Tom that he didn't know me, but it was unlucky for me that I didn't know much about him. But I was soon to learn more about him and what kind of a Man of God he is. I jokingly told how Rotary, and other Service Clubs, would only allow membership to one profession only, like one Banker, one Attorney, one Dentist, one Shoe Store owner, etc. However, the Rotary Founders made one exception and that was for the Ministry. Rotary must have felt that a Rotary Club could never have too many Ministers.

I reminded the audience that back in 1987 AIDS was just making the news in the U. S. It had already hit other countries and was Big News there but the U.S. really hadn't been giving much attention to it since it hadn't made a big impact here. In Zambia, Africa 1 out of 9 people were HIV + and in Haiti 1 out of 7. When it began to appear in the U.S., first in San Francisco and New York City, the media began to publicize it and there were all sorts of miss-conceptions on how contagious it was. There were possibilities that one who was HIV+ could spread it as easily as sneezing on someone, or someone drinking out of the same glass or shaking hands or even drinking out of the same water fountain. Some hospitals were being extremely cautious and they put all AIDS patients in a special wing of the hospital, and then no one was allowed access to them unless they had gotten permission and were informed of the unknown risks and provided hospital gowns, masks, gloves and foot cover, all of which were burned or destroyed after use.

Miscellaneous

With all of these unknowns, Tom made front page news (either right before or right after he joined Rotary, I couldn't remember). With all the unknown risks Tom went right ahead and opened a Ministry to AIDS patients and was visiting them. God was using Tom to help these patients who at the time were being told they may have only a few weeks to a few months to live. And God put Tom there to help me too. On Thanksgiving Day 1986, my oldest son, Doug, called me from Dallas to tell me he had AIDS. He had recently graduated from College and found a nice job in Dallas. He was embarrassed and ashamed about the AIDS and he didn't want me to tell anyone. So, for about 5 months I was battling the news alone except for a few in the immediate family. I was reading and trying to find out as much as I could about AIDS. Doug told me his first doctor told him he had only a few weeks live. Doug, knowing I had a couple of Veterinary friends, called me once and asked if I could get a certain prescription from them. Doug wanted to commit suicide. I had to explain to him that God didn't want him to do that. God wanted him to live as long as possible so he could be an inspiration to others or because God knew that something was coming to help those with AIDS.

Right after Tom came into Southside Rotary I approached him and briefly told him about Doug and how Doug was questioning his faith in God. Tom said he would be glad to talk with him and when I said unfortunately he was living in Dallas, Tom said 'no problem'. Tom was taking a Religious Course and was going to Dallas on a regular basis. Hmmm? Did God have a part in this? Tom wasn't my Pastor and Tom and I barely knew each other. Here I was dealing with one of life's most stressful events practically alone and then 3 other stressful events begin to fall upon me. But God sent Tom to help Doug and me. Doug managed to live almost 2 years after being diagnosed. During this time Tom said Doug had found peace with God again. I still didn't know Tom really well and even though Tom assured me of this, I had questions as to whether Tom was just saying this for my benefit so I would feel better or what. I needed more assurance from God and God knew this and HE took care of that.

I was visiting Doug the day before he died and the lady with Hospice pointed out to me that Doug, even though in a semi-conscious state, kept repeating over and over "Light, Light!" She and I both wondered what this might mean. I left there and later that day God directed me to a religious book store (Mardel's). As I walked in I spied a round wire display rack with a header saying "Christian Meanings of Popular Names." Right off I noticed a card that said *'Doug'* with the meaning *"seeker of Light"* right below it.

Well the next day, a Sunday, I was contacted and told to hurry over because the Hospice lady said Doug was about to go. It was a dismal, rainy, cloudy day just like the previous 4 days. Shortly after I got there and others had arrived…Doug just went to sleep. The Hospice person then exclaimed…" Look, the sun is breaking thru the clouds", and the Light shown upon Doug's face. Doug had found the 'Light' and I had found closure, Thanks to God and for God using Tom.

But God wasn't through. I never did ask Doug how he thought he might have contacted AIDS. When he first called and told me he had AIDS, all I knew at the time was that he was going to die and I needed to do whatever I could to help him through it. It was some years later, after I had joined the Kirk where Tom Pastored, a young lady approached me and asked if I remembered her. She looked familiar, but I could not think where from. She said she was Felicia, Doug's girlfriend in High School. We talked for a little bit and then she told me about the High School teacher who lead Doug and several other boys' astray.

This reminds me of the boys at the Tulsa Juvenile Detention Center that I and a few others from the Kirk visit and minister to. These boys have all been led astray in some way or another, maybe by so called 'friends' or family members, or parents, or TV shows, or no telling what. We are all susceptible to being led astray and it is people like Tom who try to keep us on the 'Straight and Narrow Road' with God's Word. And I'm hoping that now, since Tom may have some spare time, that maybe he will write a book or two or even more so that he can reach out to literally thousands upon thousands of others who are tempted to go astray. May God Bless Tom in what he does.

The KRR guy, A BIC

3 in 2 & One Missed Skillet

Hey Tom, Wayne & Dan…. the KRR guy again…

Boy Oh Boy! Praise & Worship Gatherings are popping up all over the place. I made 3 in 2 months but missed out when SKILLET came to town. I helped out again at PASSION 2014 in Houston where there were 17,000 mostly college 18 to 25-year old's in attendance. It was sold out at the Toyota Center Dome as was the one earlier in Atlanta at the Phillips Arena with 16,000. It was not as massive as the 60,000-last year in Atlanta at the Georgia Dome but there PASSION stood the risk of having to relocate at the last minute if the Atlanta Falcons wound up in the NFL Playoffs. The Falcons had priority if they needed the dome. As a result, PASSION is reaching out to smaller venues. This year it was a 2 day instead of a 3-day event. Still very impressive but many missed the smaller breakout gatherings where they could meet students from all around the country and the world. Scott and the Kirk Crew were there again and Scott figured out a way for them to get in line early so they could get seating on the main floor. When dinner break came and everyone had to rush out somewhere to eat and get back, Scott left early and went and got orders to go and brought the food back to the Crew and they ate in and around the Kirk Van and hurried back to be first in line.

Then it was WINTERJAM 2014 at the BOK Center where it was sold out with 19,000 in attendance. WINTERJAM continues to grow bigger and bigger each year. This year they will reach well over ½ million in 42 cities. They have 10 different Christian Rock groups each year attracting mainly Junior and Senior High students. Their goal is to share the Gospel with as many people as possible. This year at the BOK the unannounced Surprise Star was Oklahoma's own Carrie Underwood who appeared with Thousand Foot Krutch and performed a fantastic Praise & Worship song. What an impact a Believer like Carrie Underwood can make on these young peoples' lives.

Then it was JESUS CULTLURE this last week at the Rhema Bible Church. To me their Worship music reaches down deep in your soul and no one can help but raise their arms Up in Praise to God. About 2,000 were in attendance and all ages were present. I noticed a higher percentage of Hispanics here than at the other Worship gatherings. JESUS CULTURE originated out of a Pentecostal style church out of Redding, CA and has recently moved to Sacramento. One inspiring middle-aged woman attending the Worship & Ministry at Rhema was jumping and dancing and raising her arms for the full one and one-half hours that JESUS CULTURE started with. God definitely filled her with His Glory. JESUS CULTURE is traveling and performing all over the country and internationally too, reaching hundreds of thousands.

I tell you again, God is stirring things up and using these different Worship Teams to reach out to this generation, and the next one too. Glory Be to God! Your BIC...the KRR guy

Psalm 44:4

"You are my King and my God"

Hey Mark.... David Cox here,

Well Thanks to you Mark, God woke me up at 4:44 this morning. That's the 2nd time in the last week so I thought I had better see what He was trying to get across to me.

Anyway, at 4:44, He reminded me of the guy I prayed for on Hwy 169 the other day. At the time, I had no idea that it was you. It wasn't until a couple of days later when we were at breakfast with our small group of Christian brothers and you said something to me about my almost running into you on Hwy 169. I didn't remember the whole story at the time so God had to wake me up this morning at 4:44 a.m.

God reminded me of driving down Hwy 169 and cutting in front of someone in a pickup and then how the guy in the pickup signaled he was changing lanes and began to pass me. Then the guy signaled 3 or 4 more times whenever he was changing lanes up ahead of me. I thought how courteous that guy is. You just don't see many drivers doing that and so I wanted to catch up with him and give him a thumbs up. But, then I thought No! I better not because he might not see it plain enough and think I was giving him the 'Road Sign" instead. So, I remember just praying to God to Bless that guy's day and may his act of kindness and courtesy be seen by others and be an encouragement to them. Well it looks like God had other plans again and wanted me to personally congratulate you.

You know Mark, one of my faults is my impatience when I am behind the wheel. I am always in a hurry and it seems like I invariably get behind someone who is not paying attention to their driving. Time after time I have to ask God to give me patience and usually I ask Him to 'Hurry Up'. Hmmm! That's not a sign of impatience, is it? He takes care of me on His time and sometimes He'll have a great Christian song come up on my CD like "Holy, Holy, Holy' by Jesus Culture and it will calm me down. BUT He still does not want me to put a 'Fish' Symbol on my vehicle. Now you? I think God would say you'd be OK to put a 'Fish' Symbol on your vehicle.

Hey, Have a Great Weekend…your Brother Dave, A BIC

Christianity Today-Favorite Verses

Hmmm! Something to think about....

A recent edition from Christianity Today mentions the most popular Bible verses searched out by people around the world in 2015 on the You Version Bible app. It was interesting to see that most of the countries (5) in the Southern Hemisphere (12% of the World's population) searched for verses found in the Old Testament while the countries (6) in the Northern Hemisphere (88% of the World's population) searched for verses in the New Testament. Then as you see and read the different verses and think about the living conditions in those various countries you can sort of see why those particular verses are apropos.

New Testament verses mentioned...

Romans 12:2 ...Paul warns that we should not copy the selfish and corrupting behavior of the world but to let God transform us into a new person by changing the way we think. *The United States, Canada & the United Kingdom.*

1 Corinthians 10:13...Paul talks about temptation and as we see others craving evil things that we should seek God to help us resist those same temptations. *China*

Philippians 4:13...As we face challenges we can turn to Christ for strength. *South Korea*

Old Testament verses mentioned...

Joshua 1:9...We are told to be strong and courageous no matter what the challenge for God is with us. *Mexico, Columbia & Brazil*

Jeremiah 29:11...Do not give up hope for God has good plans for us. *Nigeria & South Africa*

Proverbs 3:5-6...Solomon's advice to young people or a young country about who to trust for advice and guidance and that is our LORD and GOD. *Australia*

Hmmm! Who's Speaking?

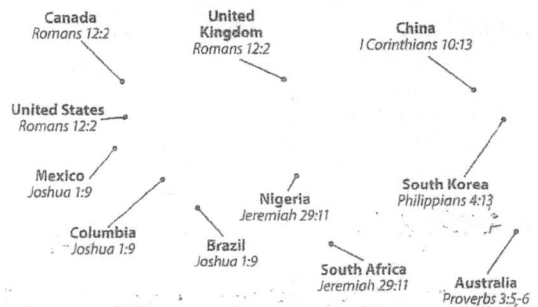

Favorite verses in 11 countries

YouVersion Bible app highlights annual user activity, discovering what has been the most popular Bible verse throughout the year. In 2015, YouVersion tracked the verses most bookmarked, highlighted, shared, and listened to in the 11 countries where the YouVersion app has been downloaded the greatest number of times.

The map above indicates favorite verses across the globe.

christianitytoday.com, 12/8/15

And another interesting article was about China which may become the number one country with the most Christians. Since 2010 the number of Christians in China has been increasing whereas the country, the United States, with the greatest number of Christians has been seeing a decrease. If the trend continues then in the next 15 to 20 years China will have more Christian Believers than the United States. Hmmm!

Football Sunday and Lakeview Baptist Church

Hey Tom, Wayne and others…the KRR guy again out & about on Football Sunday,

With the Big Game on Sunday afternoon I thought I had better get my Church visits in early so I attended www.life.church/tulsa at 8:30 and then skipped up to Lake View Southern Baptist in Skiatook at 10:30. Quiet a difference in the messages and services but both churches filled with caring and friendly members and attendees. And Oh! Free Food at both Churches. I tell you God is always looking out for me and my stomach.

At Life Church, the grills were out and hot dogs were hot and ready at all 8 services. Thousands were served at each location I'm sure. Craig Groeschels message was *30 second theology which* tied in with about 6 of his most favorite Super Bowl Sunday commercials and how he related them to Scripture. Very interesting and if interested you can pull it up on their website. The message also included testimonials of 6 of that day's Super Bowl players who are members of a Life Church or follow the Church on www.LifeChurch.tv.

And if you're not aware of **The Increase/Football Sunday** then you should check it out at www.theincrease.com/football and click on Football Sunday – An Eternal Impact. This is a powerful message by players on both of the Championship teams that share their stories of their faith journeys. This site, called Football Sunday – An Eternal Impact, has only been up a couple of years and this year it was presented in over 2,000 churches across the country and around the world.

My next stop was at Lake View Baptist in Skiatook, conveniently located across Hwy 20 from a Casino. I have a granddaughter who was invited to join in with their Contemporary Worship team and it was her 17th Birthday too. As soon as I walked in the front door I was tempted with two tables filled with home baked goodies. My Oh My! I did make it by those tables but as soon as I was seated a lady came walking up with a bag of homemade Pear Butter Jam and handed me a jar since she recognized that I was a visitor. The congregation here was of a more mature age than what I observed at Life Church and so I was a little surprised they had a Contemporary Worship team but perhaps the Minister and the congregation are looking to the future and want to attract more young families. It was Holy Communion Sunday and it was handled a little bit differently than what I am used to. I have visited many different places however and this wasn't nearly as different as some I have participated in. Here you walked to the front and picked up the elements and went back to your seat but you did not partake until everyone had been served and then everyone joined in with the Scripture prayer. I observed that it was a little awkward if you were right handed and if the cup with wine was filled to the top. You should be proud of me however since I did not spill a drop.

What a fantastic Sunday this was for me and then for my team to pull off a win, it was a Win, Win, Win Day. Your KRR guy, A BIC

'Y' God at the 'Y'

And a last name with a 'Y'

Hey Wayne, Dan and others.…. the KRR guy and the 'Y'

Well God got my attention last Sunday in one of those surprising ways. After attending Church Services at Kirk Crossing I headed home but first stopped by a Wal-Mart to pick up a couple of things. Just as I walk into Wal-Mart I almost walked into a stack of 'Sundays' Tulsa World Newspaper. Now I don't usually buy the Sunday Tulsa World because I don't have the time to read it and often their articles are biased in the wrong direction. But this time, God must have made me pick up a copy.

Now for a little prior info, I usually work out about 2 or 3 times a week at the Union High School **Y** (YMCA). A month or so ago I noticed a new young trainer helping out and working with others. I thought I heard his name was Alex and so when I'd see him I'd call him by that name. Now my hearing isn't what it used to be and I did not realize I was calling him by the wrong name and the young man didn't correct me. But God must have wanted me to get his name right because HE is using this young man to help others and HE will be using him even more in the future. This is one of the reasons **Y** (why) the **Y** (YMCA) was begun back in 1844 in London. YMCA of course stands for Young Men's Christian Association. It was established for young men living on the streets of London to give them a place for Bible Study & prayer and then went on to improve their health. Paul alludes to this in 1st Corinthians 6:19-20 and 9:24-25 and then in 2nd Timothy 4:7

God must have wanted me to get this young man's name right and HE knew a way to do it. When I got time to sit down and read the newspaper, I unwrapped it and the front page popped open and right there on the Front Page, the only picture on the page, was a picture of Alex, BUT his name wasn't Alex, it was **Nick**. And his last name was **Y**acovazzi. And the Big Headline on the front page was **Weight worry. Perception Gap** and the article was about getting healthy. And the 4th word in the article mentioned Nicks name. Now God must have wanted me to correct myself on Nicks name ASAP. On Monday mornings, I usually go to the **Y** but only occasionally will see this young man while I'm there. Well for the first time ever, here was Nick at the front door of the 'Y' and he welcomed me in. You can see the article and a video at www.tulsaworld.com and search Weight Worry-Perception Gap in the archives (July 31, 2016). You'll see and hear how Nick lost 90 pounds in two years (down from 295) with exercise and something else not mentioned in the newspaper article. Hmmm! * **(see below)**.

Talking with Nick brought back memories of my first encounter with the 'Y'. Back about 60 years ago I joined the YMCA in its new building in downtown Tulsa. I was in high school and working out and one day one of the directors came up to me and asked if I would stop by his office before I left. What in the world? When I walk in his office he said the 'Y' was looking for some counselors and he wanted to know if I could help them out with some 4th grade boys once a week and then also at summer camp. Who Me? Hey I was in High School and thought I was pretty smart and probably was kind of brazen then and so I told the director that I was not the right person. He asked why and I said I was Agnostic (one who believes the truth about God is not known & probably unknowable). I thought at the time that the director would be shocked…BUT he simply said "Oh! You'll grow out of that". Obviously, he knew a lot of high school kids got miss-directed in school and they will grow out of that belief in time. (The director was right. I grew out of it, but for me it took another 16 years and that is another story). However, since that was the director's attitude, I went ahead and volunteered to help, which I did for a couple of years.

So that's **Y** (Why) God got my attention at the **Y** about a young man named **Y**acovazzi.

That's all for now… the KRR guy,

Aug. 3rd, 2016

> 1st Corinthians 6:19-20…*Or don't you know that your body is the temple of the Holy Spirit, who lives in you and was given to you by God? You do not belong to yourself, for God bought you with a high price. So, you must honor God with your body.*
> 1st Corinthians 9:24-25…*Remember that in a race everyone runs, but only one person gets the prize. You also must run in such a way*

that you will win. All athletes practice strict self-control. They do it to win a prize that will fade away, but we do it for an eternal prize. 2nd Timothy 4:7...I have fought a good fight, I have finished the race, and I have remained faithful.

* Biased reporting is quite common and so I wasn't totally surprised when I heard Nick telling his story on the video. Nothing was mentioned in the article about how the YMCA has helped his Faith in the Lord and how God has helped him. Evidently some reporters haven't grown out of their Agnostic beliefs yet. Hey! It took me a while but God finally got my attention.

Where is Paul Harvey and the Rest of the Story?

Hey Wayne, Dan and others…. the KRR guy with some questions and comments,

With the Elections coming up soon it would be nice if we could hear what Paul Harvey would have to say.

Many of you may remember the radio broadcasts by Tulsa's own Paul Harvey. Paul was born in Tulsa on Sept. 4, 1918 and died at the age of 90 in 2009. His dad, a Tulsa Police Officer, was shot and killed by 4 robbers when Paul was only 3 years old. Paul went on to graduate from Tulsa Central High School and then attended Tulsa University.

I can still remember hearing many of his popular broadcasts entitled 'The Rest of the Story' which were broadcast from 1976 to 2009. He would start off telling about someone who was in the news at the time and almost all of us were hearing something negative about them. Well, Harvey would then go on to tell us 'The Rest of the Story' after he had thoroughly checked the information out. He would find out if the information was nothing but rumors that may have been started unintentionally or in some cases intentionally by someone with a grudge or just plain hate. Sometimes the story or rumor would get even more out of balance or context with each person it was passed on to.

Harvey expressed his concern about big government, bureaucrats who lacked common sense, permissive parents and America succumbing to moral decay. He championed love of God and country. He was a close friend of Billy Graham and would have told the 'Rest of the Story' about Billy Graham if the need arose. And the Billy Graham Association recently is quoted as saying they do not enjoy hearing the scandals about either candidate right now and they added to vote for the candidate who will appoint the right people to the Supreme Court…" *who they appoint to the Supreme Court will remake the fabric of our society for our children and our grandchildren, for generations to come."*

Today we can go check out rumors or things we hear that seem out of character, contrary or inconsistent with what we know by going to web sites such as 'Truth or Fiction.com', 'Snopes.com', 'fastcheck.org', 'buzzfeed.com' or 'politifact.com'. With the Presidential Election soon coming up we need a leader who will have the same concerns and love of God and country as Paul Harvey had. We need to check out things we hear about the candidates before we make our vote and if neither candidate seems to fit the bill, then we must remember who will be the one to most likely appoint Supreme Court Justices who will fit the bill.

And we need to remember in our daily lives if we hear something about someone we know that doesn't sound right… to check it out. And if it is right and we know that God would not like it, then we need to help God get it straightened out.

The KRR Guy…...A BIC

444 & 333 and the Anthem

March 30, 2017

Hey Wayne, Dan and others…. the KRR guy out and about

First off…God & the 444 woke me up at 4:44 a.m. on Sunday 3/19. I was having some issues about several things that night and even my dreams were disturbing and then God did His thing and repeated the 444 to me 3 times and I'm lying there thinking what in the world does this mean. When I rolled over to see what time it was on my digital clock it says 4:44. Well…this must mean something so I had better write it down and then check it out at a decent time. I put it aside and went off to Kirk Crossing for church and lo & behold, Pastor Dan was giving his message about how *Jesus would use numbers sometimes to make a contrast to help get a point across.* Dan gave the example of Mark 5:21-43 where Jesus was asked to hurry to the house of Jairus to heal his **12-year**-old daughter who was about to die. Then in the crowd of people rushing along the road with Jesus, Jesus asked? *Who touched my clothing?* And when you read the verses you find out it was a woman who Jesus knew who had been having bleeding problems for **12 years.** This slowed the crowd and Jesus down and when he reached Jairus' house his daughter had died. Well Dan's message reminded me to check out the 444. But did I? Nope! It wasn't until Tuesday afternoon that I finally checked into it. But did I remember it on my own? Nope! It took God using a pigeon to get my attention. At my office, I was busy working away in the late afternoon and a pigeon walks by my office window on the sidewalk and looks in and goes on by. I'm thinking what is that pigeon doing? I've never seen a pigeon there before in the last 20 years or so. Then the pigeon comes back walking in the opposite direction, then turns around and walks by again. 3 times this bird walks by. I had a Journey Meeting to attend that evening and I was going to need to leave around 5 p.m. so I glanced at a digital clock to see what time it was and Lo & Behold it was showing 4:44, and things started to click.

    OK! OK! I got the message God! So, I go to my computer and Google and type in 444 Biblical or Spiritual Views. And what pops up at the top? Spiritual Views and Lo & Behold it explains that the 444 means that

Miscellaneous

Angels are with you for your comfort and protection and to carefully pay attention to the signs that you see around you. Hmmm!

But God wasn't through communicating with me yet. The very next Sunday in the early a.m. God wakes me up with the numbers 333. 3 times I perceived this and when I look at the clock it is 3:33 a.m. Now the night b/4 I had been asking God if I was supposed to visit a certain Church in Broken Arrow. Two people had suggested I visit this Church as something did not seem right there. I had pre-determined on my own to visit that particular church but I could not find what time their Church service or services were. I made an educated guess and figured it would probably be around 10:30 or 11:00 a.m. So, I make an early visit to Kirk of the Hills and skip out early to make it to the Broken Arrow Church around 10:30. As I arrive, they did not have any signage out front saying what time their Services were but the back-parking lot was pretty full. As I drive in I finally see a small sign that says Church Service at 9:15 a.m. and Bible Classes at 10:30. WELL! I was a little over an hour late. Evidently, I went there on my thinking alone, BUT God got my attention then and His thoughts were to get me down the road a few miles to a New Church, the Anthem Church at 7777 So. Garnett. Now I didn't know what time their Services were, but when I arrived they had two services, one at 9:30 and the 2nd one at 11:00. It was then 10:50, perfect timing. Hmmm? How did that happen?

Well the New Anthem Church is where the previous Liberty Church was and where the Gathering Church down the road away was going to join up with them so they could be "Better Together". I had visited each one them several months ago, and I had been wanting to see how things were working out for them and I can now say after this most recent visit.... that things couldn't be any "Better". They added a new service and from what I observed at the 11 a.m. service they will need to soon add a third service and start thinking about enlarging. Brad Jenkins is now the Lead Pastor and his message was how Jesus can make a Way when there is No Way from John 6:1-15. There was no way to feed 10,000 or more people (5,000 men plus women & children), but Jesus knew what He was going to do in advance. So, Jesus provided and there were still 12 Baskets full of food after everyone had all they needed for that day. And the 12 Baskets? One for each of the 12 Disciples who had not eaten. Hmmm!

Hmmm! Who's Speaking?

Brad went on to quote from John 6:35.... *Where Jesus says... he is the bread of life, come to me and never be hungry again.*

And Oh! After my 3 Church visits I go by my office & pull up on Google... 333 Spiritual Meaning. And I find that it is a sign of the **Trinity.** Hmmm! The Church I had planned on visiting was **Trinity** Lutheran. It also means that Angels are with us as we seek the Truth.

And FYI... some info some other Churches might want to check out. At the Kirk of the Hills it was <u>SOUPer Sunday</u> where the High School youth were raising money for their summer Mission Trips. They were offering Home Made soup to eat there or take with you and they had a selection of about **12 different** varieties of soup and they were absolutely delicious. And then at the Anthem they had a decorative wall in their foyer where you could write a short anonymous testimony how God had Blessed and Helped you thru a trying time in your life. And by sharing you could help someone else who may be experiencing the same thing right now.

And also... if you plan on visiting the Anthem Church turning South from 71st St., Do not turn into the first or second appearing entryways. They are not the Right Way and they quickly turn into a Dead End. Turn east into the 3rd entryway. That is the Right Way to your Final Destination.

Hey, you all have a 444 and a 333 day.... your KRR guy, A BIC

Post Oak Sewer Station

July 31, 2017

Hey Wayne, Dan and others…. the KRR guy out and about,

Maybe some of you are aware of the Post Oak Lodge www.postoaklodge.com just northwest of downtown Tulsa about 5 miles. A spectacular place where you can hold business and church retreats and feel like you are hundreds of miles away from any major city. The Tulsa Botanic Garden www.TulsaBotanic.org is just about a mile north and it is really special too if you've never been there. The Lodge is located on the eastern edge of Osage County which is famous for its rolling hills and history of hiding some of Oklahoma's early outlaws.

I'm with a small group of men that are involved in a Mission to transform lives through The Journey, a Global Ministry thru the Influencers, www.influencers.org.

Part of our agenda was to get away someplace where we could experience some quite time alone and enjoy the beauty and creations that God has provided. Little did I know that could be found just 10 minutes from downtown Tulsa. The hills and the woods are alive with God's creations. You can't see or hear anything that can distract you from your quite time.

After meeting at 8 a.m. on a Saturday morning and enjoying a great breakfast we were sent on our way out into the trails and woods. It was 8:30 and we were asked to check back around 11 a.m. to share what we experienced and enjoy a lunch.

There were 8 of us and each headed off in different directions. When we returned we each started sharing our experiences? The 4 or 5 that shared their experiences before me had found some spots that sounded utterly fantastic. I was almost embarrassed when I told them God sent me to the 'Sewer Station'. I explained that when I left the Lodge I just asked God to guide me to where He wanted me. He guided me to the end of a road leading out North & West from the Lodge. I passed by some beautiful cabins and went on down the road. Soon I came upon a sign that said 'Trail No. 1' that led off into the woods full of oak and pine trees and bushes of all kinds. But I felt I was being led on down the road, maybe to another

Hmmm! Who's Speaking?

trail. Soon I came upon a sand Volleyball court and horseshoe corral and an open-air barn type structure. I passed by and continued on down the road where I soon detected the road was ending. Before me I could see a tall, 8' chain link fence with 3 strands of barb wire above it bent outwards toward anyone approaching it. A large sign was posted on the entry gate that said 'City of Tulsa Pump & Sewer Station'. Inside this fenced area of about 2 acres, all the trees and bushes had been cut down and taken out. Only asphalt, short cut dry grass and a small pump building were enclosed. Just outside the fence, all the way around it, were lush trees and bushes and birds.

I opened up my portable folding chair and sat down thinking I would leave in a few minutes. But God had different plans. I was there for almost 2 hours.

Looking into the area where the Sewer Station was it was kind of like God saying – 'At the end of the Road – I do not want you to enter into the Sewer for Eternity. I want you with Me so you can always enjoy the beauty of things I have created'. I had parked myself in the shade of some trees and a cool breeze was blowing thru the woods with a fresh scent to it.

I begin to reflect upon a book by Phillip Keller 'A Shepherd Looks at Psalm 23'. Keller grew up in East Africa and in his early years was an actual Shepherd being a sheep owner and rancher. His story brings out the true meaning of the 23rd Psalm and what it meant to those living at the time it was written. Keller mentions how some sheep may be fenced-in in an area where their Shepherd-Master doesn't give a hoot about them. No good grass, no water, no shelter from storms or foxes or other prey. Longingly they look thru wire fences to the other side where there is a Good Shepherd-Master. Which master do we want to have – the Evil Master or the Good Master? Keller goes on to explain that some of his sheep (like some people) -No Matter How Good their life is… think or feel that the grass is always greener on the other side of the fence. Some of his sheep would find a way to get to the other side of the fence and then realize how much better it was where they had been. Keller would then have to retrieve them.

The barren, uninviting 2-acre tract of land where the Sewer Station is, has a gate with a large chain and padlock on it and one could not get out unless they had a key. This reminded me that if you feel locked into a place like this – then turn to God. He has the Key to let you out even when you wander away from Him.

After I grasped why God sent me to the Sewer Station an even bigger, cooler and more comforting breeze came blowing across me. Hmmm! I felt I got His message.

Hey, enjoy your day and Thank God for His Blessings… Your KRR guy, A BIC

The Epilogue

It is my hope that something in a story in this book may have clicked on a light for you. Probably some of you already know God but something new may have been brought to light. God can use each and every one of us and He wants to use us.

You don't have to know a 100 or so Bible verses by heart. You don't have to know all about each and every Book in the Bible. You don't have to wear certain clothes to Church or wear them in a certain way. You don't have to speak in tongues or raise your arms in praise a certain way. Don't be turned away from God because you feel you don't fit in. God has a place for you where you can feel comfortable and get to know Him in a personal way. He has given each of us certain Gifts to use for Him. Peter, Paul, and John mention some of the different gifts- prophesying, serving, teaching, encouraging, generosity, leading, healing, interpreting, helping others, kindness and others. Just accept Him and then get to know Him and then you will know when He is communicating with you and wanting you to share His Good News of Hope and Eternal Life with others around you through the Gift He has given you.

GOD'S WAY
IS THE ONE WAY
ALWAYS

CPSIA information can be obtained
at www.ICGtesting.com
Printed in the USA
LVHW010834271118
598075LV00001B/6/P